MW00474564

CHRISTIAN FREEDOM
FAITH WORKING THROUGH LOVE

CHRISTIAN FREEDOM
FAITH WORKING THROUGH LOVE

by Martin Luther and Philip Melanchthon

A Reader's Edition

Edited by Edward A. Engelbrecht
and Charles P. Schaum

Translations by Christopher J. Neuendorf
and J. A. O. Preus II et al.

CONCORDIA PUBLISHING HOUSE • SAINT LOUIS

15-5184
ISBN 10: 0-7586-3102-2
ISBN 13: 978-0-7586-3102-2
Christian Living / Spiritual Formation

Copyright © 2011 Concordia Publishing House
3558 S. Jefferson Ave., St. Louis, MO 63118-3968
1-800-325-3040 · www.cph.org

Quotations marked LW in this publication are from *Luther's Works*, American Edition (vols. 1–30, 58, 69 St. Louis: Concordia, and vols. 31–55 Philadelphia: Fortress Press, 1955–2010).

Quotations marked WA are from the Weimar Ausgabe ("edition") of Luther's Works. *Luthers Werke: Kritische Gesamtausgabe.* 65 vols. Weimar: Hermann Böhlau, 1883–1993.

Unless indicated otherwise, Bible references are translated from the Latin Vulgate.

Quotations marked *TLWA* are from *The Lord Will Answer: A Daily Prayer Catechism*, copyright 2004 Concordia Publishing House. All rights reserved.

Quotations marked *Concordia* are from *Concordia: The Lutheran Confessions*, second edition; edited by Paul McCain, et al., copyright © 2006 Concordia Publishing House. All rights reserved.

Manufactured in the United States of America

Library of Congress Cataloging-in-Publication Data

Luther, Martin, 1483-1546.
  [Selections. English. 2011]
  Christian freedom : voices from Wittenberg / by Martin Luther and Philip Melanchthon ; a reader's edition edited by Edward A. Engelbrecht and Charles P. Schaum ; translations by Christopher J. Neuendorf and J.A.O. Preus II.
      p. cm.
  Includes bibliographical references and indexes.
  ISBN 978-0-7586-3102-2
  1. Liberty--Religious aspects--Lutheran Church. 2. Lutheran Church--Doctrines. I. Engelbrecht, Edward. II. Schaum, Charles P. III. Neuendorf, Christopher J. IV. Preus, Jacob A. O. (Jacob Aall Ottesen), 1920-1994. V. Melanchthon, Philipp, 1497-1560. Loci communes rerum theologicarum. Locus 24. English. VI. Title.
  BR331.E5 2011
  230'.41--dc23   2011031450

1 2 3 4 5 6 7 8 9 10   20 19 18 17 16 15 14 13 12 11

TABLE OF CONTENTS

ABBREVIATIONS

AC Augsburg Confession
Ap Apology of the Augsburg Confession
Ep Epitome of the Formula of Concord
FC Formula of Concord
LC Large Catechism
SA Smalcald Articles
SC Small Catechism
SD Solid Declaration of the Formula of Concord
Tr Treatise on the Power and Primacy of the Pope

Citation Examples

AC XX 4 (Augsburg Confession, Article XX, paragraph 4)
Ap IV 229 (Apology of the Augsburg Confession, Article IV, paragraph 229)
FC SD X 24 (Solid Declaration of the Formula of Concord, Article X, paragraph 24)
FC Ep V 8 (Epitome of the Formula of Concord, Article V, paragraph 8)
LC V 32, 37 (Large Catechism, Part 5, paragraphs 32 and 37)
SA III I 6 (Smalcald Articles, Part III, Article I, paragraph 6)
SC III 5 (Small Catechism, Part III, paragraph 5)
Tr 5 (Treatise, paragraph 5)

Other Abbreviations

c.   circa (approximately)
fl.   floruit (flourished)
LW   Luther's Works, American Edition
WA   Weimar Edition of Luther's Works

LIST OF CHARTS AND ILLUSTRATIONS

Forty-Day Reading Guide

——•◆•——

The following guide will walk you through Luther's teaching on Christian freedom and conclude with Melanchthon's summary on freedom. Each day's reading includes about 3–5 pages of text, which may take about 10–15 minutes to read. The reference numbers in the charts below are to page numbers.

This schedule may be followed at any time or during the forty days of Lent, beginning on Ash Wednesday, which would be an excellent plan for congregational reflection. Conclude each day's reading by reciting the appointed prayer for the week, voicing personal prayers, journaling your thoughts, or doing freely whatever your devotion may suggest.

Week 1

Day 1/Wed	An Open Letter to Pope Leo X 27–29
Day 2/Thurs	29–32
Day 3/Fri	32–36
Day 4/Sat	36–39

1. Prayer for Pure Faith

O Father of all mercy, You have begun Your work in us. Endow us more and more with all fullness of wisdom and knowledge. Then we may be assured in our hearts and fully know how the Spirit, who has raised up our Lord, also enlivens the faith within us with the same power and strength. Through Him we have also risen from the dead by His mighty power, which works in us through Your holy Word. Help us to grow in the knowledge of Your dear Son, our Lord Jesus Christ, and to remain firm in the confession of His blessed Word. Give us the love to be of one mind and to serve one another in Christ. Then we will not be afraid of that which is disagreeable, nor of the rage of the arsonist (Satan) whose torch is almost extinguished. Dear Father, guard us so that his craftiness may not take the place of our pure faith. Grant that our cross and sufferings may lead to a blessed and sure hope of the coming of our Savior Jesus Christ, for whom we wait daily. Amen. (Martin Luther; *TLWA* 35)

WEEK 2

Day 5/Mon	Christian Freedom 47–50
Day 6/Tues	50–53
Day 7/Wed	53–55
Day 8/Thurs	55–57
Day 9/Fri	57–63
Day 10/Sat	63–65

2. PRAYER FOR FAITH AND FREEDOM

O Lord, increase faith in us. Gladly and truly I would think of You as my dearly beloved Father, and Christ as my brother. But alas, my flesh will not follow. Therefore, help my unbelief, so I may receive Your Word as truth and glorify Your name by Your Holy Spirit. O Lord, end our captivity. Redeem us, for we are the firstborn of Your new creation. As redemption has been perfectly and sufficiently accomplished through Christ, so may we fully and truly know and accept it. As by Your mighty hand the sea was dried up by the parching wind, so let everything that remains of our bondage vanish. Amen. (Martin Luther; *TLWA* 185)

WEEK 3

Day 11/Mon	Christian Freedom 65–68
Day 12/Tues	68–70
Day 13/Wed	70–75
Day 14/Thurs	76–78
Day 15/Fri	78–83
Day 16/Sat	83–86

3. Prayer for Communion with God

Dear God, how shall I, a poor and offensive person, receive such great honor to think that my soul is the bride of God, and the Son of God its bridegroom? The eternal Majesty has lowered itself to come into my poor flesh and blood and actually unite Himself with me. This is an honor not even bestowed on the angels in heaven. From head to foot I am full of pollution, corruption, leprosy, sin, and offense before God. How can I be considered His beloved, and be one in body with the high, eternal, glorious Majesty? Since You want it so, praise and thanks be unto You in eternity. Amen. (Martin Luther; *TLWA* 207)

Week 4

Day 17/Mon	Luther on Freedom 92–94
Day 18/Tues	94–96
Day 19/Wed	98–102
Day 20/Thurs	102–108
Day 21/Fri	109–113
Day 22/Sat	115–117

4. Prayer for Freedom from Suffering

Grant, dear Lord God, that the blessed Day of Your holy advent may come soon, so that we may be redeemed from this bad, wicked world, the devil's dominion, and be freed from the terrible plague which we must suffer from without and within, from wicked people and our own conscience. Dispatch this old maggot sack that we may finally get a different body, which is not full of sin, inclined to unchasteness and to everything evil, as the present one is, but one that is redeemed from all bodily and spiritual misery and made like Your glorious body, dear Lord Jesus Christ, that we may at last come to our glorious redemption. Amen. (Martin Luther; *TLWA* 288)

Week 5

Day 23/Mon	Luther on Freedom 117–120
Day 24/Tues	120–121

Day 25/Wed	122–124
Day 26/Thurs	125–126
Day 27/Fri	126–128
Day 28/Sat	129–134

5. Prayer for Freedom through the Blood of Jesus

O my God, though I am a sinner, yet I am not a sinner. On my own and apart from Christ, I am a sinner. But in my Lord Jesus Christ and apart from me, I am no sinner. I firmly believe that He has destroyed all my sins with His precious blood. To show this, I am baptized, cleansed by God's Word, and declared absolved and freed from all my sins. In the Sacrament of the true body and blood of my Lord Jesus Christ I have received the forgiveness of sins as a sure sign of grace. This He has merited, won, and accomplished for me by shedding of His precious blood. For this I thank Him in eternity. Amen. (Martin Luther; *TLWA* 399)

Week 6

Day 29/Mon	Luther on Freedom 135–137
Day 30/Tues	138–141
Day 31/Wed	143–147
Day 32/Thurs	147–151
Day 33/Fri	152–155
Day 34/Sat	157–161

6. Prayer for Love and Faith

Behold, Lord, here is an empty cask that needs to be filled. My Lord, fill it. I am weak in faith; strengthen me. I am cold in love; warm me and fill me with fire that my love may flow out over my neighbor. I do not have a firm, strong faith; I doubt at times and cannot fully trust God. O Lord, help me; increase my faith and trust for me. In You is locked the treasure of all my possessions. I am poor; You are rich and are come to have mercy upon the poor. I am a sinner; You are righteous. I pour forth a stream of sin; but in You are all fullness and righteousness. Amen. (Martin Luther; *TLWA* 378)

Week 7

Day 35/Mon	Melanchthon on Christian Liberty 167–170
Day 36/Tues	170–173
Day 37/Wed	173–177
Day 38/Thurs	177–180
Day 39/Fri	180–183
Day 40/Sat	183–184

7. Prayer for the Holy Spirit

Almighty and Holy Spirit, the Comforter, pure, living, true,—illuminate, govern, sanctify me, and confirm my heart and mind in the faith, and in all genuine consolation; preserve and rule over me that, dwelling in the house of the Lord all the days of my life, to behold the beauty of the Lord, I may be and remain forever in the temple of the Lord, and praise Him with a joyful spirit, and in union with all the heavenly church. Amen. (Philip Melanchthon; *TLWA* 263)

TIMELINE

1500   Charles V born in Ghent, February 24; Pope Alexander VI proclaims Jubilee Year, calls for crusade against Turks

1501   Luther enters University of Erfurt (receives Master of Arts in philosophy, 1505)

1502   Frederick the Wise, Elector of Saxony, founds University of Wittenberg; work begins in Alcalá, Spain (Latin name of city, : *Complutum*) on a massive Bible in Hebrew, Greek, Latin, and Arabic (the *Complutensian Polyglot*)

1503   John Frederick the Magnanimous born at Torgau, June 30; Pope Alexander VI dies, August 18; Pope Pius III serves from September 22 to October 18, dies; Pope Julius II begins pontificate, November 1

1505   Luther enters monastery, July 17

1506   Pope Julius II lays cornerstone of St. Peter's Basilica, Rome; Luther takes final vows as Augustinian friar, autumn

1507   Luther ordained priest at Erfurt Cathedral, April 3; celebrates first Mass, May 2; begins study of theology

1508   Luther appointed substitute lecturer in moral philosophy at University of Wittenberg

1509   Luther obtains Bachelor of Theology degree, March 9; returns to Erfurt; Henry VIII becomes king of England

1510   Luther sent to Rome on mission for Augustinian order

1511   Luther sent to Wittenberg University to serve as professor, takes over chair of Staupitz at Wittenberg

1512   Luther awarded Doctor of Theology degree, October 18–19; Fifth Lateran Council begins (ends in 1517)

1513   Pope Julius II dies, February 21; Pope Leo X begins pontificate, March 11; Luther begins lectures on Psalms

1514   Albert of Brandenburg, cardinal, archbishop of Mainz, and elector, begins his reign; indulgences later sold to offset

Albert's massive debt and to fund St. Peter's Basilica; Greek New Testament of the *Complutensian Polyglot* complete

1515 Luther begins lectures on Romans; *Index of Prohibited Books* adopted at Fifth Lateran Council

1516 Erasmus publishes *Novum Instrumentum omne*, first printed and published Greek-Latin parallel New Testament; Luther begins first lecture series on Galatians

1517 Pope Leo X declares indulgence for rebuilding of St. Peter's; Luther posts Ninety-five Theses, October 31

1518 Philip Melanchthon comes to Wittenberg University; Heidelberg Disputation, April; process against Luther begins in Rome; Luther appears before Cardinal Cajetan in Augsburg, October–November; Luther appeals to a general coun-cil, refuses to recant; Frederick the Wise refuses to surrender Luther, December

1519 Charles V elected Holy Roman Emperor, June 28; Leipzig Disputation between Luther and Eck, July

1520 Leo X issues papal bull *Exsurge, Domine*, giving Luther sixty days to recant or be excommunicated, June 15; Lucas Cranach the Elder creates first portrait of Martin Luther, an engrav-ing; Luther burns the papal bull and a copy of canon law, December 10

1521 Luther excommunicated by papal bull *Decet Romanum Pontificem*, January 3; Luther appears before Diet of Worms and refuses to recant, April 17–18; Charles V issues *Edict of Worms*, declaring Luther a public outlaw and making it ille-gal to have Luther's books, May 25; Frederick the Wise hides Luther at the Wartburg Castle for eleven months; Luther trans-lates New Testament into German, from December to March 1522; Philip Melanchthon publishes first Lutheran dogmatic text, *Loci Communes*; Leo X dies, December 1

1522 Pope Adrian VI elected, January 9; Luther returns from Wartburg, March 6; Luther preaches the *Invocavit Sermons* against excesses of the Zwickau prophets; ban on Luther lifted; Luther's translation of the New Testament published, September 21; Luther writes *Personal Prayer Book*, predecessor of Small Catechism; Charles V establishes Inquisition in Spanish Netherlands, with over 2,000 killed; Ulrich Zwingli begins Reformation in Zurich; *Complutensian Polyglot* Bible finally published

1523 Escaped nuns from Nimbschen, including Katharina von Bora, arrive in Wittenberg, April 7; Heinrich Voes and John Esch, first Lutheran martyrs, burned at stake in Antwerp, July 1; Luther's translation of the Pentateuch published, summer; Luther writes his first hymn; Luther writes *The Baptismal Booklet*; Adrian VI, last non-Italian pope until John Paul II, dies, September 14; Pope Clement VII elected, November 18

1524 Peasants' War begins, led in part by Thomas Münzer; Luther's translation of Psalter published; Luther resumes lecturing in Wittenberg; Luther stops wearing monk's clothing, October; *Achtliederbuch (A Book of Eight Hymns)*, first Lutheran hymnal, published by John Walter and Luther; John von Staupitz dies, December 28

INTRODUCTION

BRAVE HEARTS YEARN FOR FREEDOM

Who shall defend thee now, and make thee free?
Alas! in war, who shall thy leader be!
Who shall thee now rescue from Saxon rage,
And who their wrath and fury can assuage?
I say no more, but beg God of his grace,
May thee in haste restore to wealth and peace:
Brave Wallace now shall thee govern no more,
Who to thy rights restor'd thee thrice before.
—*Blind Harry's* **Wallace**[1]

In 1508, Blind Harry's poem about freedom fighter William Wallace came to press in Edinburgh, Scotland. There Scottish patriots questioned who would deliver them from the Saxons—the English—who persistently trespassed their borders. Across the channel in Germany's Electoral Saxony, a young friar took up residence in the Augustinian cloister at Wittenberg. This young Saxon would also crave freedom and struggle for it. But the freedom sought by this brave heart was markedly different from the national and economic freedom sought by William Wallace, Blind Harry, and other medieval persons.

Martin Luther's hope and cry stand out among the other medieval voices. To understand why Luther's message stands out, we begin with a brief survey of the hopes and causes of freedom that preceded

---

1   William Hamilton of Gilbertfield, ed. (Edinburgh: Luath Press, 1998), 220.

Luther's greatest treatise, *Christian Freedom* (1520). Then we shall turn to hear the Wittenberg cry.

THE FREEDOM OF THE CHURCH (1079)

Among rugged hills in northern Italy stands the castle of Canossa. Here, in January 1077, Holy Roman Emperor Henry IV walked barefoot through the snow on three separate days to appear before the castle walls. Inside was Pope Gregory VII, who had excommunicated Henry nearly a year earlier for meddling in church affairs. Gregory was now planning to cross the Alps, meet with Henry's subjects at Augsburg, and work for Henry's removal from the throne. Henry came barefoot in the snow as a penitent, seeking pardon from Gregory in order to strengthen his political position at home. He had only recently quelled the Saxon Uprising (1073–75) and could little afford further conflict. His exceptional pleading worked. Gregory granted him pardon in a year that dramatically showed the tensions between the growing power of the medieval papacy as a priestly authority and the long-held belief in the divine right of kings to exercise authority, even over leaders of the churches in their territories.

Tensions between these two leaders would persist, causing Gregory in 1079 to draft a letter entitled "The Freedom of the Church." In this letter and other documents, Gregory sought to confirm the authority of the papacy over earthly rulers. He sought a church that was "free, chaste, and catholic": (1) free from kings appointing or "investing"[2] churchly leaders; (2) chaste or celibate so as to be free from the influence of family ties with the nobility, who would manipulate church affairs; and (3) catholic or universal rather than subject to local kingdoms of the world. Gregory's declaration of the church's freedom did not end the struggles between papacy and empire—far from it. But he established a precedent that guided the beliefs and actions of church leaders and kings for centuries to come. Gregory's cry for the "freedom of the church" represented one medieval quest for freedom.

THE GREAT CHARTER (1215)

Another example of the medieval quest for freedom can be seen in the *Magna Carta* or the Great Charter of the Freedoms of England. The introduction and first legal clause of the charter describes the freedom

2   The eleventh-century conflict is known as the Investiture Controversy.

Different Visions of Freedom

Thomas Murner's poem "Concerning the Great Lutheran Fools" (1522) satirized Luther's teaching about Christian freedom as a call to revolt. Note that this woodcut from Murner's book shows a man carrying the freedom banner while also bearing a sword.

of English churches, drawing on agreement between the bishops and the barons who sided against King John (1166–1216). The king had meddled in the appointment of the archbishop of Canterbury and perpetuated corruption that angered his subjects. As a result, the bishops reasserted the church's freedom and sided with the political leadership to support greater freedoms for "all free men of our kingdom." The charter itself was hastily compiled and did not last long as a legal document. Yet it embodied principles of economic and political freedom to which people would return again and again.

CRIES FOR SPIRITUAL FREEDOM

In the thirteenth century, laypeople increasingly formed devotional groups that imitated monastic piety, yet without the usual vows. These lay organizations became significant havens for mystical and even heretical ideas. Influential teachers, such as the philosopher Amalric of Bene (d. c. 1207), apparently held that when the soul was united with God, it could no longer sin. In other words, true believers became free from sin and even free from moral constraints on what they could do with their bodies. These ideas of spiritual freedom spread and were attributed to a variety of groups, such as the Beguines, a guild for women. Medieval writers at times refer to "Brethren of the Free Spirit" when describing adherents of these mystical ideas, though no formal organization of such a group is known. (An organization of free spirits would certainly seem contradictory!) The Inquisition attempted to stop the spread of these ideas. At Vienna in 1312, a church council drew up a list of abuses by advocates of the "spirit of freedom."

Other groups, such as the Waldenses and later the Hussites, asserted their freedom from control by churchly authorities. Among other things, the Waldenses wanted freedom to preach from the Bible without permission from a bishop, and the Hussites wanted freedom to receive both the host and the chalice in the Lord's Supper.

Another interest in spiritual freedom was the ongoing effort to explain the powers and limits of the human will. However, the ancient positions of classical philosophers and the debate between Pelagius and Augustine largely guided these interests.

Major Peasants' Revolts (1323–81)

As early as the ninth century, nobles in Europe expressed concerns about the peasants conspiring for greater liberties. Numerous regional revolts threatened medieval feudalism as peasants sought economic advantages and as feudal masters sought their own advantages. The chart on page 6 provides examples of local, regional, and national revolts that took place throughout the medieval period.

However, in the fourteenth century, the number of revolts reached a crescendo that threatened to overthrow feudal civilization completely. The longing for greater economic freedom and societal change flowed from the devastating effects of the Black Death, which passed through Europe at that time. The plague greatly reduced the number of peasants who could work fields and maintain their lords' estates. As a consequence, the services of the peasants became more and more valuable and they began to demand greater freedoms in return for their service. These demands for freedom grew violent in numerous revolts, such as the Flanders Peasants' Revolt (1323–28), the Jacquerie Revolt in France (1356–58), and the Great Peasants' Revolt in England (1381).

Bundschuhfahne

Rebelling peasants surround a knight while raising a banner featuring a peasant shoe (*Bundschuh*) as the symbol that the peasants are stepping forward to claim their rights. This woodcut appeared in a 1539 edition of *Remedies for Fortune Fair and Foul* (German title: *Trostspiegel*) by the early Renaissance humanist Petrarch.

EXAMPLES OF MEDIEVAL REVOLTS

997	Peasants' Revolt in Normandy
1073–75	Saxon Uprising
1102	Monks of St. Arnoul de Crépy experience rebellion
1189	Abbot of Croyland experiences rebellion
1207–35	Archbishop leads Stedinger Crusade against peasants
1220	Chartres Serfs' Rebellion
1229	Dunstable tenants rebel against monks
1246	Bondfolk of Esmans rebel against abbot of St-Germain-des-Prés
1323–28	Flemish Peasants Revolt
1336	Dernehale and Overe bond tenants rebel
1350–1415	Remensas' Revolts
1356–84	Tuchins' Revolt
1357/8	Jacquerie Revolt
1378–82	Wool Carders' (Ciompi) Revolt
1381	Great Peasants' Revolt in England
1419–34	Hussite War in Bohemia
1431	Worms Peasants' Revolt
1438	*The Reformation of Kaiser Sigismund* calls for societal changes
1468–75	Elsass (Alsace) Peasants' Revolt
1467–70	Great Irmandino (Brotherhood) Wars in Galicia, Spain
1478	Kärnten (Carinthia) Peasants' Revolt
1486	Strassburg Peasants' Revolt
1493	Schlettstadt Revolt
1502	Breisgau Peasants' Revolt
1508	Joseph Grünpeck publishes *Mirror of Natural, Heavenly, and Prophetic Observations of All Affliction*, which predicts the upheaval of all society.

Events drawn from "Revolte," in *Lexikon des Mittel Alters*, and G. G. Coulton's *Medieval Village, Manor, and Monastery* (1925).

Freedom's Chorus

As this brief survey shows, medieval people voiced many cries for freedom—some of them worthy, some of them open to dispute. They sought freedom from church and state authorities, greater economic opportunities, and even spiritual and intellectual freedoms. As mentioned in the introduction, the dashing character of William Wallace seeking national freedom for Scotland is only one example among many. Blind Harry, who celebrated Wallace's efforts, saw and described the dilemma most clearly. At the close of the medieval period, he pleaded that God, by His grace, would send a new champion.

When Luther raised his voice to describe Christian freedom in 1520, he joined a chorus of other medieval people who longed for change. Yet Luther's message was unique and uniquely rooted in the teachings of Holy Scripture, especially St. Paul's Letter to the Galatians. Luther would call for freedom, but he would also call for a voluntary return to service. It is to Luther's story that we now turn.

Luther's Passion for Freedom (1508–1520)

Luther, as a medieval man, was as interested in freedom as other people of that day. But when he entered the Augustinian Order of Eremites (hermits) in 1508, his interest in freedom received a new focus. The last chapter of the *Rule of St. Augustine*, which Luther vowed to follow, focused on living as "free children under the liberty of grace."[3] The chapter also emphasized that Augustine's rule was to be read to the monks once a week. Luther must have heard this brief message of freedom many, many

---

3   "May our Lord grant that you, as lovers of spiritual beauty, may observe all these things through a motive of love, and become fragrant with the sweet odour of Christ by a holy conversation, not as slaves under the servitude of the Law, but as free children under the liberty of grace." See Hugh of St. Victor, *Explanation of the Rule of St. Augustine*, translated by Dom Aloysius Smith (London: Sands, 1911), 116. The rule originated with Augustine's *Letter 211*, written in AD 423 to the convent of nuns that had been led by his sister and was causing trouble for her successor. Augustine's letter gave the nuns several points of advice and instruction designed to establish a better framework for communal life (Philip Schaff, ed., *A Select Library of Nicene and Post-Nicene Fathers of the Christian Church*, Series 1 [New York: The Christian Literature Series, 1886–89; reprint, Grand Rapids, MI: Eerdmans, 1956], 1:563–68). The earliest mention of the "Rule of Augustine" for a male order of clergy occurs with Lutosdus, dean of Toul, in 1095; see T. Scott Holmes, "The Austin Canons in England in the Twelfth Century," *Journal of Theological Studies* 19 (1904): 343–56 (specifically p. 348).

times in his early years, which perhaps makes his personal struggles for freedom all the more painful for us to read about today.

LUTHER'S STRUGGLE FOR A FREE CONSCIENCE

Luther described his early years in a preface written near the end of his life. In the year before he died, he reflected back on his early struggles:

> Though I lived as a monk without reproach, I felt that I was a sinner before God with an extremely disturbed conscience. I could not believe that he was placated by my satisfaction. I did not love, yes, I hated the righteous God who punishes sinners, and secretly, if not blasphemously, certainly murmuring greatly, I was angry with God, and said, "As if, indeed, it is not enough, that miserable sinners, eternally lost through original sin, are crushed by every kind of calamity by the law of the decalogue, without having God add pain to pain by the gospel and also by the gospel threatening us with his righteousness and wrath!" Thus I raged with a fierce and troubled conscience. Nevertheless, I beat importunately upon Paul at that place, most ardently desiring to know what St. Paul wanted [in Romans 1]. (*Preface to Latin Writings* [1545] LW 34:337)

Along with this memory, students and guests at Luther's home recorded a number of Table Talk statements about Luther's early struggles over God's righteousness based on Romans 1:17.[4] Luther similarly struggled over the meaning of "repentance" and the doctrine of predestination.[5] Many scholars have proposed a variety of dates for these events in Luther's life without settling the timing.[6]

What is certain is that Luther's struggles led him to focus on Holy Scripture like no one else. Things he read in Scripture repelled him with great fear, while at the same time what he read absorbed his thoughts

---

4   Uuras Saarnivaara, *Luther Discovers the Gospel* (St. Louis: Concordia, 2005), 35–38.

5   Saarnivaara, *Luther Discovers the Gospel*, 19–21.

6   For example, Luther biographer Martin Brecht and Saarnivaara believed Luther's evangelical breakthrough took place in 1518 after the start of the indulgence controversy. Franz Posset proposes an earlier time in Luther's life; see his chapter "In the Context of the Late Medieval 'Bernard Renaissance,'" in *The Real Luther: A Friar at Erfurt and Wittenberg* (St. Louis: Concordia, 2011). Given that Luther describes breakthroughs on repentance, predestination, righteousness, and even other topics, it is perhaps best to conclude that Luther experienced numerous breakthroughs even as he also experienced numerous struggles.

and fostered hope for a merciful Father in heaven. Luther's colleague Melanchthon commented on Luther's struggles in his memoirs of Luther's life. He described an example of when Luther faced great stress during a disputation over doctrine.[7]

> **Often, when he thought more intently about the wrath of God or the awesome examples of punishments, great terrors so suddenly overcame him that he almost died. When he was overcome by tension in a certain disputation about doctrine, I myself saw him going into the nearby room to lay down on the bed, where he repeatedly called upon God and mixed the following verse into his prayer: "For God delivered all to disobedience, that he might have mercy upon all" [Rom 11:32].[8]**

This example and Luther's testimony show that the freedom Luther sought was not political, economic, moral, intellectual, or philosophical. It was deeply personal. It is this spiritual longing that distinguishes Luther from so many others who wrote about freedom in that day. He longed for freedom from fear and death at a time when plagues and terrors abounded. But what is more, the church teaching and practice of that time focused sinners not so much upon the mercy of God and the free promise of forgiveness in Jesus Christ as upon their own efforts to afford such peace. In his early years, this was for Luther a living hell. His keen mind so readily recognized and remembered his faults. Although St. Augustine's rule commended life as a free child under grace to friars like Luther, this freedom eluded him even as he prepared for the priesthood in 1507 and professorship in 1512.

In the same preface where Luther explained his early struggles, he also explained how God changed his life through the study of Holy Scripture. He reported the following realization that came to him after intense study:

> **At last, by the mercy of God, meditating day and night, I gave heed to the context of the words [in Romans 1], namely, "In it the righteousness of God is revealed, as it is written, 'He who through faith is righteous shall live.'" There I began to**

---

7   Melanchthon did not name or date the event, but it was certainly after 1518 when Melanchthon arrived at Wittenberg. This example shows that Luther underwent such struggles even after the indulgence controversy was well underway.

8   Franz Posset, *The Real Luther: A Friar at Erfurt and Wittenberg* (St. Louis: Concordia, 2011), 154.

understand that the righteousness of God is that by which the righteous lives by a gift of God, namely by faith. And this is the meaning: the righteousness of God is revealed by the gospel, namely, the passive righteousness with which merciful God justifies us by faith, as it is written, "He who through faith is righteous shall live." Here I felt that I was altogether born again and had entered paradise itself through open gates. There a totally other face of the entire Scripture showed itself to me. Thereupon I ran through the Scriptures from memory. I also found in other terms an analogy, as, the work of God, that is, what God does in us, the power of God, with which he makes us strong, the wisdom of God, with which he makes us wise, the strength of God, the salvation of God, the glory of God. (LW 34:337)

These changes for Luther likely took some years to realize. Yet when he more clearly understood God's grace and righteous power to save, Luther's life was changed. His earlier writings show his growing understanding of Christian freedom.

Early Teaching on Freedom

Luther clearly taught a new understanding of freedom already in his 1515 *Lectures on Romans*. In the following quotation, the words in italic are from St. Paul's letter to the Romans. The other text is from Luther.

> *And having been set free from sin,* so that we do not do what sin demands; you are still not entirely free in all respects, but *you have become slaves,* so that we do the things which are according to faith. (Gloss on Romans 6:18; LW 25:54)

Luther described how God changes our status by granting us freedom from sin so that we may, by faith, become slaves of righteousness. Those who trust in God are not "entirely free" so that they can wallow in sin as they choose but are free to walk in God's ways according to faith. In commenting on Romans 13:1, Luther wrote:

> [Paul] calls the other kind of servitude the very best of all, Galatians 5:13: "Through love be servants of one another." About this kind of love he says that though he was free, yet he made himself the servant of all. This kind of servitude is the highest freedom, for it lacks nothing and receives nothing, but

rather gives and bestows. Thus it is truly the best freedom and one which is the peculiar property of Christians. (*Scholia on Romans* [1515?] LW 25:474)

Luther imagined a day when the message of the churches might change, when the churches would free people from superstitious practices so that they would come to church freely and with a free conscience. Although he also knew that such freedom would have incredible consequences, he still longed to see these changes (LW 25:493).

In a June 23, 1516, letter to Michael Dressel, the prior of the Augustinian order in Neustadt, Luther expressed his hope for a peace that the world could not give. He had realized that such peace did not come by retreating from the world or from our struggles for it. It came through the cross of Jesus Christ:

> You are seeking and craving for peace, but in the wrong order. For you are seeking it as the world gives, not as Christ gives. Know you not that God is "wonderful among His saints," for this reason, that He establishes His peace in the midst of no peace, that is, of all temptations and afflictions. It is said "You shall dwell in the midst of your enemies." The man who possesses peace is not the man whom no one disturbs—that is the peace of the world; he is the man whom all men and all things disturb, but who bears all patiently, and with joy. You are saying with Israel, "Peace, peace," and there is no peace. Learn to say rather with Christ: "The Cross, the Cross," and there is no Cross. For the Cross at once ceases to be the Cross as soon as you have joyfully exclaimed, in the language of the hymn, "Blessed Cross, above all others, One and only noble tree."[9]

How boldly Luther instructed a fellow leader of his order about God's peace and the cross! We see in this passage how confident Christ has made him. Christ provided Luther with a reformation of his character before he set out for reform in the church. The letter shows how Luther was applying what he learned from Scripture about the kind of peace and freedom God gives through the cross of Christ.

---

9   Cited from Henry Wace, *First Principles of the Reformation* (London: John Murray, 1883), xviii. The English has been updated to current usage. See WA Br 1:47.

The Challenge of Public Controversy
(1517–20)

When Luther posted his 1517 *Disputation on the Power and Efficacy of Indulgences*, commonly known as the *Ninety-five Theses*, he challenged popular, late medieval notions about forgiveness, authority, and freedom. Here are just two examples of what he wrote:

> 21. Thus those indulgence preachers are in error who say that a man is absolved from every penalty and saved by papal indulgences.

> 84. Again, [the laity ask] "What is this new piety of God and the pope that for a consideration of money they permit a man who is impious and their enemy to buy out of purgatory the pious soul of a friend of God and do not rather, because of the need of that pious and beloved soul, free it for pure love's sake?" (LW 31:27, 32)

The sale of indulgences brought the issues of freedom to public interest and debate. Luther declared a freedom from the suffering of purgatory through the mercy of God and His love in Christ rather than human efforts to satisfy God. Luther's challenges and questions connected with the concerns of the laity about what the papacy and its representatives taught and did. Printers took Luther's statements and multiplied them until people throughout Europe were drawn into a discussion of indulgences.

To many, Luther looked and sounded like a revolutionary, though it appears that Luther never aspired to such a calling or imagined that his statements would arouse such broad interest. Luther was very interested in churchly reforms, especially for the six friaries that he oversaw as an Augustinian superior and supervisor. However, he thought and acted with spiritual concerns.

In a letter of early November 1517, Luther expressed concern to his friend George Spalatin that the uproar over indulgences might spill over into politics and get their Duke, Frederick, into trouble. Luther did not at all seek this political involvement. Interestingly, in this same letter, Luther signed his name as "Martin Eleutherius" (Greek: "freed man") as an expression of his evangelical outlook. On November 11,

Luther again signed his name this way in a letter to John Lang and added with irony that he was in truth a slave and captive,[10] a statement that anticipated his famous opening paradox in the opening words of *Christian Freedom*. Luther continued to sign his name as "freed man" until the summer of 1518, when he returned to signing simply as Martin Luther.

In the 1519 *Lectures on Galatians*, one finds Luther's continuing reflections after the issue of freedom went public. He warned about those who believe that freedom in Christ means they can do anything (LW 27:325), likely referring to the medieval "free spirits" and those who believed that indulgences gave them freedom to indulge their sinful passions. Luther explained St. Paul's view of freedom:

> "Christ," he says, "has made us free with this freedom." It is a spiritual freedom, one to be preserved in the spirit. . . . It is freedom from the Law, but in a way contrary to what usually takes place among men. For it is human freedom when laws are changed without effecting any change in men, but it is Christian freedom when men are changed without changing the Law. Consequently, the same Law that was formerly hateful to the free will now becomes delightful, since love is poured into our hearts through the Holy Spirit (Romans 5:5). In this freedom, he teaches us, we must stand strongly and steadfastly, because Christ, who fulfills the Law and overcomes sin for us, sends the spirit of love into the hearts of those who believe in Him. This makes them righteous and lovers of the Law, not because of their own works but because it is freely bestowed by Christ. If you move away from this, you are both ungrateful to Christ and proud of yourself, since you want to justify and free yourself from the Law without Christ. (LW 27:325–26)

Luther saw that it was the Gospel that truly changed people, not new laws of social order. The Law remained important and essential as God's means for teaching right and wrong, and for convicting people of their sins. But only the Gospel of Jesus Christ gave genuine spiritual freedom, since Christ fulfilled the Law and granted the Holy Spirit so that those in Christ may love their neighbors joyfully.

When one comes to Luther's treatise on the *Freedom of the Christian* (1520), one finds Luther spelling out the implications of

10   See WA Br 1:118, 122; also LW 48:55.

what he learned about the freedom Christ grants through justification. Luther taught this in a remarkable opening paradox:

> A Christian is the freest lord of all, subject to none.
> A Christian is the most dutiful servant of all, subject to all.

Notice that Luther speaks here about the personal freedom granted in Christ. The idea of personal or individual freedom was important and essential to Luther's God-given insight. Yet it cannot be separated from his Christian faith to create a romantic notion of freedom or a declaration of individual human rights—tunes people love to sing in the modern era. Nor can Luther's statement be used to justify the oppression of one person by another. In Luther's thought, a Christian is both free and slave. To exalt in one aspect of this truth to the neglect of the other is to lose the insight and make it false. God calls us to embrace the full paradox that *in Christ* we are free, yet slaves to one another due to love. Luther did not teach a humanist ideal but *Christian* freedom, rooted in justification by grace through faith.

Reception of Luther's Tract

After publishing his treatise on Christian freedom, Luther witnessed how people abused and exploited this good news of freedom through the Gospel. He saw it take place in his own community and congregation. However, Luther was determined not to become a herdsman for the Wittenberg "swine." He implemented efforts for church discipline and concluded sermons with practical exhortations on right and wrong.

At the beginning of January 1530, frustration with libertine attitudes caught up with Luther. For months, he hardly preached, and then only when no one else was available to fill the pulpit. Some time away from his congregations seems to have helped. Yet after Luther returned to the pulpit, he still recalled these frustrations. For example, while lecturing to future pastors, Luther said:

> When Paul saw that some were opposing his doctrine while others were intent on the freedom of the flesh and became worse because of his doctrine, he comforted himself with this, that he was an apostle of Jesus Christ for the proclamation of faith to the elect of God (2 Timothy 2:10); in the same way we today are doing everything for the sake of the elect, to whom we know our

Courtesy of the Pitts Theology Library, Candler School of Theology, Emory University

Later Ideas of Liberty

By the nineteenth century, Liberty was represented as an armed and helmeted woman triumphing over the yoke of slavery. Nevertheless, she does not represent limitless individual freedom. She sits enthroned upon the motto *"pro aris et focis,"* "for God and country" (literally: "for altars and hearths"). She represents corporate, political freedom.

> doctrine is beneficial. I am so bitterly opposed to the dogs and swine, some of whom persecute our doctrine while others tread our liberty underfoot, that I am not willing to utter a single sound on their behalf in my whole life. I would rather that these swine of ours, together with those dogs, our opponents, still be subjected to the tyranny of the pope than that the holy name of God be blasphemed on their account. (LW 26:306)

The precious message of Christian freedom was readily misunderstood by those whose focus was on the things of this world rather than Christ and the cross.

Supporters of Rome likewise misunderstood Luther. Jerome Aleander, a humanist who assisted Pope Leo, charged that Luther's treatise of freedom followed the teachings of John Wycliffe in rejecting the binding character of the Law. Franciscan satirist Thomas Murner had at first welcomed Luther's reform effort. But in 1520, he attacked Luther for disrupting the social order and church authority. Erasmus, too, saw in Luther's treatises of 1520 a reason to break away from the reform. From then forward, Erasmus would oppose Luther.

Renaissance humanist Ulrich von Hutten reacted strongly to Luther's teaching in a different way. In 1520, Hutten wrote pamphlets against the papacy and even expressed a willingness to start a military conflict to free the Germans from Rome. Luther's colleague Andreas Carlstadt, along with Thomas Müntzer, trod a similar path toward violence. They saw in Luther's treatise a call to arms that ultimately led to tragic destruction of church art (iconoclasm) and the Peasants' War in 1525. Although Luther clearly and carefully stated his doctrine of Christian freedom, those around him still had medieval issues and approaches to freedom ringing in their ears.

In the treatises *Temporal Authority: To What Extent It Should Be Obeyed* (1523; LW 45:75–129) and *Dr. Martin Luther's Warning to His Dear German People* (1531; LW 47:3–55), Luther did teach resistance—ultimately armed resistance if necessary—of tyrannical political authority that suppressed the Gospel or persecuted the faithful. But he did not teach or encourage citizens to revolt. The latter treatise gained new importance after Luther's death when Charles V sought to end the Reformation by force. During a siege in 1550, the Magdeburg Lutheran pastors published *The Magdeburg Confession*, which embodied Luther's teachings on resistance of tyranny and biblical arguments that called on the emperor to recognize that he was persecuting good, law abiding citizens rather than punishing the wicked (cf. Psalm 119:46; Romans 13:3; and Acts 9:4, which appeared on the title page). The Lutherans survived the siege, preparing the way for The Peace of Augsburg (1555) that ensured the survival of the Lutheran churches. The confession of the Magdeburg Lutherans became an influential and foundational document for modern political views on the responsibilities of civic leaders and citizens.[11] For example, David M. Whitford has demonstrated that there is a clear stream of influence from the Magdeburg Lutherans, to English Bishop John Ponet of Winchester, to American political theorist John Adams,[12] though such influence should not be used to "Lutheranize" doctrines of political revolution today.

Getting Freedom Right

In subsequent generations, Puritans and Rationalists have appealed to Luther's treatise to support their own ideals. Marxists and Liberationists have complained that Luther's teachings about Christian freedom held Germany back from genuine social progress. People hear "freedom" and conclude, "Anything goes!" These interpretations require readers today to exercise greater caution as they study this most widely read tract from Luther, which has also been most widely misunderstood. As you read Luther's treatise, take careful account of his message and its context. The introductions that follow will guide you; the citations of Luther's writings and that of his closest colleague, Philip Melanchthon, are also included for your benefit.

---

11 See David Mark Whitford, *Tyranny and Resistance: The Magdeburg Confession and the Lutheran Tradition* (St. Louis: Concordia, 2001). See also Whitford's article, "The Duty to Resist Tyranny: The Magdeburg Confession and the Reframing of Romans 13," in *Caritas et Reformatio* (St. Louis: Concordia, 2002), 89–101; John Witte, *The Reformation of Rights* (Cambridge: Cambridge University Press, 2007), 106–15; Robert Kolb, *Lutheran Ecclesiastical Culture, 1550–1675* (Leiden: E. J. Brill, 2008), 402–403.

12 "John Adams, John Ponet, and a Lutheran Influence on the American Revolution," *Lutheran Quarterly*, vol. XV (2001): 143–57.

An Open Letter to Pope Leo X

MARTIN LUTHER, 1520

An Open Letter to Pope Leo X

But that I may speak further, neither did this ever enter into my heart: that I should attack the Roman Curia or that I should discuss anything that concerns her. For seeing that all remedies for her health were hopeless, I held her in contempt. When the bill of divorce had been given, I said to her, "He that is filthy, let him be filthy still. And he that is unclean, let him be unclean still" [Revelation 22:11]. I devoted myself to the peaceful and quiet study of Holy Scripture, that by this I might be of use to the brethren living about me.

—Martin Luther

Leo X, or Giovanni de' Medici of the infamous Florentine Medicis, served as a cardinal and papal legate before being elected pope when he was thirty-eight years old. Leo was sincerely religious but was such a poor manager of his office that he bankrupted the papacy within a few years. Leo's efforts to satisfy the Roman Curia and to recover financially led him to support the special indulgences that provoked Luther's writing of the Ninety-five Theses in 1517.

REFORMATION CONTEXT

In the year before Luther published his great treatise on *Christian Freedom*, he wrote on spiritual topics such as righteousness, the Sacraments, the

Courtesy of the Richard C. Kessler Reformation Collection, Pitts Theology Library, Candler School of Theology, Emory University

Martin Luther

Two men who captured tidal forces in the Church and society faced each other in 1520. Martin Luther (1483–1546) had little financial or political power, but he used the press to unleash two centuries of frustration about corruption and reform. The devotional treatise, *Christian Freedom*, was a final effort for peace and reconciliation with the papacy.

Courtesy of the Pitts Theology Library, Candler School of Theology, Emory University

Pope Leo X

Leo X (1475–1521) came from the wealthy, powerful Medici family and commanded archbishops and kings. However, Leo spent the Vatican into bankruptcy, while his power failed against Luther's "one little word."

Lord's Prayer, and the passion of Jesus. But by the middle of 1520, Luther's publications revealed a very different focus. He released sharp treatises: *On the Papacy in Rome, To the Christian Nobility of the German Nation,* and *The Babylonian Captivity of the Church.* Luther suddenly pressed for broader reform, appealing to a broader audience.

In this letter to Pope Leo X, Luther explained the agitation he felt in early 1520 as the Ingolstadt theologian John Eck harassed and accused him. The Roman Curia sought to distance Prince Frederick from Luther. Papal nuncio Karl von Miltitz needed to demonstrate that he was making progress on the Luther issue and reengaged politic efforts to isolate Luther from his order and from other supporters. Finally, Leo himself listened to the critics and threatened excommunication in the June 12, 1520, bull *Exsurge Domine* ("Rise Up, O Lord"), which Luther received in October.

Under formal threat of excommunication, Luther heeded the counsel of the Augustinians and Miltitz, who wanted Luther to write a cordial letter explaining that he never intended to attack Leo. They saw the wisdom in distinguishing the pope from his many servants who had poorly represented him. With the letter, Luther wrote a treatise more like those penned in the previous year. He turned away from the issues of authority and from polemical style. This devotional treatise, *Christian Freedom*, was a final effort for peace and reconciliation.

LETTER OF DEDICATION

Luther dedicated this famous treatise to Pope Leo. Such dedications were a common means of showing respect in that day. However, Luther's letter of dedication failed to charm the pope. As one reads the letter, one wonders how earnestly Luther attempted to please Leo, since Luther's arguments amplified Leo's weaknesses. One can see that over three years of controversy, these men had finally worn out their patience for one another.

Luther wrote the treatise in Latin but also prepared a loose translation into German. The differences between the Latin and German editions will be described on page 44. Luther sent the German version of the treatise to Hermann Mühlphordt, mayor of Zwickau, along with a letter of dedication to him.

OUTLINE

I. Reasons for Writing to Leo

II. Warnings against the Roman Curia

III. The Controversy and Three Attempts for Peace

IV. Appeal for Leo to Exercise His Limited Authority

V. Dedication of *Christian Freedom* to Leo

LUTHER'S LETTER TO LEO THE TENTH, SUPREME PONTIFF

JESUS.

To Leo the Tenth, Roman Pontiff, Martin Luther [sends] greetings in Christ Jesus our Lord. Amen.

[REASONS FOR WRITING TO LEO]

In the midst of the monsters[1] of the present time, with whom the affair and controversy surrounding me has now entered its third year, I am compelled from time to time to look also to you and to be mindful of you, most blessed father Leo. Or rather, since you alone are everywhere considered the cause of the controversy surrounding me, I cannot at any time fail to remember you. I have been compelled by your godless flatterers, who rage against me without cause, to appeal from your see to a future council. I remain unafraid of the futile decrees of your predecessors Pius and Julius, who in their foolish tyranny prohibited that very thing. Even so, I have never been so estranged from Your Beatitude that I have not wished, with all my might, all the best to you and your see, and sought them from God in my prayers with diligent groanings to the best of my ability. But as for those who so far have attempted to terrify me with the majesty of your authority and renown, I have begun practically to despise and to triumph over them. One thing I see remaining that I cannot despise—and this was the reason of my writing anew to Your Beatitude—namely, that I understand that I stand accused. People

------
1   Luther refers to his opponents as "monstrous men."

have judged my rashness to have spared not even your person, and have represented it as a great vice.

In fact, [I wish] to state the matter plainly. As far as I am aware, whenever it has been necessary to mention your person, I have said nothing but the best and most splendid things about you. If indeed I had done otherwise, I myself could by no means have approved of it and would have supported wholeheartedly[2] the judgment of those men concerning me. Nothing would have been more pleasing than to recant such rashness and godlessness on my part. I have called you Daniel in Babylon, and every reader knows quite well with what exceptional zeal I defended your well-known innocence against your slanderer Sylvester. Of course, the opinion voiced in so many works of such great men and the repute of your blameless life are too celebrated and revered throughout the world to be capable of being attacked with any stratagem by anyone, even of the greatest renown. I am not such a fool that I would attack someone whom no one fails to praise. On the contrary, it has been and always will be my desire not to attack even those whom public opinion disgraces. For I am not one who delights in the faults of any man, since I myself am conscious enough of my own great beam in my own eye [Matthew 7:3], nor can I be the first to cast a stone at the adulteress [John 8:7].

In general, to be sure, I have sharply attacked godless doctrines. It is not because of the bad morals of my adversaries, but because of their unrighteousness that I have not been slow to bite into them. I am so far from being sorry for [my actions] that I have resolved (despising the judgments of others) to persevere in this intensity of zeal, according to the example of Christ. In His zeal, He calls His adversaries a generation of vipers [Matthew 23:33], blind [Matthew 23:17], hypocrites [Matthew 23:13], sons of the devil [John 8:44]. Paul, too, charges [Elymas] the magician with being a son of the devil, full of all guile and malice [Acts 13:10]; he ridicules certain men as dogs [Philippians 3:2], deceitful [2 Corinthians 11:13], and peddlers [2 Corinthians 2:17]. If you give in to those delicate listeners, nothing will be more biting and intemperate than Paul. What is more biting than the prophets? The ears of our own time doubtlessly have been rendered delicate by the raving multitude of flatterers. As a result, as soon as we notice that people

2   Literally, with every vote, every stone cast to show support or opposition to a given position.

28

disapprove what we say, we cry out that we are being bitten. When we are unable to repel the truth by any other pretense, we flee on the pretext of biting language, impatience, intemperance. What good is salt if it does not bite? What good is the edge of the sword if it does not cut? "Cursed is the man who does the work of the Lord with slackness" [Jeremiah 48:10]. Wherefore, most excellent Leo, I beg of you to allow that by this letter I have been cleared of all charges, and to persuade yourself that I have never thought any evil concerning your person. Furthermore, [I wish to persuade you] that I am such a one as to wish the best things to befall you for eternity, and that I have no dispute with any man concerning morals, but only concerning the Word of truth. In all other things, I will yield to anyone, but I am neither able nor willing to forsake and deny the Word. He who thinks otherwise of me, or has imbibed my words in another sense, does not think rightly, and has not imbibed the truth.

[Warnings against the Roman Curia]

Your see, however, I have of course denounced [the institution] that is called the Roman Curia. Neither you nor any man can deny it to be more corrupt than any Babylon or Sodom. As far as I can tell, it has that kind of deplorable, desperate, and lamentable unrighteousness. I have been filled with indignation that the people of Christ should be deceived under your name and the pretext of the Roman Church, and so I have resisted, and will resist, as long as the spirit of faith lives within me. Not that I am striving after impossibilities, or hoping that any good can be accomplished in that most disorderly Babylon by my work alone, with the fury of so many flatterers standing against me. Rather, [I am hoping] that I recognize myself to be a debtor to my brethren. In their interest, it is necessary for me to consider in what way fewer of them may be ruined, or how they may be less ruined, by the Roman plagues. For nothing else from Rome has flooded the world for many years now—of which you yourself are not ignorant—than the laying waste of goods, of bodies, of souls, and the worst examples of all the worst things. For these things are clearer than light to everyone. From the Roman Church—at one time the most holy church of all—there has been fashioned the most lawless den of thieves, the most shameless brothel of all, a kingdom of sin, death, and hell, so

The pope sits at the head of the Roman hierarchy. However, he is dependent upon his counselors (the Curia, which included cardinals and papal officials) for making decisions and implementing plans for the bishops, abbots, parish priests, and laity.

that not even Antichrist, if he should come, would be able to think of anything to add to its wickedness.

Meanwhile you, Leo, are sitting like a lamb in the midst of wolves, like Daniel in the midst of lions. You dwell with Ezekiel among scorpions.[3] What can you alone do against these monsters? Add to yourself three or four of the most learned and best of the cardinals. What are these among so many? You would all perish by poison before you could undertake to decide on a remedy. The Roman Curia is finished. The wrath of God has come upon her to the uttermost. She hates councils, she dreads being reformed, she cannot calm the fury of her impiety, and she fills up the sentence passed on her mother, of whom it is said, "We treated Babylon, but she is not healed; let us forsake her" [Jeremiah 51:9]. It had been, of course, your duty and that of your cardinals to apply a remedy to these evils. But that gout mocks the physician's hand, and neither chariot nor horse obeys the reins. Touched by these feelings, I have always grieved that you, most excellent Leo, were made pontiff in these times, since you were worthy of better. For the Roman Curia deserves not you and your like, but Satan himself, who in truth reigns in that Babylon more than you do.

Oh, would that you would lay aside that which your most reckless enemies boast to be your glory, and live instead on a private priestly appointment or on your paternal inheritance! In that glory [of Rome] none are worthy to glory except the descendants of Iscariot, the sons of perdition. For what are you accomplishing in your Curia, my dear Leo? Only this: the more criminal and hateful any man is, the more gladly he uses your name and authority for the ruin of people's property and souls, for the multiplication of crimes, for the oppression of faith and truth together with the whole Church of God. Oh, Leo, you who are really most unfortunate, and sitting on a most perilous throne, I tell you the truth because I wish you well. For if Bernard felt compassion for [Pope] Eugenius III when the Roman see (though even then most corrupt) was as yet ruling with better hope than now, why should not we lament? So much further corruption and ruin has been added in three hundred years to the Roman see. Is it not true that there is nothing under the vast heavens more corrupt, more pestilential, more

---

3   Luther separates the person "Leo" from the institution to which Leo is normally very much attached, thus criticizing the papacy while suggesting that he is wishing well the person holding that office.

hateful, than the Roman Curia? For she incomparably surpasses the impiety of the Turks. So, in actuality, she who was once the gate of heaven is now lying open as a sort of mouth of hell. She is such a mouth as cannot be blocked up. Due to the pressing wrath of God, one course alone is left to us pitiable men: to call back and save some few, if we can, from that Roman abyss, as I have called it.

Behold, Leo my father, with what intent, with what cause I have raged against that seat of pestilence. I am far [removed] from having raged against your person. I even hoped that I would win favor and establish your safety, if I were to strike energetically and sharply at that prison of yours, or rather at your hell. For whatever assault contrived by any gifted men that can be mounted against the confusion of this godless Curia will be beneficial to you and to your safety, and to many others with you. They do their duty to you who do harm to her. They glorify Christ who in every way curse her. In short, they are Christians who are not Romans.

[The Controversy and Three Attempts for Peace]

But that I may speak further, neither did this ever enter into my heart: that I should attack the Roman Curia or that I should discuss anything that concerns her. For seeing that all remedies for her health were hopeless, I held her in contempt. When the bill of divorce had been given, I said to her, "He that is filthy, let him be filthy still. And he that is unclean, let him be unclean still" [Revelation 22:11]. I devoted myself to the peaceful and quiet study of Holy Scripture, that by this I might be of use to the brethren living about me. While I was making some advance in these studies, Satan opened his eyes. He incited his servant John Eck, that notorious adversary of Christ, with an uncontrollable lust for fame, so that he might drag me into an unexpected arena.[4] Eck would catch me in one little word concerning the primacy of the Roman Church that had fallen from me in passing. When that happened, that boastful Thraso,[5] foaming and gnashing his teeth, proclaimed that he would dare all things for the glory of God, for the honor of the holy Apostolic see. Being puffed

---

4   The Leipzig Disputation of 1519.
5   Thraso was a braggart soldier in the *Eunuchius* of Terence. Luther shows here his extensive education in the works of classical writers.

up over your power, which he was preparing to abuse, he was expecting nothing with more certainty than victory. He was seeking not so much the primacy of Peter as his own preeminence among the theologians of the present time. For that purpose, he considered it to be of no small significance if he should lead Luther in triumph. But now that this has turned out poorly for the sophist, an incredible rage torments the man. For he feels that whatever discredit to Rome has arisen through me has been caused completely by his own fault.

And so permit me now at last, I pray, most excellent Leo, both to plead my own cause and to accuse your true enemies. I believe that it is known to you in what way the Cardinal of St. Sixtus,[6] your legate, who was imprudent and unfortunate, or rather unfaithful, dealt with me. On account of my reverence for your name, I had placed myself and all that was mine in his hands. Yet he did not act so as to establish peace. He could easily have established that by one little word, since I at that time promised silence. I promised that I would make an end of my case, if he would order my adversaries to do the same. But that man of pride, not content with this agreement, began to justify my adversaries. He granted them license and ordered me to recant, something which he certainly did not have in his orders. It was precisely when the case was in the best position [to be resolved amicably] that it came through that man's savage tyranny into a much worse one. For that reason, whatever has followed after these things is the fault not of Luther, but entirely of Cajetan. He did not suffer me to be silent and remain quiet, for which at that time I was begging with all my might.[7] What more ought I to have done?

Karl von Miltitz followed, himself also a nuncio from Your Beatitude. With much and varied exertion he ran back and forth. He left out nothing that might help toward the restoration of the position of the case, which the rashness and pride of Cajetan had upset. Even with the help of the most illustrious prince, the Elector Frederick, Miltitz had difficulty. At last he worked it out, that once and again he spoke on friendly terms with me, at which time I yielded anew to your name. I was prepared to keep silence, even accepting as judge either

---

6   Thomas Cajetan.
7   By blaming Cajetan, Luther could drive a wedge between Leo and Cajetan, who were already at odds. Cajetan campaigned vigorously for the election of Charles V, to whom Leo was first opposed.

the Archbishop of Trier or the Bishop of Naumburg. When it had thus been done and concluded, while these things were being carried out with good hope, behold, that other and greater enemy of yours, Eck, rushed in with his Leipzig Disputation. This he had undertaken against Dr. Carlstadt. When a new question was taken up concerning the primacy of the pope, he turned his weapons against me when I was not expecting it, and he utterly destroyed this plan for peace. Meanwhile, Karl von Miltitz is waiting, the disputation is held, judges are chosen, and at this point nothing is decided. Nor should one marvel at this. By Eck's lies, pretenses, and devices, everything was everywhere in a state of utmost turmoil, aggravation, and confusion. So, whichever way the sentence might lean, a greater conflagration was sure to arise. For it was glory, not the truth, that he was seeking. Even at this point, I omitted nothing that was necessary for me to do.

IOHANNES ECKIVS THEOLOGVS.

IOhannes Eckius natus eſt 13 Nouemb.anno 1486 in Sueuia ſub ditione epiſcopi Auguſtani. Octo annorum puer Rotenburgi potiſsimum literis imbui cœpit, apud patruum ſuum ſacerdotem non in doctum. Cum uerò à patruo domi,& à magiſtro in ſchola diligēter erudiretur, eò intra trienniȷ ſpaciū peruenit, ut Dialecticā aliqua ex parte deguſtaret, & priuata lectione pulcherrimarum rerum cognitioni inhiaret.iam enim ſuo patruo ſub tempus prā diȷ & cœnæ biblicas hiſtorias, & quædam in Auguſtino, demū & in decretalibus, & in aliȷs nouis ſcriptis,ſelectioribus tamen(quantum eius ſeculi ſalebras ſubterfugere licebat)articulatè legere cogebatur.Vnde quidem conſumpto prius in academia Haidelbergēſi unico ſolùm anno,& Tubingæ menſibus quincȷ,artium baccalaureus dignè creatur,quod accidit anno 1499,prima die Octobris.Mox adiunctis neceſſariȷs ſtudiȷs,præterlapſo alio adhuc anno & trimeſtri tempore,etſi ętate minor eſſet permiſſu tamen profeſſorum,liberalium artium magiſter creatur,anno ætatis 15. Quo gradu ſuſcepto ſtatim Theologiam diſcere cœpit: hoc quidem tempore,etſi natura quodammodo abſtemius eſſet, cœpit bibere uinū: ſed Tubingæ graſſante iā peſte,extorſa prius à patre & patruo pecunia,anno 1501 menſe Octob. Coloniam conceſsit,quod is locus Theologię ſtudio celebraretur:ibi auditis utiliſsimis quibuſdā lectionibus,anno ſequenti, ſpectatis prius Aquiſgranenſibus reliquiȷs,in patriam & Rotenburgum eſt reuerſus. Delectocȷ mox ſibi firmiore loco,Friburgi Theologiæ amplius operam dare,& docendo in philoſophia ſeſe ſuſtentare animo conſtitutum habet. quæ res iam quidem benè cœpta erat,cum ecce ibi quocȷ,ingruente peſte,quiete ei frui non licet,ſed ut aliȷ fecerant magiſtri, Kitzingam ſuas transfert Muſas: non abſtinens interim ab inuiſendis parentibus,quod in uita ſæpiſsime fecit, pręter alias frequentiſſimas peregrinationes,quæ nullo modo omnes annotari potuerunt.

Luther before Cardinal Cajetan and John Eck

Cardinal Cajetan examined Luther's teaching in October 1518 and urged him to recant. Luther instead appealed to the pope and a general council. John Eck persistently attacked Luther, which inhibited peaceful negotiation of the issues.

I confess that on this occasion, not a little of the Roman corruptions came to light. But if there is any sin in this, it is the fault of Eck. He, in taking up a burden beyond his strength while furiously snatching at his own glory, unveiled the disgrace of Rome throughout the world. This man is that enemy of yours, my dear Leo, or rather of your Curia. By the example of this man alone, we can learn that there is no enemy more harmful than a flatterer. For what did he accomplish by his flattery except an evil that no king could have accomplished? For today the name of the Roman Curia is a stench throughout the world, and papal authority languishes. Its remarkable ignorance is in disrepute, none of which we would have heard about if Eck had not disturbed the plans of Karl [Miltitz] and me for peace. This is a fact of which—it is no secret—he too is aware, since he has been angered, too late and in vain, at the publication of my books. He ought to have thought of this back when, like a whinnying stud horse,[8] he was driven completely mad for

---

8   The Latin and German versions both speak of Eck as "a brazen, lustful stallion." In the Middle Ages the Latin term *emissarius* meant an uncastrated male horse sent

glory. He was seeking in your cause nothing but his own objects, and that with the greatest peril to you. That vainest of men was hoping that, from fear of your name, I would yield and keep silence. (I do not think that he was relying on his talents and learning.) Now, he sees that I am too confident and am speaking aloud. So with tardy repentance for his rashness, he has learned that there is One in heaven who resists the proud and humbles the presumptuous, if indeed he has [yet] learned it.

And so, now that we have accomplished nothing by this disputation except the greater confusion of the Roman cause, Karl von Miltitz for the third time approaches the fathers of the [Augustinian] order assembled in their chapter. He seeks their advice for the settlement of the case, which has now come to be most troubled and perilous. Since, by the favor of God, there is no hope of proceeding against me by force, some of the more renowned of their number are sent from this place to me. They beg that I at least show respect to the person of Your Beatitude and show in a humble letter, on the basis of both your innocence and my own, that the affair was not as yet in the utmost position of hopelessness. That is, if Leo the Tenth, for the sake of his innate goodness, would put his hand to it. Thereupon I have always both offered and wished for peace. I not only willingly yielded, but even accepted [their suggestion] with joy and gratitude, as the greatest kindness and benefit, if our hope should prove to be fulfilled. I did this in order that I might attend to calmer and more useful pursuits. It was for this very purpose that I have been stirred up with such spirit. I would restrain, by the strength and passion as much of my words as of my heart, those whom I saw to be very far from equal to myself.

[APPEAL FOR LEO TO EXERCISE HIS LIMITED AUTHORITY]

Thus I come, most blessed Father. Having prostrated myself, I ask, if it can be done, that you apply your hand and fasten a bridle upon those flatterers who are enemies of peace, while they make a show of peace. Furthermore, there is no reason, most blessed Father, for anyone to expect

---

out among the mares for breeding purposes. The thirteenth-century philosopher Ramon Llull, in his *Ars brevis*, relates in detail the story of a soldier whose mule is attacked by such a stud, resulting in the animals brutally fighting until the stallion dies (X.1.5). Such an animal is crazed and out of control.

that I should recant, unless he prefers to involve the case in still greater turmoil. Moreover, I do not tolerate laws for the interpretation of the Word of God. For the Word of God, which teaches liberty in all other things, ought not to be bound. With the exception of these two things, there is nothing that I am not able and most freely willing to do or to tolerate. I hate contentions. I will provoke no one, but I in turn do not wish to be provoked. If I am provoked, with Christ as my Teacher, I will not remain speechless. For Your Beatitude will be able to command silence and peace on both sides by one brief and simple word, when those controversies have been brought before you and snuffed out, something which I have always desired to hear.

Therefore, Leo, my father, beware of listening to those sirens. They make you out to be not simply a man, but partly a god [Acts 12:22], so that you can command and require whatever you wish. It will not happen so, nor will you prevail. You are the servant of servants, and more than any other man, you are in a most pitiable and perilous position. Let not those men deceive you who pretend that you are lord of the world, who allow no one to be a Christian without your authority, who prate that you have some kind of power over heaven, hell, purgatory. These men are your enemies. They are seeking the destruction of your soul. As Isaiah says, "My people, they who call you blessed are themselves deceiving you" [3:12]. Those who raise you above councils and the universal Church are in error. Those who assign to you alone the right of interpreting Scripture are in error. For these men are all seeking to confirm within the Church their own impieties under your name. Unfortunately, Satan has accomplished much through them among your predecessors. In brief, trust none of those who exalt you, but trust those who humble you. For this is the judgment of God: "He has cast down the mighty from their seat and exalted the humble" [Luke 1:52]. See how different Christ was from His successors, although they would all like to be His vicars.[9] And I am afraid that in truth very many of them have been all too seriously His vicars. For a person is the vicar of a prince who is absent. Now if a pontiff rules while Christ is absent

---

9   The Latin term *vicarius* refers to someone who acts in the place and authority of another, to whom the rights and privileges of an office properly belong. Consider the parable of the wicked tenants (Matthew 21:33–44). The son especially is a vicar of the father. The father is absent, thus making the presence of a vicar necessary. Luther argues from this idea that the papal claim to be the vicar of Christ implies the absence of Christ. That is contrary to Scripture (Matthew 28:20).

and does not dwell in his heart, what else is he but a vicar of Christ? And then what is that Church but a multitude without Christ? What indeed is such a vicar but an antichrist and an idol? How much more rightly did the apostles speak, who call themselves servants of a present Christ, not the vicars of an absent one!

Perhaps I am immodest. For I have seemed to teach so great a head, by whom all men ought to be taught, and from whom, as those plagues of yours boast, the thrones of judges receive their sentence. But I am imitating St. Bernard in his book *On Consideration*, addressed to Eugenius III. This book ought to be known by heart to every pontiff. I am not doing this from any desire to teach, but as a duty proceeding from that pure and faithful concern that compels us to be anxious for all that belongs to our neighbors, even if it is secure. That duty does not allow considerations of worthiness or unworthiness to be entertained, being intent only on the dangers and advantages of others. For I know that Your Beatitude is driven and storm-tossed at Rome. In other words, the depths of the sea are pressing upon you with infinite perils from every direction. You are laboring under such a condition of misery that you need even the least help from any of the least of your brothers; I do not seem to myself to be out of line if in the meantime I forget your majesty until I have fulfilled the obligation of love. I do not wish to flatter in so serious and perilous a matter. And if in this you do not see that I am your friend and most subject to you, there is One who sees and judges.

[DEDICATION OF *CHRISTIAN FREEDOM* TO LEO]

Finally, that I may not approach you empty-handed, blessed Father, I bring with me this little treatise. Published under your name, it is a good omen of the establishment of peace and of good hope. By this, you may be able to have a taste of the kinds of pursuits that I would prefer and with which I would be able to be more fruitfully occupied, if it were permitted and I had until now been permitted by your impious flatterers. It is a small affair, if you regard the paper. Unless I am mistaken, it is a summary of the Christian life put together in a small compendium, if you grasp its meaning. Nor do I, pauper that I am, have anything else to present to you, nor do you need anything else than to be enriched by a spiritual gift. And with that I commend myself to your Paternity and Beatitude, which I pray the Lord Jesus may preserve forever. Amen.

Wittenberg on the sixth of September, 1520.

June   1520 *On the Papacy in Rome*
August   1520 *To the Christian Nobility of the German Nation*
c. Sept.   1520 *The Babylonian Captivity of the Church*
Sept.   1520 *Christian Freedom*
Dec.   1520 *Why the Books of the Pope and His Disciples Were Burned*

CHRISTIAN FREEDOM

MARTIN LUTHER, 1520

EDITOR'S INTRODUCTION TO
CHRISTIAN FREEDOM

———•••———

For Christ is God and man. And that person not only has neither sinned, nor dies, nor is damned, but actually cannot sin, die, or be damned. . . . By the wedding ring of faith, [Christ] makes the sins, death, hell of His Bride common to both. In other words, He makes them His own. As far as those things are concerned, He does not conduct Himself otherwise than as if they were His own and He Himself had sinned, toiling, dying, and descending to hell, that He may overcome all things. . . . Thus the believing soul, through the pledge of its faith in Christ, its Bridegroom, becomes free from all sin, secure from death, and safe from hell. It is endowed with the eternal righteousness, life, and salvation of its Bridegroom, Christ.

—Martin Luther

Luther began the treatise on *Christian Freedom* with a paradox, a form of reasoning that is characteristic of his thought. He explained that a Christian is at the same time a free lord (servant to none) and a slave (servant to all). God makes this so in working with mankind's two natures—the inner man and the outer man. This paradox of freedom and slavery is like other parallel ideas Luther would use in his teaching. For example, he taught that a Christian is a saint and a sinner at the same time (Latin: *simul justus et peccator*), a Christian has both passive righteousness and active righteousness, and also that the pairing and distinguishing of Law and Gospel can be used to explain and apply the Scriptures.

Luther presented the body of the treatise in two parts, which expound the paradox. In the first part, Luther explained that Christ sets the inner man[1] free through the Gospel, which includes a multitude of benefits. Christ makes each believer a priest by sharing His priesthood with him. On the other hand, the outer man needs the Holy Spirit to keep him in check, since the Christian is constantly subject to temptation. The treatise illustrates these ideas with numerous examples and arguments, relating the believer's freedom and obedience to the Reformation issues of faith, good works, and the Christian life in communion with Christ and one another. In the last section of the treatise, an "addition" on ceremonies, Luther explained how ceremonies can be beneficial when used in faith.

Latin and German Editions

Luther wrote the treatise for Leo in Latin. This is the longer, official version and the basis of our translation. Including a nine-paragraph "Addition" on ceremonies, the Latin version runs seventy-three paragraphs in the Weimar edition.

In contrast, the more widely disseminated German edition is loosely based on the original treatise, being a translation that Luther prepared himself. The German version omitted the added material on ceremonies and focused on presenting the body of the treatise in freer style. It appears in thirty-six large paragraphs, divided into thirty numbered divisions. It is almost as long as the main parts of the Latin treatise (points I–III in the outline below).

Outline

I. Introduction to the Paradox of Christian Freedom and Bondage
II. First Part: The Inner Man Set Free by Faith in the Gospel
    A. Introduction
    B. First Power or Benefit of Faith
    C. Second Power or Benefit of Faith
    D. Third Power or Benefit of Faith
    E. Christian Priesthood and the Public Ministry of the Word

---

[1] For further explanation of the use of "man" in Luther's treatise, see Appendix A.

III. Second Part: The Outer Man Subject to the Holy Spirit
    A. Introduction
    B. Four Comparisons
    C. Faith and Good Works
    D. Good Works Serve One's Neighbor
    E. Christian Freedom in Society and Church
IV. Addition on the Matter of Ceremonies

A Treatise of Martin Luther on Christian Freedom

[The Paradox of Christian Freedom and Bondage]

Christian faith has appeared to many an easy thing, which not a few even reckon among the social virtues, as it were. They do this because they have not tested it by experience, nor have they ever tasted of what great virtue it is. For it is not possible for anyone to write well about it or understand well what has been rightly written, if that person has not at some time tasted of its spirit with tribulations pressing upon him. But he who has tasted even a little bit of it can never write, speak, think, hear enough about it. For it is a living fountain springing up into eternal life, as Christ calls it in John 4. Now, although I cannot boast of my abundance and I know how short my supply is, I still hope that I have attained some little drop of faith and can speak about it after having been vexed by great and various temptations. I still hope that I can speak—if not more elegantly—then certainly more soundly than those learned[2] and overly precise disputants that have discussed it until now, who have not understood their very own words. And so, in order that I may open an easier way for the unlearned—for it is they alone that I serve—I first lay down these two propositions concerning the liberty and servitude of the spirit:

---

2   Oswald Bayer supports this understanding of the Latin in *Gott als Autor: zu einer poietologischen Theologie* (Tübingen: Mohr Siebeck, 1999), 261.

A Christian is the freest lord of all, subject to none.
A Christian is the most dutiful servant of all, subject to all.

Although these statements appear to contradict each other, nevertheless, when they are found to agree, they will serve our purpose beautifully. For both are the statements of Paul himself, who says in 1 Corinthians 9[:19], "Though I be free, I have made myself the servant of all"; in Romans 13[:8], "Owe no one anything except that you love one another." Now love is by its own nature dutiful and obedient to that which is loved. Thus even Christ, though Lord of all things, was nevertheless made of woman, made under the Law [Galatians 4:4]. He was at the same time free and a servant, at the same time in the form of God and in the form of a servant.

Let us step back a moment and begin more simply than at that starting point. For mankind is composed of a twofold nature, spiritual and bodily. According to the spiritual nature, which they[3] refer to as the soul, he is called the spiritual, inward, new man. According to the bodily nature, which they refer to as the flesh, he is called the fleshly, outward, old man, and concerning this the apostle [says] in 2 Corinthians 4[:16], "Although our man who is on the outside is wasting away, nevertheless the one who is within is being renewed day by day." This contradiction makes opposing things to be said in the Scriptures concerning the same man, since these very two men oppose one another in the same man, as long as the flesh desires against the spirit, and the spirit against the flesh, Galatians 5[:17].

[FIRST PART: THE INNER MAN SET FREE BY FAITH IN THE GOSPEL]

Now the first topic that we are taking up is the inward man, as we prepare to see by what means one becomes righteous, free, and truly a Christian, that is, a spiritual, new, and inward man. And it is certain that absolutely nothing from among outward things—under whatever name they may be reckoned—has any bearing on the production of Christian righteousness or liberty, nor likewise of unrighteousness or servitude. This can be shown by an easy argument. For what can it profit the soul if the body is

---

3   Theologians.

doing well, is free and full of life, eats, drinks, and does as it pleases, when even the most impious servants of all vices abound in these things? Again, what harm to the soul is poor health or captivity or hunger or thirst or any other outward misfortune, when even the most pious of people and the freest in the purity of their conscience are troubled by these things? Neither of these conditions affects either the liberty or the servitude of the soul. Thus it will profit nothing if the body should be adorned with sacred vestments in the manner of priests or dwell in holy places or be occupied with sacred duties or pray, fast, abstain from certain foods, and do whatever work can be done through the body and in the body. There is need of something far different for the righteousness and liberty of the soul. For the things that have been spoken of can be done by any god-less person, and from these efforts nothing but hypocrites result. On the other hand, it will be no harm to the soul if the body should be clothed in secular clothing, dwell in secular places, eat and drink in the common manner, refrain from praying aloud, and omit all the things spoken of above, which can be done by hypocrites.

And so that we may reject everything, the following profit nothing: even speculations, meditations, and whatever can be done through the effort of the soul. There is need of one thing, and of that thing alone, [in order to sustain] life, righteousness, and Christian liberty. That is the most Holy Word of God, the Gospel of Christ, as He says in John 11[:25], "I am the resurrection and the life; he who believes in Me shall not die for eternity," likewise 8[:36], "If the Son makes you free, you shall be free indeed," and Matthew 4[:4], "Man does not live on bread alone, but on every word that proceeds from the mouth of God." Let us therefore consider it certain and firmly established that the soul can do without everything except the Word of God, without which absolutely nothing is any help to it. But when it has the Word, it is rich, lacking nothing. For it is the Word of life, truth, light, peace, righteousness, sal-vation, joy, liberty, wisdom, virtue, grace, glory, and every good thing, and in ways beyond counting. This is why the prophet, throughout the entire collection of octaves [i.e., Psalm 119], and in many other places, sighs for and calls upon the Word of God with so many groanings and words. Again, there is no fiercer blow of the wrath of God than when He sends a famine of hearing His Word, as He calls it in Amos [8:11–12]. In the same way, there is no greater favor from Him than if He should send forth His Word, as Psalm 107[:20] says: "He sent His Word and healed them, and delivered them from their destructions." Nor was Christ sent for any other office than that of the Word. The apostolic order, the order of bishops, and the general order of the clergy has not been called and instituted for anything but the ministry of the Word.[4]

[Faith's First Benefit: Absorbing the Word]

But you will ask, "What is this Word, and in what way should one employ it, since there are so many words of God?" I answer: The apostle, in Romans 1[:1–4], explains what it is, namely, the Gospel of God concerning His Son, who became incarnate, suffered, was raised, and was glorified through the Spirit, the Sanctifier. For to preach Christ is to feed, justify, free, and save the soul, if it believes the preaching. For faith alone is the saving and efficacious[5] use of the Word of God—Romans 10[:9]: "If you confess with your mouth that Jesus is Lord, and believe in your heart that God raised Him from the dead, you shall be saved," and again [v. 4], "Christ is the end of the Law for righteousness to every one who believes." And Romans 1[:17 says], "The righteous shall live by his faith." For the Word of God can be received and honored not by any works, but only by faith. So it is clear that as the soul has need of the Word alone for life and righteousness, so it is justified by faith alone and not by any works. For if it could be justified by any other means, it would have no need of the Word, and consequently neither of faith. But this faith absolutely cannot coexist with works, that is, if you presume to be justified through works at the same time, whatever they are. For this would be to waver between two opinions, to worship Baal and kiss the hand, which is a very great iniquity, as Job [31:27] says. Therefore, when you begin to believe, you learn at the same time that all that is within you is nothing but guilt, sin, and things worthy of damnation. This accords with that [saying] in Romans 3[:23], "All have sinned and are lacking in the glory of God," and Romans 3[:10–12], "There is no righteous man, there is no one who does good, they have all turned aside, they have all become useless at the same time." For when this has been learned, you will know that Christ is necessary for you. He has suffered and risen again for you, so that by believing in Him you might by this faith become another man,

---

4   See also AC V and XIV (*Concordia*, 33, 38–39).
5   "Efficacious" means that the salvation is truly delivered by what the Gospel says.

with all your sins having been remitted and you having been justified by the merits of another, namely, of Christ alone.

Since therefore this faith cannot reign except in the inward man, as Romans 10[:10] says, "With the heart one believes for righteousness," and since it alone justifies, it is evident that the inward man can be justified, become free, and saved by absolutely no outward work or effort. No works whatsoever have anything to do with him. In the same way, on the other hand, it is solely by impiety and unbelief of the heart that he becomes guilty and a slave of sin worthy of damnation, not by any outward sin or work. For this reason, the first concern of any Christian ought to be that, when his esteem for works has been laid aside, he should strengthen his faith alone more and more. He should grow by it in the knowledge, not of works, but of Christ Jesus, who has suffered and risen again for him, as Peter teaches in the last chapter of 1 Peter [5:10]. For no other work makes a Christian. Thus Christ in John 6[:28–29], when the Jews asked Him what they should do that they might perform the works of God, rejected the multitude of works with which He saw that they were swelling. He prescribed for them one thing only, saying, "This is the work of God, that you believe in Him whom He has sent, for this is He whom God the Father has sealed."

Hence a right faith in Christ is an incomparable treasure. It carries with it all salvation and preserving from all evil, as it says in the last chapter of Mark [v. 16], "He who believes and is baptized shall be saved. He who does not believe shall be damned." Isaiah, contemplating this treasure, predicted in 10[:22–23], "The Lord shall make upon the land a word cut short and consuming, and when the cutting short has been completed, it shall overflow with righteousness." This is as if he were saying, "Faith, which is the brief and complete fulfilling of the Law, will fill those who believe with such righteousness that they will have need of no other thing for righteousness." Thus also Paul says in Romans 10[:10], "For with the heart one believes for righteousness."

But you ask: How can it be that faith alone justifies and grants without works a treasury of so many good things, when so many works, ceremonies, and laws are prescribed for us in the Scriptures? I answer: Before all things, be mindful of this, which has already been said, that faith alone without works justifies, frees, and saves. This is something that we shall make clearer below. Meanwhile, one should note that the whole Scripture of God is divided into two parts: commands and promises. The commands, to be sure, teach good things, but the things which have been taught do not happen immediately. For they show what it is necessary for us to do, but do not give the power to do it. Yet they have been ordained for this purpose, that they may show a person to himself, through which he may learn his own powerlessness for good and despair of his own strength. For this reason, they are not only called the Old Testament, but they actually are so. For example, "You shall not covet" [Exodus 20:17] is a precept by which we are all convicted of being sinners, since no one is able not to covet, however he may struggle to the contrary. In order, therefore, that he may not covet and may fulfill the command, he is compelled to despair of himself and to seek elsewhere and through another the help that he has not found in himself. As it says in Hosea [13:9], "Destruction is yours, O Israel; only in Me is your help." Now the same despair that is caused by this one command is caused by all, for they are all equally impossible for us.

Now when [the sinner] has been taught his own powerlessness through the commands, he becomes troubled concerning the means by which he may satisfy the Law. For it is necessary for the Law to be satisfied, so that not a single jot or tittle may pass away—otherwise he will be damned without any hope. Having been truly humbled and brought to nothing in his own eyes, [the sinner] does not find in himself the means by which to be justified and saved. Here the other part of Scripture is at hand—the promises of God. They announce the glory of God and say, "If you wish to fulfill the Law, not to covet, as the Law requires, look ([I say] to you), believe in Christ. In Him are promised to you grace, righteousness, peace, and liberty. If you believe, you shall have all these things. If you do not believe, you shall lack them." For what is impossible for you by all the works of the Law, which are many and yet useless, you shall fulfill by an easy route through faith. For God the Father has put all things in faith. So whoever has this has all things, while he who does not have faith has nothing. For He has locked all people under unbelief, that He might have mercy upon all, Romans 11[:32]. Thus the promises of God give that which the commands require. They fulfill what the Law commands, so that they are all God's alone, both the commands and their fulfillment. He alone commands. He alone also fulfills. Hence the promises of God belong to the New Testament, or rather they are the New Testament.

Now, these promises of God are words that are holy, true, righteous, free, peaceful, and full of all goodness. Therefore, it happens that the soul, which clings to them with a firm faith, is so united to them (or rather is so thoroughly swallowed up by them) that it not only partakes in but is also saturated and intoxicated by every one of their virtues. For if the touch of Christ is used to heal, how much more does this most tender touch in the spirit—or rather this swallowing up of the Word—communicate to the soul all the things that belong to the Word? In this way, therefore, the soul, through faith alone, without works, is justified, sanctified, made true, put at peace, freed, and filled with every good thing by the Word of God. The soul is truly made the daughter of God, as John 1[:12] says, "He gave to them power to become the sons of God, to those who believe in His name."

From all this, it is easy to understand why faith is capable of so much and why no good works—nor even all of them—can compare with it. For no work can cling to the Word of God or be in the soul, but faith alone and the Word reign within it. As the Word is, so also the soul becomes by the Word. [It is clear that] iron exposed to fire glows like fire, on account of its union with the fire. In the same way, it is clear to a Christian that his faith is enough for everything, and that there will be no need of works for him to be justified. And if he has no need of works, neither does he have need of the Law. If he has no need of the Law, he is certainly free from the Law. The saying is true, "The Law has not been laid down for the righteous" [1 Timothy 1:9]. And this is that Christian liberty, our faith, that brings it about—not that we should be lazy or lead a bad life, but that no one should need the Law or works for righteousness and salvation.

[Faith's Second Benefit: Genuine Worship and Obedience]

Let this be the first virtue of faith. Let us also consider a second. For this too is a function of faith, that it honors Him in whom it believes with the most pious and highest esteem of all, namely, that it holds Him to be truthful and trustworthy. For neither is there any honor like that estimation of truth and righteousness with which we honor Him whom we believe. What greater thing can we ascribe to anyone than truth and righteousness and sheer absolute goodness? On the other hand, it is the greatest insult to brand someone with an estimation of falsehood and iniquity, or to hold him suspect, which we do as long as we do not believe him. Thus the soul, as long as it firmly believes God when He promises, holds Him to be true and righteous. It can show to God no more outstanding esteem than this. This is the highest worship of God, to grant to Him truth, righteousness, and whatever ought to be ascribed to one whom we believe. Faith shows itself by this to be prepared for all that He wills. It hallows His name and allows itself to be dealt with as it may be pleasing to God. For when faith clings to His promises, it does not doubt that He is true, just, wise, and will do, arrange, and take care of all things in the best way. And is not such a soul, by this its faith, most obedient to God in all things? What commandment is left, therefore, which has not been abundantly fulfilled by such obedience? What fulfillment is more full than complete obedience? But it is not works, but faith alone that shows this. On the other hand, what rebellion, what impiety, what insult to God is greater than not to believe Him when He promises? For what is this other than either to make God a liar or to doubt that He is true, that is, to attribute truth to oneself, but to God falsehood and vanity? And by this act, does one not deny God and raise up the self as an idol for oneself in the heart? What, therefore, is the advantage of works done in that impiety, even if they should be angelic or apostolic works? Rightly, therefore, God has locked all not in wrath or lust but in unbelief, lest any who pretend that they are fulfilling the Law by chaste and gentle works (as are the political and human virtues) presume that they will be saved. For being caught in the sin of unbelief, they should either seek mercy or be justly damned.

But when God sees that truth is ascribed to Him, and that by the faith of our hearts He is honored with such great honor, of which He Himself is worthy, then in return He Himself honors us. He ascribes also to us truth and righteousness on account of this faith. For faith brings about truth and righteousness by rendering to God what is His. So God in return renders glory to our righteousness. For it is true and righteous for God to be true and righteous, as well as to attribute this to Him and confess it. That is, [we say] that He is true and righteous. Thus 1 Samuel 2[:30 says], "Whoever honors Me, I will glorify him, and those who despise Me shall be of no renown." Thus Paul in Romans 4[:3] says of Abraham that his faith was reckoned as righteousness. For through faith, he most plentifully gave glory to God. And to us, for the same reason, faith will be reckoned as righteousness, if we believe.

[FAITH'S THIRD BENEFIT: UNION WITH CHRIST]

The third incomparable grace of faith is this, that it joins the soul with Christ, as a bride with a bridegroom [Ephesians 5:30–32]. By that mystery, as the apostle teaches, Christ and the soul become one flesh. And if they are one flesh, and if a true marriage is consummated between them, or rather by far the most perfect of all marriages—since human marriages are feeble types of this one great marriage—then it follows that all that belongs to them becomes common to both. [They share] the bad as well as the good so that whatever Christ has, the faithful soul can take to itself and boast of as its own. And whatever is the soul's, Christ claims for Himself. Let us compare those things, and we shall see that they are immeasurably [different]. Christ is full of grace, life, and salvation. The soul is full of sin, death, and damnation. Now, let faith intervene, and it comes about that sin, death, and hell are Christ's, and grace, life, and salvation are the soul's. For it is necessary for Him, if He is a Bridegroom, to accept that which His Bride possesses, and at the same time to impart to His Bride that which is His. For how could He who gives her His own body and His very self not give all that is His? And how could He who receives the body of His wife not receive all that is His Bride's?

Now this affords a most pleasing illustration not only of communion but also of a salutary strife and victory and salvation and redemption. For Christ is God and man. And that person [of Christ] not only has neither sinned, nor dies, nor is damned, but actually cannot sin, die, or be damned. His righteousness, life, and salvation are invincible, eternal, and almighty. By the wedding ring of faith, [Christ] makes the sins, death, and hell of His Bride common to both. In other words, He makes them His own. As far as those things are concerned, He does not conduct Himself otherwise than as if they were His own and He Himself had sinned, toiling, dying, and descending to hell, that He may overcome all things. I say, when such a person [as Christ] does this—and since it is so—sin, death, and hell cannot swallow Him up. They are necessarily swallowed up by Him in a conflict at which we

Parable of the Bridegroom

Christ the Bridegroom enters to find five wise virgins prepared to meet Him (Matthew 25:1–13). This parable of faith anticipates Luther's teaching on the soul's union with Christ.

marvel. For His righteousness is higher than the sins of all men, His life more powerful than all death, His salvation more unconquerable than all hell. Thus the believing soul, through the pledge of its faith in Christ, its Bridegroom, becomes free from all sin, secure from death, and safe from hell. It is endowed with the eternal righteousness, life, and salvation of its Bridegroom, Christ. Thus He presents to Himself a glorious Bride, without spot or wrinkle, cleansing her with a washing in the Word of life, that is, through faith in the Word of life, righteousness, and salvation. Thus He betroths her to Himself in faith, in mercy, in righteousness, and in judgment, as Hosea 2[:19–20] says.

Who, then, can value highly enough these royal nuptials? Who can comprehend the riches of the glory of this grace? Here Christ, this rich and pious Bridegroom, takes as a wife this little poor person, an impious little harlot, redeeming her from all her evils and adorning her with all His goods. For it is now impossible that her sins should destroy her. They have been laid upon Christ and swallowed up in Him. She herself has her righteousness in Christ, her Bridegroom, a righteousness that she may claim as her own and set with confidence against all her sins, in opposition to death and hell, and say, "If I have sinned, still my Christ has not sinned, in whom I believe, whose goods are all mine, and all that is mine is His." As [it says] in the Song of Solomon [2:16], "My beloved is mine, and I am his." This is what Paul says in 1 Corinthians 15[:57]: "Thanks be to God, who has given us the victory through Jesus Christ our Lord," victory, that is, over sin and death. For he begins that passage, "The sting of death is sin, and the power of sin is the Law" [1 Corinthians 15:56].

From all this, you will again understand why so much is ascribed to faith, so that it alone fulfills the Law and justifies without any works. For you see that the First Commandment, where it is said, "You shall worship the one God," is fulfilled by faith alone. For even if you yourself were nothing but good works from the soles of your feet to the crown of your head, you would still not be righteous. Nor would you be worshiping God, nor would you be fulfilling the First Commandment, since God cannot be worshiped unless the glory of truth and of all goodness is ascribed to Him, as it ought in truth to be ascribed. Works do not do this, but only the faith of the heart. It is not by working but by believing that we glorify God and confess Him to be true. On this ground, faith alone is the righteousness of a Christian and the fulfillment of all the commandments. For he who fulfills the first fulfills all the rest by this easy work. But works, since they are insensible things, cannot glorify God. Yet they may, if faith be present, be done to the glory of God. But at present, we are asking not of what sort the works are that are done, but about him who does them, who does the glorifying and produces good works. This is the faith of the heart, the head and substance of all our righteousness. Hence it is a blind and perilous doctrine that teaches that the commandments are fulfilled by works. For before all good works, it is necessary for the commandments to have been fulfilled, and the works follow the fulfillment, as we shall hear.

[CHRISTIAN PRIESTHOOD AND THE PUBLIC MINISTRY OF THE WORD]

But we may view more broadly this grace that that inward man of ours has in Christ. To this end, one should recognize that in the Old Testament

God consecrated to Himself every firstborn male, and the birthright was of great value, being prized above all for the double portion, the priesthood and the kingship [Genesis 49:3; Deuteronomy 21:17].[6] For the firstborn brother was priest and lord of all the rest. By this figure, Christ was foreshadowed, truly and solely the firstborn of God the Father and the Virgin Mary, and truly King and Priest, not according to the flesh and the world. For His kingdom is not of this world [John 18:36]. He reigns over and consecrates heavenly and spiritual things, which are righteousness, truth, wisdom, peace, salvation, and such. Not that all things, even those of earth and hell, are not subject to Him. (Otherwise, how could He defend and save us from them?) But it is not in these, nor of these, that His kingdom consists. Thus neither does His priesthood consist in the outward pomp of vestments and gestures, as was that human priesthood of Aaron and our ecclesiastical priesthood of today. But His kingdom consists in spiritual things, through which, in His invisible office, He intercedes for us before God in heaven. There He offers His very self and does all the things that it are necessary for a priest to do, as Paul describes Him to the Hebrews under the figure of Melchizedek [Hebrews 6–7]. Nor does He only pray and intercede for us, but He also teaches us inwardly in the spirit with the living teachings of His Spirit. These are properly the two offices of a priest, which is figured by fleshly priests with visible prayers and sermons.

Now Christ, by His birthright, has obtained these two portions. He imparts and makes them common property to every one of His faithful under that law of matrimony already spoken of, by which whatever is the bridegroom's is also the bride's. Hence we are all kings and priests in Christ, whoever among us believes in Christ. As 1 Peter 2[:9] says, "You are a chosen race, a people of His possession, a royal priesthood, and a priestly kingdom, that you may tell of the virtues of Him who called you out of darkness into His marvelous light." And these two things stand out. First, regarding that which pertains to the kingship, every Christian is so exalted above all things by faith that he is lord of absolutely all things with spiritual power. This happens in such a way that nothing whatsoever can harm him at all. On the contrary, all things,

---

6   We have added the reference to Deuteronomy 21:17 because it speaks of the "double portion" due the firstborn. Luther interprets the "double portion" not as twice the number of goods as the other children receive, but as the double office of priest and king.

Courtesy of the Richard C. Kessler Reformation Collection, Pitts Theology Library, Candler School of Theology, Emory University

Resurrection Lordship

Christian freedom is based on the historical fact of Jesus' resurrection and lordship. It is tied unbreakably to His exalted body, in which Christians are spiritual members and in whom Christians find their Head and Source. Christians show the humble, obedient Christ now in their life and death. Yet they shall be like Him in the general resurrection and reign forever (1 Corinthians 15:42–58).

being subject to him, are compelled to serve for his salvation. Thus Paul says in Romans 8[:28], "All things work together for the good of the elect," and again in 1 Corinthians 3[:22–23], "All things are yours, whether death or life, or things present or things to come, but you are Christ's." Not that in bodily power anyone among Christians has been appointed over all things to possess and rule them, a madness with which certain ecclesiastics carelessly rave—for this belongs to kings, princes, and men upon the earth.[7] For in the very experience of life, we see that we are subject to all things. We suffer many things, even to the point of death, or rather the more of a Christian anyone is, the more evils, sufferings, and deaths he is subject to. We see this in the firstborn Prince Himself, Christ, and all His holy brethren. This kingship is a spiritual power, which rules in the midst of enemies and is powerful in the midst of oppressions. It is nothing other than strength made perfect in weakness. In all things, I can profit for my salvation, to the point that the cross and death are compelled to serve me and to work together for my salvation. For this is a lofty and splendid dignity and a true and almighty power, a spiritual rule, in which nothing is so good, nothing so bad, as not to work together for my good, if only I believe. And yet I have need of nothing. For faith alone suffices for my salvation. Expect that in salvation, faith may exercise the power and rule of its liberty. Behold, this is the fathomless power and liberty of Christians.

Nor are we only the freest kings over all things, but also priests forever. This is far more excellent than kingship, because through the priesthood, we are worthy to appear before God, to pray for others, and to teach one another in turn the things of God. For these are the duties of priests. They cannot be granted to any unbeliever whatsoever. Christ has thus brought it about for us, if we believe in Him. Just as we are fellow brethren, fellow heirs, and fellow kings, so also we should be fellow priests with Him, daring with confidence, through the spirit of faith, to come into the presence of God and cry, "Abba, Father." We dare to pray for one another and do all the things that we see done and figured in the visible and corporeal office of priests. But whoever does not believe, to him nothing serves or works together for good. He himself is the servant of all things, and all things turn out badly for him, because he impiously uses all things for his own advantage, not

---

7   See also AC XVI (*Concordia*, 39–40).

for the glory of God. And thus he is not a priest, but a secular person. His prayer is turned into sin, nor does he ever appear before God, because God does not hear sinners. Who then can comprehend the loftiness of that Christian dignity, which through its royal power rules over all things, death, life, sin, and so forth? Through its priestly glory, it is capable of all things before God, since God does what He Himself seeks and wishes. As it is written, "He will do the will of those who fear Him, and He will hear their cry and save them" [Psalm 145:19]. It is certainly not by any works that one attains to this glory, but by faith alone.

From this, anyone can clearly see in what way a Christian is free from all things and over all things, such that he needs no works in order to be righteous and saved. Instead, faith alone abundantly bestows all these things. But if he were so foolish as to presume to become righteous, free, saved, and Christian by means of any good work, he would immediately lose faith together with all its benefits. Such foolishness is beautifully represented in the fable about a dog, running along the water and carrying in his mouth a real piece of meat. When he has been deceived by the reflection of the meat that is visible in the water, he loses the real meat together with the image in trying to seize it with his open mouth.

Here you will ask, "If all who are in the Church are priests, by what name are those whom we now call priests to be distinguished from the laity?" I reply: By the use of those terms "priest," "cleric," "spiritual," "ecclesiastic," an injustice has been done. For they have been transferred from the rest of the Christians to those few who are now, by a harmful usage, called churchmen.[8] For Holy Scripture makes no distinction between them, except that those who are now vaunted as popes, bishops, and lords, it calls ministers, servants, stewards. They are to serve the rest in the ministry of the Word for the teaching of the faith of Christ and the liberty of the faithful. For even if it is true that we are all equally priests, nevertheless we cannot, nor should we (if we could) all publicly serve and teach. Thus Paul [says] in 1 Corinthians 4[:1], "Thus let a man consider us as ministers of Christ and stewards of the mysteries of God."

---

8   Luther enhances this criticism in the Smalcald Articles. See also *Concordia*, 264–70.

But that arrangement [of churchmen] has now resulted in such a pompous display of power and such tyranny that no empires, either of the nations or of the world, can be compared to it. It is as if the laity were anything other than Christians. This is a perversity that has caused the knowledge of Christian grace, faith, liberty, and the entire Christ, utterly to perish, with an intolerable captivity of human works and laws taking its place. We have become, according to the Lamentations of Jeremiah [1:11], the slaves of the vilest men on earth, who abuse our misery for all the disgraceful and shameful purposes of their own will.

To return where we began—I think that through these observations, it has become clear that it is not enough, nor Christian, if we preach like those who are now [considered] the best preachers. They preach Christ's works, life, and words in a historical manner as certain accomplishments, which it is enough to know about as an example for the conduct of life. Even more so, we should avoid speaking of Christ at all as these preachers do, [wherein they] teach instead [of Christ] the laws of men and the decrees of the fathers. There are at this time many who preach and read about Christ with the intention of moving the human emotions to sympathy with Christ, to indignation against the Jews, and other childish and womanish absurdities of that kind. But it is necessary that one should preach according to the goal of promoting that faith in Him. [The goal is] that He may be not only Christ, but also Christ for you and for me. [Also] that what is said of Him and what He Himself is called may be worked in us. But this faith is produced and preserved if one preaches why Christ has come, what He has brought and given, and for what use and fruit He is to be received. This is done when the Christian liberty that we have from Christ Himself is rightly taught, as well as the reason why we Christians are all kings and priests, how we are lords of all things, and why we are confident that whatever we do is pleasing and acceptable before God, as I have already said.

For whose heart, upon hearing these things, would not rejoice in all its depths? And when such a great consolation has been received, whose heart would not sweeten into the love of Christ, a love to which it can never attain by any laws or works? Who is there who can do harm to such a heart or frighten it? If the consciousness of sin or the horror of death rushes in, it is prepared to hope in the Lord. [Such a heart] is not terrified by that evil sound or unsettled, as long as it despises its enemies. For it believes that the righteousness of Christ is its own, and that its sin is no longer its own, but Christ's. But it is necessary on account of faith in Christ that all sin be swallowed up from before the face of the righteousness of Christ, as I have said above. And [the heart] learns with the apostle to scoff at death and sin, and to say, "Where, death, is your victory? Where, death, is your sting? But the sting of death is sin, and the strength of sin is the Law. But thanks be to God, who has given us the victory through Jesus Christ our Lord" [1 Corinthians 15:55–57]. For death has been swallowed up in the victory not only of Christ, but ours also, since through faith it becomes ours and in it we, too, conquer.

[SECOND PART: THE OUTER MAN SUBJECT TO THE HOLY SPIRIT]

Let this be said concerning the inward man, concerning his liberty, and concerning the chief righteousness of faith, which has need of neither laws nor good works. They are even harmful to it, if anyone presumes to be justified by them.

Now let us turn to the second part, to the outward man. For here we shall give an answer to all those who take offense at the Word of faith. At what has been said, they say, "If faith does everything and is enough for righteousness on its own, then why are good works commanded? We therefore shall remain idle and do no works, being content with faith." I reply: Not so, godless men, not so. That would really be the case, to be sure, if we were thoroughly and completely inward and spiritual. That will not happen until the last day of the resurrection of the dead. As long as we live in the flesh, we are doing nothing but beginning and making progress in that which shall be completed in the life to come. On account of that, the apostle in Romans 8[:23] calls what we have in this life the firstfruits of the Spirit. For we shall have the tithes and the fullness of the Spirit in the future. To this part relates what has been stated above, that the Christian is the servant of all and subject to all. For in that part in which he is free, he does no works. But in that part in which he is a servant, he does all works. Let us see in what sense this is so.

As I have said, a person inwardly is justified abundantly enough through faith, according to the spirit. He has whatever he ought to have, except that it is necessary that this very faith and wealth increase from day to day until the life to come. Although this is true, nevertheless he remains in this mortal life upon the earth, in which it is necessary that he rule his own body and have dealings with people. Here works finally begin. Here one must not remain idle. Here one must certainly take care of one's body, by fasts, vigils, labors, and other regular disciplines. One must be exercised and subjected to the Spirit, so that the outward man may obey and be conformed to the inward man and faith, nor rebel against it or impede it, as is its nature if the outward man is not restrained. For the inward man is conformed to God and created in the image of God through faith, and rejoices and delights on account of Christ, in whom such great blessings have been conferred upon him. Hence he has only this task before him, that he serve God with joy and freely in unfettered love.

While he is doing this, behold, he comes upon a contrary will in his own flesh, which is striving to serve the world and to seek that which is its own. The spirit of faith cannot and will not bear this contrary will. It undertakes with cheerful zeal to restrain and repress it, as Paul says in Romans 7[:22–23], "I delight in the Law of God according to the inward man. But I see another law in my members fighting against the law of my mind and bringing me into captivity to the law of sin," and elsewhere, "I discipline my body and bring it into subjection, lest perhaps when I have preached to others I myself should be rejected" [1 Corinthians 9:27], and in Galatians 5[:24], "Those who are Christ's have crucified their flesh with its desires."

But it is necessary that these works not be done with the idea that through them anyone can be justified before God—for faith, which alone is righteousness before God, will not bear this false notion. These works should be done only with the idea that the body may be brought into subjection and purified from its evil desires, so that one may have in view only the purging away of desires. For when the soul has been cleansed through faith and made to love God, it wants all things to be cleansed in the same way, especially its own body, so that all things may join with it in loving and praising God. Thus it comes about that a man, because his own body requires it, cannot remain idle. He is compelled by it to do many good works, that he may bring it into subjection. Yet neither are these works the reason he is justified before God. With unfettered love, he does them in obedience to God, attending to nothing other than the divine good pleasure, which he desires to obey most dutifully in all things.

On this principle, each may easily instruct himself in what measure or discretion, as they call it, he ought to discipline his own body. For he will only fast, keep vigil, and labor, as much as he sees to be enough for the suppression of the lustfulness and desire of the body. But those who presume to be justified by works are looking not to the mortification of desires. They look only to the works themselves. They think that, if only they do as many and as great of works as possible, all is well with them, and they are made righteous, sometimes even injuring the brain and destroying nature, or at least rendering it useless. This is enormous folly and ignorance of Christian life and faith, to want to be justified and saved without faith through works.

[Four Examples of Good and Valid Works]

Now in order that the things that we have said may be more easily grasped, let us demonstrate them with illustrations. The works of a Christian, who is justified and saved through his faith out of the pure and free mercy of God, ought to be regarded in no other way than would have been the works of Adam and Eve in paradise and of all their children if they had not sinned. Of them it is said in Genesis 2[:15], "God placed the man whom He had formed in paradise, that he might work and take care of it." But Adam had been created by God righteous and upright and without sin so that he did not have need of being justified and becoming upright through his work and caretaking. But that he might not be idle, the Lord gave him the business of keeping and cultivating paradise. These would indeed have been the freest of works, done for the sake of nothing but the divine good pleasure, not for the obtaining of righteousness. He already had that to the full, which would also have been innate in us all.

It is the same with the works of the individual who believes. Through his faith, he has been newly placed in paradise. Being created anew, he does not need works in order that he may become or remain righteous, but that he may not be idle and that he may exercise and preserve his own body. These works are for him works of the freest sort.

They are done only with a view to the divine good pleasure, except that we are not yet fully created anew in perfect faith and love. These ought to be increased, though not through works, but through themselves.

Another [illustration]: A sacred bishop, when he consecrates a church, confirms children, or performs any other duty of his office, is not consecrated as bishop by these works themselves. On the contrary, unless he had been previously consecrated as bishop, not one of those works would avail anything and they would be foolish and childish and ridiculous. Thus a Christian, having been consecrated by his faith, does good works. But he does not become more sacred or Christian through

Courtesy of the Richard C. Kessler Reformation Collection, Pitts Theology Library, Candler School of Theology, Emory University

Faith, Love, and Then Works

Within "Four Examples of Good and Valid Works," Luther appeals to Christ's teaching about the good tree (Matthew 7:18) as the basis for the Reformation teaching about how faith leads to love and good works, which are the fruit of faith.

these works, since this is [the effect] of faith alone. On the contrary, unless he previously believed and was a Christian, all his works would not help at all and would really be godless and damnable sins.

And so these two sayings are true: "Good works do not make a good man, but a good man does good works. Bad works do not make a bad man, but a bad man does bad works." Thus it is always necessary that the substance itself[9] or the person[10] be good prior to any good works, and that good works follow and come forth from a good person. As even Christ says, "A bad tree does not make good fruits; a good tree does not make bad fruits" [Matthew 7:18]. Now it is clear that the fruits do not bear the tree, nor does the tree grow on the fruits. On the contrary, the trees bear the fruits, and the fruits grow on the trees. As it is necessary that trees exist prior to their fruits, and as the fruits do not make the trees either good or bad—on the contrary, the same sorts of trees make the same sorts of fruits—so it is necessary that the person itself of the man[11] be good or bad first before he does a good or bad work. His works do not make him bad or good, but he himself makes his works either bad or good.

It is possible to see similar cases in all handicrafts. A bad or good house does not make a bad or good builder. But a bad or good builder makes a bad or good house. And in general, no work makes the workman like the work itself is, but the workman makes the work like he himself is. It is the same way with human works: as the individual himself is of a certain kind, whether a person in faith or in unbelief, so also his work is of the same kind, good if done in faith, bad if in unbelief. But the converse is not true, that the work of a certain kind is that which the individual becomes in faith or in unbelief. Since works do not make a person faithful, so neither do they make him righteous. But since faith makes a person faithful and righteous, so also it makes his works good. Since works therefore justify no one, and it is necessary

---

9   A *substance* is the underlying stuff that makes an object. It is not merely the abstract idea of what something is, its *essence*. It is the concrete instance of what something is, usually its essence plus matter.

10   Luther uses the word *person* here in a philosophical sense, a "self-subsisting intelligence" that is attached to a particular substance. Thus, a human person has a human substance consisting of a human body and a natural soul.

11   Here again, this expression refers to the guiding intelligence existing in that individual's body. Yet the person is never separate from the body, as if one could falsely separate human personhood from being human.

that a person be righteous before he does good, it is most evident that it is faith alone which, by the pure mercy of God through Christ in His Word, worthily and sufficiently justifies and saves the person. A Christian needs no work, no Law, for salvation. For through faith he is free from all Law, and in pure liberty does all things freely, whatever he does, seeking nothing either of profit or of salvation, but only the good pleasure of God. For by the grace of God he is already enriched and saved through his faith.

[The Effects of Faith and Good Works on Christians]

So, too, no good work is of any advantage to an unbeliever for righteousness and salvation. On the other hand, no bad work makes him bad or damned. The exception is unbelief, which makes the person and the tree bad, makes his works bad and damned. Wherefore, when anyone is made good or bad, this does not arise from his works, but from his faith or unbelief. As it says in Wisdom [Ecclesiasticus 10:12], "The beginning of sin is to fall away from God," and that means not to believe. And Paul says in Hebrews 11[:6], "It is necessary for him who approaches to believe." And Christ says the same thing: "Either make the tree good, and its fruits good, or else make the tree bad, and its fruits bad" [Matthew 12:33], as if He should say, "He who wishes to have good fruits will begin with the tree and plant a good one." Thus he who wishes to do good works should begin, not by working, but by believing, which makes the person good. For nothing makes the person good except faith, nor bad except unbelief.

This is certainly true, that in the public sphere a person becomes good or bad by his works. But this becoming is the same as showing and recognizing who is good or bad, as Christ says in Matthew 7[:20], "By their fruits you shall recognize them." But all this stops at appearances and externals, a matter in which many are deceived. They presume to write and teach about good works, by which we are supposed to be justified. In the meantime, they do not even mention faith. They walk in their own ways, ever deceived and deceiving, progressing for the worse, blind leaders of the blind. They weary themselves with many works, and yet never attain to true righteousness. St. Paul says of them in 2 Timothy 3[:5, 7], "Having indeed a form of piety, but denying its power, ever learning and never attaining to the knowledge of the truth."

Whoever therefore does not wish to go astray with those blind men, it is necessary that he look beyond works, laws, or doctrines of works. On the contrary, with his attention diverted from works, it is necessary that he consider the person, and how the justified individual may be justified and saved not by works, nor by laws, but by the Word of God—that is, by the promise of His grace. One should do this so that the glory of the divine majesty may be upheld, which has saved us who believe. It does so not by works of righteousness which we have done, but according to His mercy through the Word of His grace.

From this, it is easy to learn on what principle one ought to reject or embrace good works, and by what rule all men's teachings put forth concerning works are to be understood. For if works are joined to righteousness and are done with that perverse leviathan and under the false persuasion that you presume to be justified through them, they then impose necessity upon us. They extinguish liberty along with faith. By this very addition, they are no longer good and are actually damnable. For they are not free, and they blaspheme the grace of God, to which alone belongs the ability to justify and save through faith. That is something that works attempt to accomplish, not with the actual ability to do so, but with godless presumption through this folly of ours. Thus [godless works] violently seize upon the office of grace and its glory. We therefore do not reject good works, but on the contrary we embrace and teach them as much as possible.[12] For it is not on account of the works themselves but on account of this godless addition and the perverse notion of seeking righteousness that we condemn them, by which it happens that they only outwardly appear good. In fact, they are not good, [these] works by which men are deceived and deceive like ravening wolves in sheep's clothing.

Now this leviathan and perverse notion about works is invincible when sincere faith is lacking. For this notion cannot be absent from those saintly doers of works until faith, its destroyer, comes and reigns in the heart. Nature on its own cannot expel this notion. Indeed, it is rather more so that nature cannot even recognize this notion. Instead, nature considers such an idea the most saintly will, since, if custom steps in and strengthens this depravity of nature (as has been done by godless teachers), then the evil is incurable and irreparably seduces

---

12   See also AC VI and XX (*Concordia* 33–34, 41–44).

and destroys countless people. Therefore, even if it is good to preach and write about penitence, confession, and satisfaction, nevertheless, if one should stop there and not go on to the teaching of faith, without doubt those teachings would be deceitful and devilish. For thus Christ, together with His own dear John [the Baptist], not only said, "Do penance," but added the word of faith, saying, "The kingdom of heaven is at hand" [Matthew 3:2; 4:17].

For not only one or the other, but both words of God should be preached. New and old things are to be brought forth from the treasury, the voice of the Law as well as the Word of grace. The voice of the Law should be brought forth that hearers may be terrified and brought to a knowledge of their sins. From this, they will be converted to repentance and a better manner of life. But one must not stop here. For this would be to wound only and not to bind up, to strike and not to heal, to kill and not to make alive, to bring down to hell and not to bring back up, to humble and not to exalt. Therefore also, the Word of grace and of the promise of forgiveness ought to be preached for the teaching and building up of faith. Without the Word of grace, the Law, contrition, repentance, and all other things are done and taught in vain.[13]

Preachers of repentance and grace still remain, to be sure. But they do not explain the Law and the promise of God with such a goal [in mind], and in such a spirit, that it may be possible to learn the source of repentance and grace. For repentance comes forth from the Law of God. But faith or grace comes from the promise of God, as it says in Romans 10[:17], "Faith comes from hearing, and hearing from the Word of Christ." Thus it happens that a person who has been humbled and brought to knowledge of himself by the threats and terror of the divine Law is consoled and raised up through faith in the divine promise. Thus Psalm 29 [30:6 says], "weeping will tarry in the evening and [there is] joy in the morning."

[Good Works Serve One's Neighbor]

Let this be said concerning works in general, and at the same time concerning those that the Christian practices with regard to his own body. Lastly, we will speak also of those works that a Christian does toward his

---

13   C. F. W. Walther also writes extensively on this. See Walther, *Law and Gospel: How to Read and Apply the Bible* (St. Louis: Concordia, 2010).

neighbor. For man does not live for himself alone in that mortal body only to work on its account, but also for all people on earth, or rather he lives only for others and not for himself. For it is to this end that he brings his own body into subjection, that he may be able to serve others more sincerely and freely, as Paul says in Romans 14[:7–8], "No one lives for himself and no one dies for himself. For he who lives lives for the Lord, and he who dies dies for the Lord." Thus it cannot come about that he should be idle in this life and without activity toward his neighbors. For it is necessary that he speak, act, and have dealings with others, just as Christ, made in the likeness of humans, was found in fashion as a man and had dealings with men, as Baruch 3[:38] says.

Nevertheless, a Christian needs none of these things for righteousness and salvation. That is why in all his works, he ought to be informed by this view and look only to this: In whatever he does, he may serve and be of help to others in all things, having nothing before his eyes but the necessity[14] and advantage of his neighbor. For thus the apostle commands, that we work with our hands so that we may give to him who has need. Although he could have said, "that we may support ourselves," he says, "but that he may give to him who has need" [Ephesians 4:28]. For it is also Christian to take care of the body for this very purpose, that by its soundness and well-being we may be enabled to labor, acquire goods, and secure the livelihood of those who are in need. Thus the stronger member may serve the weaker member, and we may be the sons of God, each concerned and active for the other, bearing one another's burdens and thus fulfilling the Law of Christ.[15] Behold, this is truly the Christian life, here faith is truly active through love, that is, when one goes forth with joy and love to the work of the freest servitude. By this, one serves another freely and willingly, and this service is itself abundantly satisfied with the fullness and richness of its own faith.

Thus, when Paul had taught the Philippians how they had been made rich through faith in Christ, in which they had obtained all things, he teaches them further. He says,

---

14   *Necessity* here means "a real need, something more than just a perceived need or desire."
15   Luther's understanding of "fulfilling the Law" here refers to sanctification and the third, teaching use of the Law.

> If there is any consolation of Christ, if there is any comfort of love, if there is any fellowship of the Spirit, fulfill my joy by being like-minded and having the same love, being of one accord, of one mind, nothing through strife or empty boasting, but each in humility deeming the other superior, considering not the things which are his own, but the things which are of others. [Philippians 2:1–4]

Here we clearly see that the life of Christians has been ordered by the apostle according to this rule, that all our works should be directed to the advantage of others. For through faith, each is so abundantly supplied so that all other works and the entirety of life are more than he needs, so that by his works he can serve and benefit his neighbor in spontaneous goodwill.

To this end, he gives Christ as an example, saying:

> Think among yourselves that which was also in Christ Jesus, who, although He was in the form of God, did not deem it robbery to be equal with God, but emptied out His very Self, taking the form of a servant, being made in the likeness of men; and being found in fashion as a man, He became obedient to the point of death. [Philippians 2:5–8]

Of course, they who have completely failed to understand the expressions "form of God," "form of a servant," "fashion," and "likeness of men" have obscured this saying of the apostle, so salutary for us. They have transferred them to the natures of the divinity and the humanity. What Paul intended was that Christ was filled with the form of God. He abounded in all good things, so that He had need of no work or suffering to be righteous and saved—for He had all these things right from the beginning. Although He had all this, nevertheless, He was not puffed up with these things. He did not exalt Himself above us and claim for Himself some kind of power over us, though He might lawfully have done so. On the contrary, His manner of action in laboring, working, suffering, and dying showed that He was like the rest of us. He was nothing other than a man in fashion and conduct, as if He were in need of all things and had none of the forms of God. All of this, nevertheless, He did for our sakes, that He might serve us, and that all the works that He did under this form of a servant might become ours.

Thus a Christian, being filled and complete like Christ, his Head through his faith, ought to be content with this form of God obtained through faith. Yet as I have said, he ought to increase this very faith until it is perfected. For this is his life, righteousness, and salvation, preserving his person itself and making it acceptable, and bestowing all that Christ has, as I have said above, and as Paul affirms in Galatians 2[:20], saying, "Now what I live in the flesh I live by faith in the Son of God." And although he is thus free from all works, nevertheless he ought in return to empty himself of this liberty. He ought to take the form of a servant, be made in the likeness of men, be found in fashion as a man, and serve, help, and in every way deal with his neighbor as he sees that he has been dealt with and is dealt with by God through Christ. This very thing [he should do] freely, and with regard to nothing but the divine pleasure. He should reason thus: "Look at me, an unworthy and damned creature. Apart from all merit and by pure, free mercy, my God has given me in Christ all the riches of righteousness and salvation. So I no longer need anything at all, except faith, which believes that this is so. For such a Father as this, therefore, who has overwhelmed me with these infinite riches of His—why should I not freely, cheerfully, with my whole heart, and with willing eagerness do whatever I know to be pleasing and acceptable before Him? And so I shall give myself as a sort of Christ to my neighbor, as Christ has given Himself to me. I shall intend to do nothing in this life except what I see will be necessary, advantageous, and salutary for my neighbor, since through faith I abound in all good things in Christ."

Behold, in this manner from faith there flows love and joy in the Lord. From love there flows a cheerful, willing, free spirit for the voluntary service of the neighbor, such that it has no basis in gratitude or ingratitude, praise or blame, gain or loss. For neither does it do this that men may be obliged to it, nor does it distinguish between friends and enemies. Nor does it seek to determine who is grateful and who is ungrateful. But most freely and willingly, it spends itself and its goods, whether it wastes them among the ungrateful or is deserved. For thus its Father did also, distributing all things to all men abundantly and freely. He makes His sun to rise upon the good and the bad. So the son does and endures nothing except from the free joy with which he delights through Christ in God, the giver of such great things.

You see, therefore, that, if we recognize the things that have been given to us, great and precious, then, as Paul says [in Romans 5:5], there is soon poured out in our hearts through the Spirit the love by which we are made free, joyful, all-powerful workers. [We are] victors over all tribulations, servants to our neighbors, and yet no less lords of all things. But as for those who do not recognize what has been given to them through Christ, for them Christ has been born in vain. They walk by works. They will never attain to the taste and feeling of those things. Therefore, just as our neighbor experiences necessity and has need of our abundance, so also we experienced necessity before God and were in need of His mercy. That is why, as our heavenly Father has freely helped us in Christ, so also we ought to help our neighbor freely through our body and its works. Each ought to become to the other a sort of Christ, so that we may be Christs to one another. So Christ may be the same in all, that is, [that all may be] truly Christians.

Who, therefore, can comprehend the riches and glory of the Christian life? This life is capable of and has all things and lacks nothing—a lord over sin, death, and hell, and yet at the same time a servant both obedient and useful to all. Unfortunately, this life is today unknown throughout the world. It is neither preached nor sought after, to the point that we ourselves are completely ignorant about our own name. That is, [we are ignorant about] why we are and are called Christians. We are certainly called Christians because of Christ. He is not absent, but dwells among us, that is, as long as we believe in Him and are reciprocally and mutually each the Christ of the other, doing to our neighbors as Christ does to us. But now, with the doctrines of men, we are taught to seek after nothing but merits, rewards, and those things that are ours. So we have made of Christ nothing but a taskmaster far more severe than Moses.

The Blessed Virgin, beyond all others, also afforded an example of the same faith. As it is written in Luke 2[:22–24], she was purified according to the Law of Moses, in keeping with the custom of all women. Although she was not bound by such a law, nor was there need for her to be purified, yet she submitted herself to the law voluntarily and in unbound love. She became like the rest of women, lest she offend them or show them contempt. She was not, therefore, justified by this work, but having been justified, she did it freely and without coercion. So also ought our works to be done. [We do not act] for the sake of being justified, since, having been justified already by faith, we ought to do all things freely and cheerfully for others.

St. Paul, too, circumcised his disciple Timothy [Acts 16:3]. This was not because he needed circumcision for righteousness, but that he might not offend or show contempt for those Jews, weak in faith, who had not yet been able to grasp the liberty of faith. But on the other hand, when [the Judaizers] despised the liberty of faith and were insisting that circumcision was necessary for righteousness, Paul resisted and did not permit Titus to be circumcised, Galatians 2[:3]. Paul wanted not to offend or show contempt for anyone's weakness in faith, so he yielded for a time to their will. [With the same concern for faith], on the other hand, Paul did not want the liberty of faith to be offended or held in contempt by hardened judges.[16] He took a middle way, bearing with the weak for a time and resisting the hardened at all times, that he might convert all to the liberty of faith. We also should act with the same zeal. Then we may care for the weak in faith (as Romans 14:[1–15:7] teaches), yet we boldly resist the hardened teachers of works, of whom we shall speak at greater length below.

Even Christ, in Matthew 17[:24–27], when the two-drachma [tax] was sought from His disciples, discussed with St. Peter whether the sons of a king were not free from taxes. Peter agreed to this, yet Christ commanded that he go to the sea, saying, "Lest we offend them, go and take up the fish that first comes up, and when its mouth has been opened, you will find a two-drachma piece;[17] take it and give it for Me and for you." This example is beautifully suited to what has been set forth, for in it Christ calls Himself and His free men the sons of a King. They are in need of nothing. Yet Christ willingly submits Himself and pays the tax. To the same extent that this work was necessary or useful to Christ for righteousness or salvation, so much do all His other works

---

16   Literally, "justiciars," men appointed in the Middle Ages to discharge laws in the place of the ruler. Luther's emphasis is not on these men's attempt to prove themselves righteous by their works but on their audacity and presumption in passing judgment on others.

17   Both the Greek and Latin Bible texts have the word *stater*. In New Testament times, the *didrachma* (two-drachma coin), minted by the successors of Alexander the Great, was the standard currency in the Middle East. Its value equaled about two days' wages. Although staters were distinct from the didrachma, the general term *stater* often applied to both types of coin. Some Bible versions translate *stater* as *shekel*. Luther translates it in his Bible with *Zweigroschenstück*, a two-dime piece.

or those of His [disciples] benefit for righteousness. For they all come subsequently to righteousness and are free, done only in obedience to others and as an example for them.

[CHRISTIAN FREEDOM IN SOCIETY AND CHURCH]

Such are the things that Paul also taught in Romans 13[:1–7] and Titus 3[:1], that they should be subject to the authorities and prepared for every good work. Not that they might be justified through this (since they were already righteous by faith) but that in liberty of spirit they might serve others and the authorities, and obey their will out of selfless love. Such, too, ought to have been the works of all colleges, monasteries, and priests, that each should do the works of his own profession and station for this purpose alone. They should not do such works that through them they might be justified, but that they may practice the subjection of their own bodies as an example to others, who themselves also have need of the disciplining of their bodies. They should also do such works that they may merely be obedient to the will of others out of selfless love. They should observe at all times and with the utmost care lest vain confidence believe that anyone is justified, earns merit, or is saved through [the works] themselves. That is [the office] of faith alone, as I have so often said.

If anyone, therefore, has this knowledge, he can easily conduct himself without danger among those innumerable commands and precepts of the Pope, bishops, monasteries, churches, princes, and magistrates. Some foolish pastors urge [the precepts] as if they were necessary for righteousness and salvation, calling them precepts of the Church, although nothing is further from the truth. For the Christian, who is free, will say, "I will fast. I will pray. I will do this or that which has been commanded by men. This is not because I have need of that for righteousness or salvation, but that I may oblige the Pope, the bishop, the community, this or that magistrate, or my neighbor as an example. I will do and suffer all things, just as Christ did and suffered much more for me. He Himself had need of none of these things at all. He was made to be under the Law for my sake, although He was not under the Law." And however much tyrants may do violence or injustice in requiring this, still it will not hurt, as long as it is not done against God.

From all this, each will be able to attain a sure judgment and faithful discrimination between all works and laws, and to know who are blind, foolish pastors, and who are true and good ones. For whatever work is not directed to this alone, that it be done either for the disciplining of the body or for the service of the neighbor—provided he require nothing contrary to God—is neither good nor Christian. For this reason, I am terribly afraid that few or no colleges, monasteries, altars, or ecclesiastical offices today are Christian. This is true of both fasts and special prayers to certain saints. I am afraid, I say, that in all these, nothing is being sought except that which is our [own interest], as long as we fancy that through these things our sins are purged away and salvation is found. Thus, Christian liberty is utterly snuffed out, which happens because of ignorance of Christian faith and liberty.

Very many pastors, and these the blindest of all, diligently promote this ignorance and suppression of liberty whenever they stir up and urge the people to zeal for these things by praising them and puffing them up with their indulgences. But they never teach faith. Now I would advise you, if you have any wish to pray, to fast, or to establish foundations in churches (as they call it), that you take care not to do so with the goal that you may gain some advantage, either temporal or eternal. For you will do an injustice to your faith. Faith alone bestows all things upon you. That is why it alone is to be attended to, that it may increase either by works or by sufferings. But what you give, give freely and selflessly, that others may prosper and be well off from you and your goodness. For thus you will be truly good and Christian. For what to you are those good works of yours? They are no more than you need for the disciplining of the body. For you have enough for yourself through your faith, in which God has given you all things.

Behold, by that rule, it is required that the good things, which we have from God, should flow from one to another and become common to all. Then each one may become his neighbor and so behave toward him as if he himself were in his place. The [good things] flowed and do flow from Christ to us, who has so put us on and acted for us as if He Himself were what we are. From us, they flow to those who have need of them, so that it is necessary for my faith and righteousness to be laid down before God as a covering and intercession for the sins of my neighbor. I take [them] upon myself, and so labor and serve in them as if they were my own. For so Christ has done for us. For this is true love and the genuine rule of the Christian life. But it is only true and genuine where faith is true and genuine. Hence the apostle in 1 Corinthians 13[:5] attributes to love that it does not seek the things that are its own.

And so we conclude that a Christian does not live in himself, but in Christ and in his neighbor, or else he is not a Christian: in Christ through faith, in his neighbor through love. Through faith, he is caught up above himself into God. Through love, he sinks back down below himself into his neighbor, though always remaining in God and His love, as Christ says in John 1[:51], "Amen, I say to you, from now on you will see heaven opened and the angels of God ascending and descending upon the Son of Man."

And this is enough concerning liberty, which, as you see, is spiritual and true, making our hearts free from all sins, laws, and commandments. As Paul says in 1 Timothy 1[:9], "The Law has not been laid down for the righteous man," who is above all other external liberties, as far as heaven is above earth. May Christ make us to understand and preserve it. Amen.

[AN ADDITION: THE MATTER OF CEREMONIES]

Finally, for the sake of those to whom nothing can be said so well that they will not distort it by poorly understanding it, something must be added—if indeed they can understand even that. There are very many who, when they hear of this liberty of faith, immediately turn it into an occasion for the flesh. They think that everything is now permitted to them. They do not want to show themselves free and Christian in any other way than by their contempt and rebuking of ceremonies, traditions, and human laws. They do this as if they were Christians merely because they do not fast on the established days. Or they devour meat while others are fasting. Or they omit the customary prayers, scoffing at the precepts of men with upturned nose, while they utterly neglect everything else that pertains to the Christian religion. On the other hand, those who strive to be saved by the mere observance of and reverence for ceremonies most stubbornly resist this first group of men. The latter act as if indeed they were saved because they fast on the established days or abstain from meat or pray certain prayers. They show off the precepts of the Church and of the Fathers, and do not care one bit about those things that belong to our genuine faith. Both are plainly at fault, because while matters that are weightier and necessary for salvation are being neglected, they fight with an enormous uproar over matters that are of little weight and not necessary.

[THE APOSTLE PAUL TEACHES A MIDDLE COURSE]

How much more rightly does the apostle Paul teach us to take the middle way. He condemns both sides, saying, "Let him who eats not despise him who does not eat, and let him who does not eat not judge him who eats" [Romans 14:3]. You see here that those who omit ceremonies and censure them out of mere contempt instead of piety are rebuked when the apostle teaches us not to despise, since knowledge puffs up. On the other hand, he teaches the stubborn that they should not judge the others. Neither side observes toward the other the love that edifies. Hence, Scripture must be listened to on this point, which teaches that we should turn aside neither to the right nor to the left. [We should] follow the righteous judgments of the Lord, which gladden our hearts. For just as no one is righteous merely because he serves and is devoted to works and ceremonial rites, so neither will he be accounted righteous merely because he omits and despises them.

For it is not from works that we are free through faith in Christ, but from opinions concerning works. That is, we are free from the foolish presumption of seeking justification through works. For faith redeems our consciences, makes them upright, and preserves them, since by it we recognize that righteousness is not in works. Yet good works neither can nor ought to be absent, just as we cannot exist without food and drink and every work of this mortal body. Yet our righteousness is not found in them, but in faith. Still, works are not on that account to be despised or omitted. Thus in this world, we are compelled by the needs of this bodily life, but we are not righteous because of this. "My kingdom is not from here or of this world" [John 18:36], says Christ, but He did not say, "My kingdom is not here or in this world." Paul, too, [says,] "Though we walk in the flesh, still we do not do battle according to the flesh" [2 Corinthians 10:3], and in Galatians 2[:20], "What I live in the flesh I live by faith in the Son of God." Thus, the necessities of this life and the concern of ruling our bodies brings about what we do, how we live, and who we are in works and ceremonies, yet we are not righteous by these things, but by faith in the Son of God.

The Apostle Paul

The Letters of Paul were key to the Reformation insights about the relationship between faith and good works. Paul's letters are distinguished in the New Testament for their careful and extensive explanation of doctrine.

The Christian must therefore take the middle way and set before himself these two kinds of men. For he will either meet the stubborn, hardened ceremonialists, or he is met by the simple, the dull-witted, the ignorant, and the weak in faith. The ceremonialists are like deaf adders. They refuse to listen to the truth of liberty. They vaunt, enjoin, and urge their ceremonies, as if they could justify without faith. They are as the Jews of old, who refused to understand, that they might act well. It is necessary to resist these people—to do the opposite, and to offend them boldly—lest by that godless notion they deceive many along with themselves. Before the eyes of these people, it is appropriate to devour meat, to break fasts, and to do on behalf of the liberty of faith other things that they hold to be the greatest sins. And it should be said of these ceremonialists, "Let them alone, they are blind and leaders of the blind" [Matthew 15:14]. For in this way, Paul also would not have Titus circumcised, though they were urging it [Galatians 2:3]. And Christ defended the apostles, because they were plucking heads of grain on the Sabbath [Matthew 12:1–8], and many similar instances. The simple and weak in faith, as the apostle calls them, are not yet able to grasp that liberty of faith, even if they wanted to. One must spare these people, lest they be offended. One must bear with their weakness until they are more fully instructed. For since these people do not act or think thus from hardened malice, but only from weakness of faith, to avoid offending them one must observe fasts and other things that they consider necessary. For this is what love requires, which injures no one but serves everyone. For it is not their own fault that they are weak; [it is the fault] of their pastors. They, by the snares and weapons of their own traditions, have led the weak into captivity and cruelly beat them, when the weak ought to have been freed and healed by the teaching of faith and liberty. Thus the apostle says in Romans 14[:15], "If my food offends my brother, I will not eat meat forever" [1 Corinthians 8:13]. And again, "I know that through Christ nothing is unclean except to him who considers it to be unclean, but it is evil for the man who eats it with offense" [Romans 14:14].

Therefore, one should boldly resist those teachers of traditions and the laws of the pontiffs, by which [such teachers] prey upon the people of God. They are to be sharply rebuked. Yet one must spare the timid crowd, which those godless tyrants hold captive with their laws, until

Source: *Dr. Martin Luther's Sämmtliche Schriften* (St. Louis: Concordia, 1898), 14:208–09

Recognize the Tyranny

"Therefore, one should boldly resist those teachers of traditions and the laws of the pontiffs, by which [such teachers] prey upon the people of God. They are to be sharply rebuked. Yet one must spare the timid crowd, which those godless tyrants hold captive with their laws, until they are set free. So fight strenuously against the wolves—but on behalf of the sheep, not against the sheep at the same time. This you will do [well] if you protest against the laws and lawgivers, and yet at the same time observe them together with the weak (lest they be offended) until they themselves also recognize the tyranny and understand their own liberty."

they are set free. So fight strenuously against the wolves—but on behalf of the sheep, not against the sheep at the same time. This you will do [well] if you protest against the laws and lawgivers, and yet at the same time observe them together with the weak (lest they be offended) until they themselves also recognize the tyranny and understand their own liberty. But if you wish to use your liberty, do it in secret. As Paul says in Romans 14[:22], "As for you, keep the faith that you have by yourself before God." But take care not to use [this liberty] in the presence of the weak. On the other hand, in the presence of tyrants and the stubborn, use it all the more constantly in spite of all of them, that they too may understand that they are godless and that their laws are nothing when it comes to righteousness, indeed, that they had no right to establish them.

[WE CANNOT LIVE WITHOUT CEREMONIES AND WORKS]

This life cannot be conducted without ceremonies and works. For the hot-blooded and those in the young age of adolescence have need of being restrained and guarded by these chains. Each one must discipline his own body by these efforts. Thus, it is necessary that the minister of Christ be prudent and faithful in ruling and teaching the people of Christ. [He must act] in such a manner regarding all these topics that their conscience and faith may not be offended, and no notion or root of bitterness may spring up among them, and so many be defiled. Paul warned the Hebrews [in 12:15] about this defilement that happens when faith is lost, that they may not begin to be corrupted by a notion about works, as if they were to be justified through them. This happens easily. It defiles very many unless faith is constantly taught at the same time, though this cannot be avoided when faith is silenced and only the ordinances of men are taught. This has been done until now by the pestilential, godless, soul-murdering tra-ditions of our pontiffs and opinions of our theologians, with countless souls having been drawn down to hell by these snares, so that you can recognize Antichrist.

In brief, like poverty amid riches, honesty amid occupations, humility amid honors, abstinence amid banquets, chastity amid plea-sures, so also the righteousness of faith amid ceremonies is imper-iled. "Can anyone," says Solomon [in Proverbs 6:27], "carry fire in his bosom, and his clothes not be burned?" It is necessary to live amid riches, amid occupations, amid honors, amid pleasures, amid sumptuous meals, so also amid ceremonies, that is, amid perils. Similarly, infant boys have the greatest need of being cherished in the bosom and by the care of girls, lest they perish. Yet when they are grown, it is a danger to their salvation for these boys to live among girls. Likewise, it is necessary for men who are young and at the hot-blooded time of life to be restrained and disciplined even by the iron bars of ceremonies, lest their powerless minds rush headlong into vice. Yet it would be death to them if they were to persist in the notion of justification by these things. They should rather be taught that they have not indeed been thus imprisoned so that through this they might be righteous or deserving of much. [They are restrained] in order that they might not do wicked things and might be more easily instructed in the righteousness of faith. Because of the passion of their time of life, they could not handle such [freedom] unless it were repressed.

Hence ceremonies in the Christian life are not to be viewed in any other way than builders and workmen view those temporary structures that are set in place for building or working [on the real job]. Such provisions are not furnished so that they may actually be anything or endure, but because without them nothing could be built or done. For when the structure is completed, the temporary provisions are laid aside. Here you see that the things themselves are not to be despised, but are especially to be sought, though we do despise a [falsely high] esteem for them. No one thinks that they constitute a real and permanent structure. But what if anyone were so clearly out of his senses that he cared about nothing in his entire life other than setting up these temporary preparations as extravagantly, diligently, and persistently as possible, but never thought about the structure itself? [He would be] pleased with himself and show off his work on those useless preparations and props. Would not everyone pity his madness and think that, with that wasted expense, something great could have been built? Thus, too, we do not despise works and ceremonies. On the contrary, we especially seek them. But we despise a [false] esteem for works, lest one consider them to constitute true righteousness, as do those hypocrites who direct and waste their entire life in these efforts, and yet never attain to that for the sake of which they are done. As the apostle says

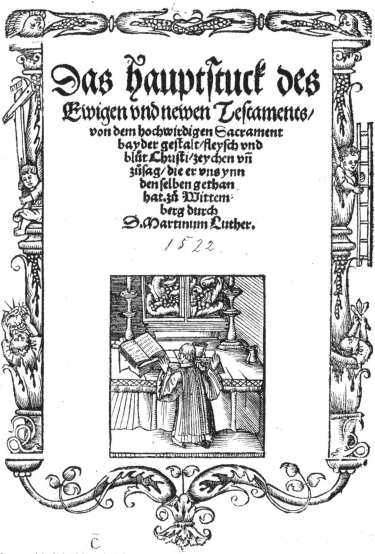

Das hauptſtuck des
Ewigen vnd newen Teſtaments/
von dem hochwirdigen Sacrament
bayder geſtalt/fleyſch vnd
blůt Chriſti/zeychen vñ
zůſag/die er vns ynn
den ſelben gethan
hat.zů Wittem-
berg durch
D.Martinum Luther.

1522.

Useful Ceremonies and Works

On the 1522 title page of Luther's *The Chief Part of the Eternal and New Testament*, a Lutheran pastor extends his hands in prayer and consecration of the Eucharistic elements. The Lutheran Reformation conserved many traditional services and ceremonies.

[in 2 Timothy 3:7], "Always learning and never attaining to the knowledge of the truth." For they seem to want to build. They make preparations. And yet they never do build. Thus they continue in a show of piety and do not attain to its power. Nevertheless, in the meantime, they are pleased with themselves for these efforts, even daring to judge all others whom they see do not shine with such a pompous display of works. Although, if they had been filled with faith, they could have done great things for their own and others' salvation with that useless expense and abuse of the gifts of God.

[THE NEED TO PRAY]

Human nature, or natural reason, as they call it, is naturally superstitious. When any laws or works are set forth, it is inclined to the notion that justification is to be attained through them. Not to mention that this reason is also exercised and confirmed in the same view by the practice of all earthly lawgivers. It is impossible, therefore, that this reason should withdraw itself on its own from that work-obsessed servitude into recognition of the liberty of faith. And so there is need for prayer, that the Lord may lead us and make us *theodidacts*, that is, "readily taught by God." May God Himself, as He has promised, write His Law in our hearts. Otherwise, we are finished. For unless He Himself should teach us inwardly this wisdom hidden in a mystery, nature can do nothing but condemn it and judge it to be heretical. For nature is offended by it. Such a mystery seems folly to nature, just as we see happened of old in the case of the prophets and apostles. Even now, godless and blind pontiffs, together with their flatterers, behave in the same manner of rejection regarding my case and of those who are like me. May God at length have mercy upon them and us. May He shine His countenance upon us [Leviticus 6:25], that we may know His way upon the earth, His salvation among all the nations, He who is blessed forever. Amen.

LUTHER ON FREEDOM

———◆•◆———

SELECTIONS FROM LUTHER'S COMMENTARIES ON THE HOLY SCRIPTURES

INTRODUCTION

Since persons during the Reformation and even today have misunderstood or misapplied Luther's teaching on freedom, we believe readers may benefit from reading more of Luther's insights devotionally and from learning more about the context of his teaching. The following pages provide a series of readings from Luther's lectures and sermons on the Bible, which illustrate and amplify the ideas he presented in *Christian Freedom*. The selections range from the beginning of the Reformation to Luther's mature years as a churchman, pastor, and professor.

In the following selections from the American edition of Luther's Works, the footnotes of a more technical nature have been removed for the sake of readability. Some cross-references have been modified or removed.

LECTURES ON GALATIANS
FROM 1519

———•◦•———

EDITOR'S INTRODUCTION

In the year before Luther published *Christian Freedom*, his pamphlets on various topics flooded the book markets of Europe. In 1519, Luther's pamphlets in print numbered in the tens of thousands of copies. Printers and distributors could not release them fast enough, as the Swiss publisher John Froben explained to Luther in a letter that year. In England, church authorities wished to keep the pamphlets out of people's hands but found the task impossible. For example, when Bishop Tunstall learned that he could not stop the flow of pamphlets, he granted Thomas More the freedom to read Lutheran publications and attempt to refute them.

At this time, Luther determined to prepare an edition of his 1516–17 lectures on Galatians for publication. The notes would require considerable work. He had delivered his lectures in about six months, through the midst of winter, while concerned that the outbreaks of plague in the region would prevent him from completing them. But the following spring found that his completed lectures provided a verse-by-verse commentary on the sacred letter. After Luther's hearing before Cardinal Cajetan in October 1518, he was ready to prepare a more thorough statement of his views. In March 1519, he set out to revise the Galatians lectures; he completed his revision in fall of 1519. Freedom is an important theme in Paul's Epistle to the Galatians and, as the following selections show, it received careful attention in Luther's publication. Luther's review of Galatians was an important step toward writing the pamphlet *Christian Freedom.*

LUTHER'S COMMENTS ON GALATIANS 2:3–5

Note: In this portion of Galatians, Paul describes the Judaizers' insistence that the Gentiles must be circumcised and keep the Law of Moses. Luther comments on Paul's exasperation with the Judaizers' lack of understanding about the salvation Christ Jesus accomplished for all people.

The Gospel and the doctrine of justification provide us with the freedom to choose among matters that God neither commands nor forbids. Luther shows here the meaning of *adiaphora*, neutral acts or institutions that may themselves be of benefit according to the Law, yet, if made compulsory, would infringe upon the Gospel by directing people to works instead of to Christ. The translation is from LW 27:202–4.

The statement [from Paul] "to these we did not yield submission even for a moment" could also have been expressed more dearly, namely, "to whom we did not yield for a time [so Jerome has it][1] into subjection" or "that we might be subjected." This means: "We stood so firmly for evangelical freedom that they were unable to get even this from us that we yielded for a time and only for this occasion. As though we would later revert, after the purpose of the followers of the Law had been accomplished with this concession, since we are accustomed to do so many things with a view of time, place, and persons—things we are later free to disregard. But let this be done in those matters where divine truth and evangelical freedom do not come into danger. Where these are at stake, time, place, and person should not be considered." So much for points of grammar.

Otherwise the whole essence of this controversy has to do with the necessity or freedom of works of the Law, not with what works of

---

1   Jerome, *Commentarius*, 359.

the Law are. . . . For when Christ came, He did away with the works of the Law in this way that they can be looked upon as immaterial but no longer binding—as Paul will show later (Gal. 4:1 ff.) with the beautiful example of the heir who is a child. Therefore the other apostles, together with the Jews who were believers, did them. Paul and Barnabas, however, sometimes did them, and sometimes they did not do them—in order to show that these deeds were simply adiaphora and were in accord with the nature of the person who did them, as Paul says in 1 Cor. 9:20–21: "To the Jews I became as a Jew, in order to win Jews; to those under the Law I became as one under the Law, though not being myself under the Law. To those outside the Law I became as one outside the Law." How could he have unfolded the freedom of the Gospel more clearly? "I came," he says, "to preach Christ to the Jews. But in order that they might listen to me it was necessary on their account for me not yet to use this freedom and show contempt for them together with their works. Therefore I did what they themselves were doing, until I could teach them that these things were not necessary but that faith in Christ was sufficient. . . .

Notice, therefore, the words of the apostle in which the essence of what he means is expressed. "Compelled," he says; likewise "freedom," "slavery," "subjection." With these words he sets forth plainly enough the fact that among them there were those who watched him closely because he sometimes observed the Law—in accordance with his liberty and freedom—and sometimes did the opposite—depending on whether he saw that it was serviceable for the gaining of souls and the preaching of the Gospel. And these people betrayed and reproached him because he did not observe the Law and did not circumcise the Gentiles. They wanted to put pressure on him. Here he calls this subjection and slavery. For the freedom of which he boasts that we have it in Christ consists in this, that we are not bound to a single outward work but are free with regard to anything you please, in regard to anyone you please, at any time, and in any manner, except where an offense is committed against brotherly love and peace, as Rom. 13:8 states: "Owe no one anything, except to love one another." Therefore a true Christian, as Paul says in the third chapter (v. 28), is neither free nor slave, neither Jew nor Gentile, neither male nor female, neither a cleric nor a layman, neither religious nor secular; he neither prays nor reads; he neither does nor leaves undone. On the contrary, he is entirely free with regard to everything. Depending on whether a thing has come to hand or has withdrawn, he does it or leaves it undone, as Samuel said to Saul (1 Sam. 10:6): "You shall be turned into another man" and (v. 7) "Do whatever your hand finds to do; the Lord is with you." But that one man takes a wife and another enters a monastery, that one man indentures himself to this work and another to that work—he does not do this under compulsion of the Law but subjects himself to servitude of his own accord. If he does this out of love, he is acting nobly; but if he does so because he is impelled by necessity or fear, he is acting in conformity with human nature, not as a Christian. Accordingly, the people of our day err most seriously, especially the clergy and the members of religious orders. On account of the pomp of external worship, on account of their rites and ceremonies—in which they have become entangled to the point of the hopeless destruction of their souls—they feel such disgust for others, who are not conspicuous by a similar outward show, that they quarrel endlessly and have the nerve to declare publicly that they are unwilling ever to agree or to make common cause with them.

Finally, in this passage "the truth of the Gospel" seems to be taken, not as the actual content of the Gospel but as the proper use of the Gospel, because the Gospel is always true, whereas its use is not seldom subverted by hypocrisy. For "the truth of the Gospel" means knowing that all things are permitted, that to the pure all things are pure (Titus 1:15), and that no work of the Law is necessary for salvation and righteousness, since the Law is dead and no longer compels; when one performs works of the Law, therefore, it is on account of love, not out of compliance with the Law.

LUTHER'S COMMENTS ON GALATIANS 5:1

Note: Having just rehearsed the story of Sarah and Hagar (Genesis 16) to illustrate the contrast between freedom and slavery, Paul states commandingly that God does not want His people to return to slavery. The abuse of freedom is spiritual backsliding from God's kingdom, which leads into the thralldom under sin. The Lord therefore limits freedom by the Gospel. Freedom is not equal to license. The translation is from LW 27:325–26.

I am driving home *ad nauseam* the fact that this is the freedom and the slavery of which Paul speaks in Rom. 6:20, 22: "When you were slaves of sin, you were free in regard to righteousness. But now that you have been set free from sin, you have become slaves of God." But let us set this up in a diagram:

Service of sin
Freedom from righteousness

Freedom from sin
Service of righteousness

For he who is free from sin has become a slave of righteousness; but he who is the slave of sin is free from righteousness, and vice versa.

I repeat all this because I know that on account of the multitude of grasshoppers and locusts the fruits of our land have reached the point that this slavery and freedom are generally not understood, so fixed and deeply rooted has the human falsehood about free will become in those who oppose and deny both. What is more, those whom the apostle was forced to oppose in the same sixth chapter of Romans also have a fleshly idea of freedom, as if in Christ it were permissible for anything at all to be done, whereas this freedom is such that because of it we do of our own accord and gladly, without regard for penalties or rewards, the things that are stated in the Law. But it is slavery when we do these things out of slavish fear or childish desire. Therefore it profits nothing. Neither is there any difference between a slave of sin and a slave of the Law, because he who is a slave of the Law is always a sinner. He never fulfills the Law except to put works on display, and a temporal reward is given to him just as it is given to children of slave women and concubines. But the inheritance goes to the son of the free woman. "Christ," he says, "has made us free with this freedom." It is a spiritual freedom, one to be preserved in the spirit. It is not that heathen kind, which even the pagan Persius knew was not enough.[2] It is freedom from the Law, but in a way contrary to what usually takes place among men. For it is human freedom when laws are changed without effecting any change in men, but it is Christian freedom when men are changed without changing the Law. Consequently, the same Law that was formerly hateful to the free will now becomes delightful, since love is poured into our hearts through the Holy Spirit (Rom. 5:5). In this freedom, he teaches us, we must stand strongly and steadfastly, because Christ, who fulfills the Law and overcomes sin for us, sends the spirit of love into the hearts of those who believe in Him. This makes them righteous and lovers of the Law, not because of their own works but freely because it is freely bestowed by Christ. If you move away from this, you are both ungrateful to Christ and proud of yourself, since you want to justify and free yourself from the Law without Christ.

---

2   Aulus Persius Flaccus, *Satires*, V, sets forth the Stoic paradox that except for Stoic philosophers, all men are slaves.

Sermons on 1 Peter from 1522

Editor's Introduction

In the politics after the Diet of Worms, Luther was a pawn. Emperor Charles V formally condemned him as an outlaw (May 1521). Men in the service of Luther's prince, Elector Frederick the Wise, kidnapped Luther and hid him in the mountain castle of Wartburg. For a year, Luther occupied himself with translating the Bible into German and writing letters to those carrying on the Reformation. But in spring of 1522, a new crisis carried Luther back to Wittenberg. His colleague Andreas Carlstadt drew to himself men of violent intentions. Luther preached a series of sermons, starting on March 9, Invocavit Sunday, for a total of eight days. Luther's *Invocavit Sermons* restored the peace.

These events demonstrated to Luther the power of the Gospel preached in sincerity and truth. After restoring peace, Luther regarded preaching as the focus of his service. Whereas in 1517–18, Luther signed his name as "Freed Man" (*Eleutherius*), he now began to sign his letters with the title "Preacher" (*Ecclesiast*). In May of 1522, he began a series of sermons on 1 Peter, which caused him to reflect on what a Christian may do with his freedom.

LUTHER'S COMMENTS ON 1 PETER 1:15–16

Note: In preaching about godly sobriety, Luther explains what servitude to sin and freedom in Christ are. He uses the proper distinction between Law and Gospel to show the futility of righteousness through the Law. Yet Luther shows how the chastisement of the flesh and the restraint of gluttony, sexual passion, and other lusts are good, physical expressions of one's faith that keep one focused on the Gospel and turned aside from the snares of the flesh. One does these good works not for merit, but to affirm one's faith. Luther again points to Scripture as the authority for the preaching of Christ and instruction in good works. Like Christian freedom, good works also point to Christ. (Compare to Luther's interpretation of Galatians 5:13 on pp. 152–55.) The translation is from LW 30:27–28, 31–33.

[St. Peter] does not want the body to be destroyed or to be weakened too much. Thus one finds many who have fasted themselves mad and have tortured themselves to death. Even though Saint Bernard was a saintly man, he, too, was afflicted for a time with such folly. He denied his body so much that his breath stank and he could not associate with people.[3] Later, however, he came to his senses and also told his brothers not to hurt the body too much. For he realized that he had made himself unable to serve his brothers. Therefore St. Peter demands no more than that we be sober, that is, that we stint the body as long as we feel that it is still too lascivious. He does not prescribe any definite length of time for fasting, as the pope has done; but he leaves it to everyone's discretion to fast in such a way that he always remains sober and does not burden the body with gluttony. He must remain reasonable and sensible, and he must see to what extent it is necessary for him to mortify the body. It does no good at all to impose a command about this on a whole crowd or community, since we are so different from one another. One has a strong body, another

---

3   Cf. the *Vita prima* of Bernard, *S. Bernardi vita et res gestae*, 22, *Patrologia, Series Latina*, CLXXXV-1, 239, 240; Luther refers to this repeatedly in his writings, as, for example, in LW 4:273; 22:360.

Andreas Bodenstein von Carlstadt

Luther's colleague of approximately ten years became impatient. His teaching led to violent destruction of images (iconoclasm) and immediate changes in practice, which troubled the laity.

has a body that is weak. Therefore one person must deny it much, and another person must deny it little, in such a way that when this is done, the body remains healthy and able to do good.

But it is also wrong for the other crowd to come along and say that they are getting on well by not fasting and by feeling free to eat meat.[4] For these people, like the others, do not understand the Gospel either and are of no importance. They do no more than disdain the pope's command. Yet they do not want to gird the mind and the understanding, as Peter says. They let the body have its way, with the result that it remains indolent and lascivious. It is good to fast. But one fasts in the right way by not giving the body more food than is needed to keep it healthy, and by letting it work and wake, in order that the old ass may not become too reckless, go dancing on the ice, and break a leg but may be bridled and follow the spirit. It should not imitate those who, when they fast, fill themselves so full of fish and the best wine at one time that their bellies are bloated.

This is what St. Peter means by being sober. . . .

Do not be conformed to the passions of your former ignorance.

That is, do not deport yourselves as you did before. One should not regard you as what you formerly were. Formerly you were idolatrous; and you lived in unchastity, gluttony, drunkenness, greed, vanity, anger, envy, and hatred. This was an evil, heathenish way of life. It was unbelief. You went along in such a way of life like the blind. You did not know what you did. Now desist from these evil lusts. Here you see how St. Peter traces all misfortune to ignorance. For where faith and the knowledge of Christ are lacking, nothing but error and blindness remain, so that one does not know what is right and what is wrong. Then people fall into vices of all kinds.

This is what has happened up to now. When Christ vanished and was eclipsed, error began. Then the whole world asked how one could be saved. This in itself is a sign of blindness or ignorance; it shows that the proper understanding of faith has disappeared and that no one any longer knows anything about it. For this reason the world is so full of many kinds of sects, and there is nothing but division; for everyone wants to devise his own way to heaven. From misfortune we must sink

---

4   Apparently a reference to Andreas Carlstadt's declaration of freedom from rules of fasting and the like; cf., for example, LW 45:72–73.

ever deeper into blindness, because we are helpless. Therefore St. Peter says: You have now been fools long enough. Now that you know and have come to a proper understanding, put an end to this.

> But as He who called you is holy, be holy yourselves in all your conduct, since it is written: You shall be holy, for I am holy.

Here St. Peter cites a verse from the Old Testament, from Lev. 19:2, where God says: "You shall be holy; for I the Lord your God am holy." That is, because I am your Lord and God, and you are My people, you must be like Me. For a true lord brings it about that his people are like him, walk in obedience, and are guided by his will. Now just as God our Lord, is holy, so His people are also holy. Therefore we are all holy if we walk in faith. Scripture does not say much about the deceased saints; it speaks about those who are living on earth. Thus the prophet David glories in Ps. 86:2: "Preserve my life, for I am godly."

But here our men of learning have misinterpreted the verse again.[5] They say that the prophet called himself holy because he had a special revelation. In this way they themselves admit that they lack faith and do not have the revelation of Christ. Otherwise they would surely feel this. For he who is a Christian feels such a revelation in himself. But those who do not feel this are not Christians. For he who is a Christian enters with the Lord Christ into a sharing of all His goods. Now since Christ is holy, he, too, must be holy, or he must deny that Christ is holy. If you have been baptized, you have put on the holy garment, which is Christ, as Paul says (Gal. 3:27).

The little word "holy" designates that which is God's own and is due to Him alone. In German we use the word *geweihet*. Thus Peter says: You have now given yourselves to God as His own. Therefore see to it that you do not let yourselves be led again into the worldly lusts. But let God alone reign, live, and work in you. Then you are holy, just as He is holy.

So far the apostle has described the grace that is offered to us through the Gospel and the preaching about Jesus Christ, and he has taught us what our attitude toward this should be, namely, that we should hold to a pure and unchanged meaning of faith, in such a way that we know that no work we are able to do or devise can be of any help

---

5   For Luther's own exegesis [explanation] of this passage, see his *Dictations on the Psalter* (WA IV 20).

to us. Now when this is preached, reason comes along and says: "Ah, if this is true, then I need not do a single good work!" Thus stupid minds seize upon this and change Christian life into carnal liberty. They think they should do what they please. St. Peter confronts these people here, anticipates them, and teaches them that Christian liberty must be exercised solely over against God. For here nothing else is necessary than faith, that I give God His due honor and regard Him as my God, who is just, truthful, and merciful. Such faith liberates us from sin and all evil. Now when I have given God this honor, then whatever life I live, I live for my neighbor, to serve and help him. The greatest work that comes from faith is this, that I confess Christ with my mouth and, if it has to be, bear testimony with my blood and risk my life. Yet God does not need the work; but I should do it to prove and confess my faith, in order that others, too, may be brought to faith. Then other works will follow. They must all tend to serve my neighbor. All this God must bring about in us. Therefore we should not make up our minds to begin to lead a carnal life and to do what we please.

Luther's Comments on 1 Peter 2:16

Note: In this passage, Luther preaches about St. Peter's teaching on government and his admonition to "live as free men." Luther points out that acts of sedition and rebellion would endanger the temporal existence of the Church. He teaches that at the point when a government requires its citizen to commit a mortal sin, then Christians must meekly show civil disobedience.

Luther also points to examples from both Peter and Paul where free Christians try to outdo one another in showing honor and serving others because that is in accord with the joy that they have received in the Gospel and the existence that they now have as part of the Body of Christ. The translation is from LW 30:73, 74–79, 81.

St. Peter proceeds in the proper order and teaches us how we should conduct ourselves in every situation. So far he has spoken only in general terms and has told us how one should conduct oneself in all positions in life. Now he begins to teach how one should conduct oneself toward the secular government. For since he has now said enough in the first place about how one should act toward God and for oneself, he now tells us how one should conduct oneself toward all people. This is what he wants to say: In the first place and above all, you should walk in a true faith and keep your bodies under discipline, lest they follow evil lusts. Therefore let obedience to the government be your first concern. . . .

For the Lord's sake.

We do not owe the government obedience for its own sake, says St. Peter, but for the sake of God, whose children we are. This must induce us to be obedient, not the thought that our obedience is a meritorious deed. For what I do for God's sake, this I must do without recompense and to serve Him. Therefore I must be willing to do for nothing everything His heart desires. But why should one be subject to the government for God's sake? Because it is God's will that malefactors be punished and that benefactors be protected, in order that in this way unity may remain in the world. Therefore we should further external peace. God wants us to do this. For since we are not all believers but the great majority are unbelievers, God has regulated and ordained matters this way in order that the people of the world might not devour one another. The government should wield the sword and restrain the wicked if they do not want to have peace. Then they have to obey. This He accomplishes through the government, so that in this way the world is ruled well everywhere. Thus you see that if there were no evil people, one would not need a government.[6] Therefore St. Peter adds the words "to punish those who do wrong and to praise those who do right." Pious people are to be commended for doing what is right. The secular government should praise and honor them, in order that the others may have their conduct as an example. But it should not be one's purpose to merit anything before God for this. Thus Paul also says in Rom. 13:3: "Rulers are not a terror to good conduct, but to bad. Would you have no fear of him who is in authority? Then do what is good, and you will receive his approval."

---

6 At other times Luther traced the origin of government to the original creation of God rather than to the fall of man; see, for example, LW 13:47, 48.

For it is God's will that by doing right you should put to silence the ignorance of foolish men.

With these words St. Peter stops the mouths of the good-for-nothing babblers who boast of the Christian name and estate. He refutes any argument they might adduce as they say: "Since a Christian's faith is sufficient, and works do not make a man pious, why, then, is it necessary to obey the secular authority and pay taxes or tribute?" This must be your reply: "Although we derive no benefit from this, we should nevertheless do it for God without recompense to stop the mouths of God's enemies, who chide us. Then they cannot charge us with anything and must say that we are pious and obedient people." Thus one reads of many saints that they went to war under pagan princes, slew the enemy, and were subject and obedient to these princes, just as we owe obedience to Christian governments, even though the opinion is current today that we could not be Christians under the Turk.[7]

Here you might say: "Yet Christ gave the command (Matt. 5:39) not to resist evil, but that if anyone strikes us on one cheek, we should turn to him the other cheek also. How, then, can we strike and kill people?" Answer: This is what the heathen formerly cast into the teeth of the Christians. They said: "If anything like this should happen, their rule would have to come to an end."[8] But to this we say: "It is true that the Christians do not resist evil for their own sakes. Nor should they take vengeance when they are harmed. But they should suffer injustice and violence. For this reason they also cannot be hard on the unbelievers." But this does not mean that the government is forbidden to wield the sword. For although pious Christians do not need the sword and law—since they live in such a way that no one can complain about them, and since they wrong nobody but do good to all and gladly suffer everything done to them—yet the sword must be wielded for the sake of the non-Christians, to punish them for the harm they inflict on the others. Public peace must be preserved, and the pious must be

---

7   In the preface to his treatise *On War Against the Turk*, dated October 9, 1528, Luther said that people had been importuning him "for the past five years" to write something about war against the Turks (WA XXX-2, 107). He may be reflecting the beginnings of that importuning here.

8   This was a stock argument of anti-Christian polemics; for example, the emperor Julian asked: "Can anyone praise this teaching when, if it be carried out, no city, no nation, not a single family will hold together?" (Fragment 5.)

protected. Here God has established another method of government,[9] which should use force to compel those who are unwilling of their own accord to abstain from doing wrong to refrain from doing harm.

Therefore God has instituted government for the sake of the unbelievers. Consequently, Christians, too, may exercise the power of the sword. They have the obligation to serve their neighbors and to restrain the wicked with it, in order that the pious may remain in peace among them. Yet the injunction of the Lord not to resist evil remains in force, so that even if a Christian wields the sword, he does not use it for himself and does not avenge himself but uses it solely for others. Thus it is also a work of Christian love to protect and defend a whole community with the sword and not to let the people be abused. Christ gives His teaching only to those who believe and love. And they observe it. But since the great multitude in the world does not believe, it does not keep the commandment either. Consequently, it is necessary to rule these as non-Christians and to check their arrogance. For if one permitted their power to run riot, no one would be able to live among them.

Thus there are two kinds of government in the world, just as there are two kinds of people, namely, believers and unbelievers. Christians let the Word of God rule them; for themselves they have no need whatever of the secular government. But non-Christians need another rule, namely, the secular sword, because they refuse to be guided by the Word of God. Otherwise, if we were all Christians and followed the Gospel, it would not be necessary or profitable at all to wield the secular sword and power. For if there were no transgressors, there could be no punishment either. But since we cannot all be pious, Christ has entrusted the wicked to the government to be ruled as they must be ruled. But the pious He keeps for Himself and rules them Himself with His Word alone.

Therefore the Christian rule is not opposed to the secular rule. Nor is the secular government in opposition to Christ. The secular rule has nothing at all to do with the office of Christ but is an external matter, just as all other offices and estates are. And just as these are outside the pale of Christ's office, so that a non-Christian administers them as well as a Christian, so it is not the office of the secular sword to make people

---

9   The term used here is *regiment*; cf. LW 30:20, n. 10.

either Christians or non-Christians. But I have often said enough about this elsewhere.[10]

Now St. Peter continues:

Live as free men, yet without using your freedom as a pretext for evil; but live as servants of God.

This is said especially to us who have heard about Christian liberty, lest we rush in headlong and misuse this liberty, that is, lest under the name and the pretext of Christian liberty we do everything we please, so that liberty becomes impudence and carnal arrogance, which, as we see, is happening in our day. This began to take place even in the times of the apostles. From the epistles of St. Peter and St. Paul one can note that at that time people did what the great multitude does today. By God's grace we have now again become acquainted with the truth, and we know that what pope, bishops, priests, and monks have so far taught, instituted, and practiced is sheer fraud. Our conscience has been rescued and liberated from the human laws and all the compulsion they imposed on us, so that we are not obligated to do what they have commanded us to do on pain of losing salvation. To this freedom we must now cling firmly, and we must never let ourselves be torn from it. In addition, however, we must also be very careful not to make this freedom a pretext for evil.

The pope did wrong by attempting to force and compel the people with laws. For in a Christian people there should and can be no compulsion, and if one begins to bind consciences with external laws, faith and the Christian way of life soon perish. For Christians must be guided and governed only in the Spirit, so that they know that through faith they already have everything by which they are saved, that they need nothing else for this, that they are not obligated to do anything more than serve and help their neighbor with everything they have, just as Christ helped them. All their works are performed without compulsion and for nothing; they flow from a happy and cheerful heart, which thanks, praises, and lauds God for all the good things it has received from Him. Thus St. Paul writes in 1 Tim. 1:9 that "the Law is not laid down for the just"; for of their own accord they do without recompense and unbidden everything God wants.

10   See, for example, LW 45:114–17.

Now when such compulsion of the teaching of men is abolished and Christian liberty is preached, reprobate hearts, which are without faith, rush in and want to be good Christians by refusing to observe the pope's laws. They use this liberty as an excuse and say that they have no such obligation. Yet they also fail to do what genuine Christian liberty demands, namely, to serve their neighbor with a cheerful heart, as true Christians do, regardless of the fact that this is commanded. Thus they make Christian liberty only a pretext under which they do nothing but disgraceful things. They sully the noble name and title of the liberty which Christians have.

St. Peter now forbids this here, for he wants to say: Even though you—if you are Christians—are free in all external matters and should not be compelled by law to be subject to the secular government, since, as we have said, no law is laid down for the just (1 Tim. 1:9), yet of your own accord you should be willing and unconstrained. It is not that you must obey the law out of necessity, but you must do so to please God and to serve your neighbor. Christ Himself did this, as we read in Matt. 17:24ff. He paid the tax, even though He did not have to do so but was free and a Lord over all things. Thus He also submitted to Pilate and let Himself be judged, even though He Himself said to Pilate: "You would have no power over Me unless it had been given you from above" (John 19:11). With these words He Himself confirms this power. Yet He submits to it because this was pleasing to His Father.

From this you see that that great multitude of those who do neither what the world nor what God wants have nothing at all in common with Christian liberty. They persist in the old careless way of life, even though at the same time they boast of the Gospel. To be sure, we are free from all laws; but we must also be considerate of the weak and unschooled Christians. This is a work of love. Therefore St. Paul says in Rom. 13:8: "Owe no one anything, except to love one another." Therefore let him who wants to boast of liberty first do what a Christian should do, namely, serve his neighbor. Then let him use his freedom in the following way: When the pope or anyone else presents his commands to him and wants to insist that they be obeyed, he should say: "Dear Junker Pope, I refuse to obey for the simple reason that you are ordering me to do so and are interfering with my freedom." For, as St. Peter says here, in our freedom we should conduct ourselves as servants of God, not as servants of men. Otherwise if someone desires from me a service I can render him, I will gladly do it out of good-will, regardless of whether it is commanded or not. I will do so for the sake of brotherly love and because service to my neighbor is pleasing to God. Therefore I do not want to be compelled to be subject to secular princes and lords; but I will be subject to them of my own accord, not because they command me but to render a service to my neighbor. All our works should be of such a nature that they flow from pleasure and love, and are all directed toward our neighbor, since for ourselves we need nothing to make us pious. . . .

Therefore if an emperor or a prince were to ask me now what my faith is, I would have to tell him, not because of his command, but because it is my duty to confess my faith publicly before everybody. But if he wanted to go beyond this and commanded me to believe this or that, I would have to say: "My dear lord, attend to your secular rule. You have no authority to meddle in God's kingdom. Therefore I refuse to obey you. You surely cannot put up with any meddling in your domain. If anyone trespasses on your territory without your consent, you shoot at him with guns. Do you suppose that God should tolerate your desire to dethrone Him and to put yourself in His place?" St. Peter calls the secular government merely a human institution. Therefore they have no power to interfere in God's arrangement and to give commands concerning faith. Let what I have just said be enough about this subject.

COMMENTARY ON 1 CORINTHIANS 7 FROM 1523

EDITOR'S INTRODUCTION

Luther had marriage on his mind in 1523, though not a marriage for himself. After the Easter Vigil on Holy Saturday, April 6, twelve nuns fled the Marienthron Cistercian convent at Nimbschen. Most of them ended up in Wittenberg, and Luther took the responsibility of finding them husbands. At about the same time, printers at Leipzig reprinted John Faber's tract against Luther, which included commentary on 1 Corinthians 7 as foundational teaching about Christian celibacy and monasticism. Although Luther did not reply directly or point-by-point to Faber, he did see the need to explain marriage and celibacy as matters of Christian freedom. He dedicated this little commentary for Hans von Löser's wedding. Luther himself did not marry until June 13, 1525, taking the hand of Katharina von Bora. She was the last of the twelve Marienthron nuns to wed.

LUTHER'S COMMENTS ON 1 CORINTHIANS 7:23–24

Note: Luther portrays Christian freedom in the Gospel as slavery to God. This true freedom stands opposed to the only other alternative: slavery to sin, evil people, and false doctrine. Luther makes the important point that Christian freedom comes from God's act of calling in the Gospel, not from one's vocation in life, such as being married or even being a priest. Christian freedom is determined exclusively by God and His Word—it is limited to choices that concern only oneself. However, once any decision involves another human being, a Christian ceases to be free and becomes bound to the Law, specifically to the command to love and care for one's neighbor.

Related to this is Luther's reference to conversion and how the willful desire to remain a sinner and continue sinning fights against one's conversion. He states that people who improperly turn this freedom to refrain from sin into a set of laws actually subvert this freedom into a captivity that directs one back toward sin instead of toward Christ. The translation is from LW 28:44–47.

---

23. You were bought with a price; do not become slaves of men.

What is the meaning of these words? Paul has just taught us that one should remain a slave and that this does not stand in the way of Christian faith; but here he forbids us to become slaves. Doubtless he says this as a general rule to contradict those teachings of men which destroy the freedom and equality of belief and place the individual conscience in a vise. For instance, when someone teaches that a Christian may not marry a non-Christian and remain with her—as the rules of the church do—he obstructs the freedom that St. Paul teaches us here and forces people to obey these rules more than God's Word. He calls this "serving men," for these people think they are slaves of God and serving Him, when in reality it is but the teaching of men they serve, and they thereby become the slaves of men. The same is true of those who preached that Christians must be circumcised and thereby canceled this same freedom. At all points we find Paul caring and fighting for true Christian freedom against the snare and dungeon of human regulations.

That this is his true meaning is demonstrated in his words: "You were bought with a price." By this he means Christ, who with His own blood bought us and set us free from all sin and law, as we see in Gal. 5:1. But this purchase does not work itself out according to the way of the world and does not affect the relations men have with one another, such as that of a servant toward his master or that of a wife toward her husband. These relationships are all left intact, and God wants them maintained. The effect of this purchase is spiritual and takes place in our conscience. Therefore before God no law any longer binds or imprisons us. We are all free from all things. Before we were bound in sin, but now we are rid of all sin. Whatever outwardly remains of relationship or freedom is neither sin nor virtue but only outward tranquility or trouble, joy or suffering, as is all other bodily good and ill, in both of which we can live free and without sin.

> 24. So, brethren, in whatever state each was called, there let him remain with God.

Here Paul repeats this conclusion concerning Christian freedom for the third time: that all outward things are optional or free before God and that a Christian may make use of them as he will; he may accept them or let them go. But here the apostle adds the words "with God." This means, to the extent that it is of importance between you and God. For you are doing no service for God if you marry, remain unmarried, whether you are in bondage or free, become this or that, eat this or that; on the other hand, you do not displease Him or sin if you put off or reject one or the other. Finally, you owe God nothing but to believe and confess; He releases you from all other things so that you can do as you please without endangering your conscience. This is so thoroughly true that He does not inquire on His own behalf whether you have let your wife go, have run away from your master, or have not kept your agreement, for what does He profit whether you do these things or don't do them?

But because in this relationship you are bound up with your neighbor and have become his servant, it is God's will that no one be deprived of what is his by means of His freedom but rather that those things of your neighbor be protected. For although God pays no attention to these things on His own account, He pays attention to them on account of your neighbor. This is what he means with the words "with God," as though He were admonishing us: "I did not make you free among men or with your neighbor, for I do not wish that which is his taken from him until he gives you permission. But you are entirely free with Me and cannot ruin yourself in My sight by keeping to or refraining from outward things." Therefore notice this and differentiate between the freedom existing in your relation to God and the freedom existing

Double portrait of Martin Luther and Katharine von Bora, 1529 (oil on panel), by Lucas Cranach the Elder (1472–1553). Galleria degli Uffizi, Florence, Italy/Alinari/The Bridgeman Art Library

Martin Luther and His Wife, Katharina von Bora

Although both Martin and Katharine had taken vows of celibacy earlier in life, the teachings of Scripture convinced them they were free to marry.

in your relation to your neighbor. In the former this freedom is present, in the latter it is not, and for this reason: God gives you this freedom only in the things that are yours, not in what is your neighbor's. There differentiate between what is yours and what is your neighbors. That is why no man can leave his wife, for his body is not his own but his wife's, and vice versa. Likewise the servant and his body do not belong to him himself but to his master. It would be of no importance to God if the husband were to leave his wife, for the body is not bound to God but made free by Him for all outward things and is only God's by virtue of inward faith. But among men these promises are to be kept. In sum: We owe nobody anything but to love (Rom. 13:8) and to serve our neighbor through love. Where love is present, there it is accomplished that no eating, drinking, clothing, or living in a particular way endangers the conscience or is a sin before God, except when it is detrimental to one's neighbor. In such things one cannot sin against God but only against one's neighbor.

And it should be emphasized that this little word "call" does not in this context mean the social status to which one is called, as when one says, "Your status is 'married,'" or, "His status is 'priest,'" and so on, as everyone has his calling from God. Here St. Paul is not speaking of this calling. He speaks instead of the evangelical call, which is as much as to say: "Remain in that calling to which you were called, that is, where you receive the Gospel; and remain as you were when you were called. If the call comes to you in the married state, then remain in that wherein you were found. If you are called in slavery, then remain in the slavery in which you were called."

But what if the Gospel calls me in a state of sin, should I remain in that? Answer: If you have entered into faith and love, that is, if you are in the call of the Gospel, then sin as much as you please. But how can you sin if you have faith and love? Since God is satisfied with your faith and your neighbor with your love, it is impossible that you should be called and still remain in a state of sin. If, however, you remain in that state, then either you were not called as yet, or you did not comprehend the call. For this call brings you from the state of sin to a state of virtue, making you unable to sin as long as you are in that state. All things are free to you with God through faith; but with men you are the servant of everyman through love.

From this you will see that monasticizing and making of spiritual regulations is all wrong in our time. For these people bind themselves before God to outward things from which God has made them free, thus working against the freedom of faith and God's order. On the other hand, where these people should be bound, namely, in their relations with other men and in serving everyman in love, there they make themselves free, serving no one and being of no use to anyone but themselves, thus working against love. Therefore they are a perverse people, perverting all the laws of God. They want to be free where they are bound and bound where they are free, and yet they hope to be seated much higher in heaven than ordinary Christian people. But they who make such a hellish prison out of heavenly freedom and such a hostile freedom out of loving service shall sit in the deepest hell.

Sermons on John
from 1526 to 1529

Editor's Introduction

While recovering from the Peasants' War, the Wittenberg Reformers began a limited visitation program to some churches in 1526. Luther introduced his German Mass, and gradually the territorial churches began to form and adopt church orders aimed at improving the services of the Gospel. In that same year, Luther suggested that John's Gospel should become the serial lectionary reading for the Saturday Vesper services at Wittenberg. From that time forward, Luther preached often on John's Gospel, which he regarded as the heart of New Testament teaching.

Luther's 1526 Comments on John 20:19–23

Note: In his sermons on John 20, Luther portrays Christian freedom as being alien to Christians themselves. It resides in the ministry of Christ for His people. When a Christian claims lordship, he or she claims the Gospel given by Christ. Yet when a Christian claims to act in Christ's name toward God and others, those actions are of complete servitude. A Christian actively seeks to be humble in everything; Christ actively seeks to exalt Christians in everything. Both sides occur simultaneously, but separately. The translation is from LW 69:347–48.

[It is as if Jesus said,] "I entrust the Gospel to you, so that you might speak and preach it to others, so that they may come to this light as you yourselves have been enlightened." And to this end He gives them the Holy Spirit, saying: "Receive [the Holy Spirit. Those whose sins you remit, their sins are remitted. Those whose sins you retain, their sins are retained]" [John 20:22–23]. He does not say that [your] sins are forgiven—because you [already] have that—but that you should give the Holy Spirit to others and remit them their sins. You are able to forgive or retain the sins of others, yet through the Holy Spirit. Many things must be preached about these words.

In brief, the gift and office of the Church does not consist in having many good works but in spreading the resurrection of Christ. For what does "Those whose sins you forgive" mean? It is removing all evil things and granting in their place all things good, and you have it in your power to distribute this to human beings. Not through money, but through the Word we all have this power of saying to the frightened sinner, "Brother, God speaks to you the forgiveness of sins," and though a man says it, it is just as much as God Himself speaking. It is not that we should boast that sins are taken away through our works, as we do in the [monastic] orders,[11] but God's Word does it, which is spoken to another: "Believe in Christ and acknowledge Him. In Him, without merits [of your own], you have the remission of sins." This is to be said in the sermon or with a brother [individually].

This Word is not ours; we only make use of it. It is for this purpose that we ought to remit the guilt; and I can retain it [as well], so that, when I see that a person does not believe in Christ, and persecutes and ridicules Christianity, and teaches a different doctrine, immediately I say, "Your sins are not remitted," and nevertheless it is as valid as if God Himself had said it, even if our judgment is laughed at. Moreover, we have the confidence that it will stand, and the confidence that when I remit someone's sins Satan cannot overturn it. If I say the opposite, "You will be condemned with all your works," he laughs at me, and yet

---

11   Cf. the form of Absolution for monks that Luther cites in the *Lectures on Galatians* (1531/1535) (LW 26:154): "May . . . the merit of your order; the burden of your [religious vows]; the humility of your confession; the contrition of your heart; the good works that you have done and will do for the love of our Lord Jesus Christ— may all this be granted to you for the forgiveness of your sins. . . ."

this judgment stands firm. This is so common [among us] that it is despised; we have it, but we do not consider how great a treasure it is.

I have a judgment, a verdict that God has taken away from the angels themselves [1 Cor. 6:3], and it is just as valid as if the divine Majesty had spoken. If Christ came with a great multitude of angels and said, "Your sins are remitted you," they would laugh for joy. Now I hear that [sins] are remitted, and I despise it. And in every mouth we have the same power that is in the mouth of Christ. It is always the same Word through which all the saints are saved: Mary the mother [of God] and the Magdalene [alike].[12] There are many different saints, but one Word. They may not see how many there are who believe. Even if God were to speak through a piece of straw, I ought to accept it and trust Him as if He Himself had spoken. This is our one consolation: that we forgive sins. We also frighten sinners. From this comes the custom in the Church that those who have set up sects and false doctrine are excommunicated. And so excommunication derives from these words, so that those who despise the Gospel may be excommunicated.

You see the Christian life: [first,] in peace toward God through faith; second, through charity toward one's neighbor, also in faith. Christ has made us lords. The Christian has a great dominion. The one who serves Him is lowly; those whom He serves are lords, even the human creature. This is a kingdom of all joy and the remission of sins.

Luther's 1529 Comments on John 19

Note: Luther stresses that the doctrine of justification alone through Christ's merit and free gift cannot stand with the assertions of popes and enthusiasts, namely, that people can work out their salvation by contributing their works. Luther thus indicates a true freedom in the Gospel over against the false freedom to grasp salvation through works. The translation is from LW 69:269–70.

St. Paul puts the two together, grace and gift, in Romans 5 [:15, 17]: "If many died through one man's sin, much more have the grace of God and

---

12   In medieval exegesis, Mary Magdalene was the exemplary penitent, identified with the sinful woman of Luke 7:37 who anointed Jesus' feet.

His gift extended to many through Jesus Christ, who alone of all men was in grace."[13] And again: "If, because of one man's sin, death reigned through that one, much more will those who receive the abundance of grace and gifts unto righteousness reign in life through the one man Jesus Christ." Through grace we are justified. For God takes us wholly and entirely into His favor for the sake of Christ's blood, so that He will not regard nor judge our sin. Through the gift we are preserved. For God gives us the Holy Spirit who sanctifies and keeps us in the true faith until sin is put to death.[14] St. John calls the grace "blood"; he calls the gift "water," that is, the Holy Spirit who cleanses and purifies our sinful flesh. And he puts these two parts together in order to show and testify what Christ has poured out into the world to redeem us from sins.[15]

Here it is announced and affirmed that the redemption from sins and righteousness and purity that avails before God does not consist in our own powers, merits, or works, but rather in the blood and water that flow from Christ's side, that is, in God's grace and gift, as St. Paul calls it. The pope along with his theologians and teachers says man is able to free himself from sins and achieve righteousness and purity or the purgation of sins with his works.[16] At the present day, our sectarians, Anabaptists, and others do the very same thing. They want to be justified and saved by their suffering, that is, by their own work. But St. John strikes them all down as though with a bolt of thunder and says that redemption from sins, righteousness, and purity, or purgation of sin, does not come through power, merit, or work of the monks, clergy, sectarians, or any other human beings, but rather through the blood and water that flowed from Christ's side. From this it follows that all who want to free themselves from sin and achieve righteousness with

---

13   This is Luther's translation of Romans 5:15 in his Bible editions from 1533 to 1545. Previously, he had translated "through the grace that extended to the one man Jesus Christ." In the posthumous 1546 Bible edition, incorporating Luther's last revisions, the translation read: "through the grace of the one man Jesus Christ" (WA DB 7:45).

14   Cf. the explanation of the Third Article of the Creed, *Small Catechism* (1529) II 4 (Kolb-Wengert, pp. 355–56; *Concordia*, p. 330).

15   On the distinction between grace and gift, see *Preface to Romans* (1522, 1546), LW 35:369–70.

16   Essential to medieval soteriology in its various forms was the premise that the human creature had to merit the reward of eternal life by working in cooperation with God's grace to become like God in purity and righteousness. See Steven Ozment, *The Age of Reform (1250–1550)* (New Haven: Yale University Press, 1980), p. 236.

Source: Dr. Martin Luther's *Sämmtliche Schriften* (St. Louis: Concordia, 1898), 14:232–33.

Riding in State

In this woodcut, the pope rides in state as a prince. Luther's text cites the decrees of Pope John XXII, especially the so-called *Extravagante,* where the pope claims lordship over all kings and nations. This relates also to the suppression of the Franciscan Spirituals in the thirteenth century. Luther contrasts this with Jesus' kingly humility.

their own blood, water, work, merit, and suffering take away the glory from Christ's suffering, death, blood, and water.

We also teach and confess that one should be obedient to God, have patience in tribulation, suffer persecution for the sake of the truth, and do good works, and we urge these things with all diligence. Yet we teach in addition that one should not commit idolatry with good works nor arrogantly presume that one is justified before God through them.[17] We make this distinction: out of grace we are saved without any merit of works; but good works should be done to honor God and to benefit the neighbor. The works-righteous, however, turn things around, deny grace, and ascribe the righteousness that avails before God to works.

LUTHER'S 1529 COMMENTS ON JOHN 20

Note: While preaching on the topic of authority, Luther speaks against the extravagancies of the papacy's temporal power that extends back to the 1079 bull *Libertas ecclesiae* of Gregory VII. Luther's point is that, for all their striving for worldly power and "freedom," the popes were neglecting the Gospel that is clearly central to their office and calling. This, in turn, leads to corruption and man-made doctrines that tread underfoot true Christian freedom in the Gospel. The translation is from LW 69:294–95.

You know quite well—for you have often heard it—what the difference is between Christ's kingdom and worldly rule. Christ's kingdom extends no further than to save the souls of men from sin, death, and hell and bringing them to God's grace and mercy so that man may be saved and live eternally. And it is in this kingdom and office that Christ's apostles are to serve Him. Now whoever does this, preaching such grace of God to the people and helping them to enter eternal life and be saved, he should rightly be called pope and supreme. But such an authority, which consists in nothing but service and slavery, is not what the pope and his sect want. Rather, he strives after worldly power and sovereignty and preaches

---

17   On justification by works as idolatry, cf. *Large Catechism* (1529) I 22–23 (Kolb-Wengert, pp. 388–89; *Concordia*, pp. 360–61).

nothing but external ceremonies and human commandments of eating, drinking, clothing, festivals, etc., as the way to salvation. That is an abdication of Christ's office and abandonment of the authority of service possessed by the apostles, martyrs, and all genuine Christians.

What do I care [for such ceremonies and commandments]? Or how can they help me against sin and death? Or what benefit are they to me in reaching eternal life, even if I have and keep all the commandments of the pope concerning ceremonies, eating, drinking, clothing, and festivals? Eating, drinking, and clothing belong to the secular government; in the spiritual [realm] I need not concern myself with such things. The soul needs neither food nor drink, neither clothing nor the like.[18] Now, if only I have someone who will faithfully and diligently preach to me how I may be freed from sin and death and be saved eternally, then I will listen to him and gladly give him the honor of being ranked far above me. But when the pope and his sect claim to be ranked highest and to be supreme in the Church, riding on luxuriously trapped asses and great, magnificent chargers, and they never once take thought for the instruction of the people so that they may know how to be delivered from sin and death and be saved (such are all the bishops in our day)—that may as well be and be called the devil's own authority and sovereignty.[19] Neither Christ nor His apostles and martyrs in His kingdom know anything about this, save that Christ and the apostles proclaimed that false christs and false prophets would arise (Matthew 24 [:24]) and that the man of lawlessness, the son of perdition, would oppose and exalt himself above everything that is called God or divine worship, so that he would take his seat in the temple of God as a god and proclaim himself to be God (2 Thessalonians 2 [:3–4]).

This diabolical authority of the pope and his adherents has now been revealed through the Gospel so that everyone who has a proper understanding of Christ's kingdom and office will not let such masks mislead and impede him. For Christian authority, concerning which Christ has given commandment in His kingdom, is and is called service, namely, the care of souls, serving human beings with the word of grace, so that they are delivered from sin, death, and hell and are saved. Whoever labors and does the most here is the best and highest.

---

18 Cf. *Christian Freedom* (1520), above.
19 Cf. Lucas Cranach's (1472–1553) depiction of the pope and bishops riding in state in the *Passional Christi et Antichristi* (1521), WA 9:709 [shown on p. 119].

LUTHER'S 1529 COMMENTS ON JOHN 20

Note: While preaching on Christ's authority, Luther speaks about the bishops' failure to fulfill their office and the abuses of the papacy. For these failures, he calls them Antichrist, a reference to their active use of authority to separate Christians from the free gifts offered by Christ. Luther describes such a state as enslavement to human laws posing as God's Law. The translation is from LW 69:367–69.

This is Christ's office, and for this He was sent and has come: to redeem human beings from the power of sins and out of the kingdom of the devil. He was not sent to destroy, but to save what is destroyed and lost. The apostles and their successors should also accomplish this very same thing after His example, removing sin, death, hell, and the wrath of God through their word and preaching and setting the consciences and the souls of men free from them. Therefore, St. Paul also calls the office of preaching an "office that preaches reconciliation," so that it makes us friends of God, and we receive grace and everything good from God through it (2 Corinthians 5 [:18]). And he boasts that the Lord has given him power to benefit and not to destroy (2 Corinthians 10 [:8]; 13 [:10]).

If only God would grant that our bishops could believe such things! They have the call and the mandate, and they are incumbent in the office. (This we must concede to them and cannot deny it.) But accomplishing through their office what Christ has accomplished, and carrying out their office as both need and the office require—this they do not do. They should be good shepherds, salutary bishops and teachers, comforting saviors and helpers, standing in Christ's stead and preserving men's souls through their office, as Christ did and commanded His disciples to do in Luke 9 [:55–56]: "Do you not know of which Spirit you are children? The Son of Man has not come to destroy men's souls, but to preserve them." Thus they are wolves and murderers who do not protect the flock of Christ and who scatter, slay, and kill the poor little sheep.[20]

---

20   Cf. N[ürnberg Codex Solger]: "That is the wolf preaching in the sheepfold."

Their office[21] is to preach repentance and the forgiveness of sins in Christ's name, that is, they should rebuke the world for sin so that the people may acknowledge what sinners they are; and, on the other hand, they should teach how they are to become free of their sins through Christ.[22] But they go and burden Christendom with new laws[23] and precepts of men about food, vows, clothing, and certain feast days, and they make sin where there is no sin. The Gospel, which Christ committed to the apostles and preachers, makes human consciences free from all laws, even from the Law of God. But the pope together with his bishops does nothing other than to trap and bind the consciences of men with new laws and dangerous snares. Christ commands us to forgive the true sin that hides in flesh and blood, with which humans are born and strive against God. But the pope forgives invented sins that he has made up through his human decrees.

Thus the pope becomes the true Antichrist and adversary of God. He makes new laws in the place of God's Law, and through these laws he makes new sins that are not sin before God. He establishes a new forgiveness in place of the true, evangelical forgiveness.[24] He is supposed to preach the Gospel to poor consciences and through it proclaim redemption from sins and freedom from all laws, as far as the conscience is concerned. But he preaches the commandment of men and thereby makes new snares to trap consciences and to bind that which he ought to loose and free. This is truly the wolf set up as preacher in the sheepfold. Every[25] Christian is a lord over all laws with respect to his conscience. But the pope burdens all of Christendom with innumerable laws,[26] which wretchedly imprison the conscience.

Therefore, the papacy is a diabolical government in which consciences are lamentably trapped with snares, bound, and tormented. The emperor in his government also has precepts, laws, statutes, and ordinances, but he places these on the people's hands and feet and ensnares their body and possessions and what they have. This

---

21 R[örer]: "The office of Christendom."
22 R[örer] adds: "and are liberated from laws."
23 R[örer]: "You see what kind of bishops they are, who rule Christendom merely by laws, since they do not rule it except by making new laws . . . "
24 R[örer] adds: "in which we learn that we are free from all laws."
25 R[örer]: "Yesterday you heard that . . ."; cf. Sandberg-Wengert, pp. 137–42 (WA 29:281–91).
26 R[örer]: "snares."

is appropriate for external things.[27] But the pope makes decrees and snares and places them not on the hands and feet but on the heart, in order to trap and ensnare their consciences within. This is the devil. This is not being sent as Christ was sent from the Father, and as He sends the apostles here, but acting directly contrary to the mission of Christ. Indeed, they are called and sent, and they are incumbents of the office as bishops and rulers of the Church, but they do not carry out the office as Christ carried it out and has mandated that it be carried out.

---

27   N[ürnberg Codex Solger]: "That would be fine and tolerable."

Lectures on Isaiah
from 1529 to 1530

Editor's Introduction

While Luther lectured on Isaiah, Sulayman the Magnificent led the troops of the Ottoman Empire westward into Europe until he besieged Vienna. Charles V, exasperated by the looming threat of the Muslim Turks and the divisions among the churches in his territories, came to the Diet of Augsburg in 1530 determined to unite his realm. He sought a resolution to the Reformation so he could turn all his forces against the Turks. The Lutheran princes would gather at the same diet to present the Augsburg Confession and their concern for evangelical truth and freedom.

Luther's Comments on Isaiah 52:6

Note: While commenting on how God's people recognize Him by His Word, Luther portrays Christian liberty as freedom to hear (and heed) Christ over against those who supplant Scripture with their own doctrine in the manner of Law and earthly force. The translation is from LW 17:209.

6. *Therefore in that day they shall know that it is I who speak.* It is as if He were saying: "I will not permit those tyrants, those false prophets, to

speak; I will throw them out of the church so that the people will hear Me alone." Here He removes Moses, the Pharisees, and the Sadducees together with their ministries and ascribes everything to Himself alone. In the New Testament through the teaching of Christ we have such great liberty that we reject the pope, the bishops, and all who make their boast in the flesh. We are nothing but sheep, and we must hear the voice of the Lord and it alone (John 10:4). In the Law, however, the Pharisees commanded people by the authority of blood. These ministries of the Word bound to the flesh Christ dismisses by means of His own word. No matter who he has been in person and in the flesh, if he has not had the Word, he must not be listened to. Rather, Christ alone is to be heard. This, then, is the rule: The true church of God does not admit the reprobate, as did the synagogue of the Jews, but "My sheep hear My voice." Thus it is very certain that the church is not governed by a heretical and ungodly seducer, but it is taught by Christ Himself, the Teacher of the Word. He is not a wailer and blasphemer of God, but He is an exquisitely delightful song, a Word comforting the conscience and filling it with joy, and then causing it to laud and praise God. This, I say, is the Christian liberty of conscience. While outwardly the body must be full of restrictions and controls on the part of lords, parents, and teachers, all of which have been set up to preserve the social order but not the conscience, liberty reigns inwardly in strength against Satan and in cheerfulness in the face of sins, etc. If you doubt that this is said concerning Christ's kingdom and Christian liberty, then the following words explain. In comparison with spiritual liberty and the reign of Christ, all outward adornments of the world, all kingdoms and crowns, are worthless scrap. The Holy Spirit has nothing to do with them.

Luther's Comments on Isaiah 61:1

Note: Luther describes the kingdom and office of Christ, taking aim at the papacy and other institutions for their abuse of privilege in Christ's kingdom or, in the case of Muhammad and Islam, for their great assault on Christ's kingdom. Luther shows that the arrow of freedom points one toward the body and kingdom of Christ, under the reign, person, office, and work of Christ. Freedom consists in being a servant of Christ; all else is a "prison." Luther properly distinguishes Law and Gospel as he builds his exposition of this verse. The translation is from LW 17:330–33.

Christ is the person sent by God and filled with the Holy Spirit to be the Preacher and Evangelist to the poor, that is, the afflicted. This was not done for Christ's sake but for our sake. Thus Paul boasts about his calling in a most ostentatious way, not for his own sake but for the purpose of strengthening us who are weak and of terrifying the ungodly. It is only this preaching and function of Christ that makes the poor and afflicted very strong in the will of God, so that they may know that all things turn out for them according to the will of God. Note this especially, that we must be content with the God of majesty when we consider His hidden but grand and terrifying offices. When we fall into this labyrinth, we become involved in speculations about divinity, and we want to become investigators of His majesty at our peril.

As for you, be content with the God incarnate. Then you will remain in peace and safety, and you will know God. Cast off speculations about divine glory, as the pope and Mohammed speculate. You stay with Christ crucified, whom Paul and others preach. . . .

To bind up the brokenhearted. "It is My office to heal, or to bind up, as the physicians do." He describes these three tasks. 1 Cor. 15:56 depicts three wounds, the Law, sin, and death. The prophet here describes the office of Christ as the cure for these wounds. Paul is speaking of the Law, whereby God's wrath is experienced and perceived, and he convinces us that we have no strength in which to excel. Then, in conformity with this, sin follows, whereby the Law troubles us. Then follows eternal death. These are the three chief things with which Christ, our Bishop, struggles. "The sting of death is sin, and the power of sin is the Law" (1 Cor. 15:56). Here no man can help. I take Christ's three tasks as applying to these three things. To heal *the brokenhearted*, this is the first. Those who are crushed by the Law I bind up and heal, so that they may not despair. Second, *the captives*, those who are captive under sin. For sins have snatched us like thieves. Then third, *opening to those who are bound.* The judge pronounces sentence, which is death. Against these three evils the knowledge of Christ is in force, if we would know

Christ to be the man who can free us from these evils. Therefore let us know that Christ is not a judge or a teacher of the Law, but He does the opposite: He heals, He consoles, He frees us from these evils.

In the second place: *To proclaim liberty to the captives.* The prophet is referring to the year of release (Deut. 15:1ff.). We are held captive under debts and are bankrupt, but Christ sets us free from them. These are two victories, over sin and over death. In the third place, *the opening of the prison to those who are bound,* namely, under the Law, for we are bound by the Law, since we are sinners. From these bonds Christ delivers us so that we may not be condemned by the Law. Summary: Note that Christ is a preacher to the poor and is sent to free us and help us, and this happens by the Word alone. "Through the Word I heal them so that they may know that they are free from sin, death, and the Law." One who could with affection and strong zeal handle this would really have accomplished something to enable him to cast aside the Law, sin, and death beyond heaven and earth, as if we had never seen either sin or death or the Law. The deliverance from these afflictions, I say, is ours through Christ, but in this respect there is a deficiency, that we cannot believe these words. We think heaven is filled with our sins, with the Law and death. Therefore these words must be carefully weighed. In them we should see life, salvation, and deliverance. This will not come to pass in this life. By faith we shall only see that the matter has been begun, not that it is completed. For here he sets forth bonds, captivity, and the anguish of death. We experience them in this life, and yet in the Word of Christ we should triumph over these things that are against us. While the Law is done away as far as the spirit is concerned, so that it does not accuse and trouble us, it is, I say, not done away as if the Law were no longer there. It is abolished in that it does not sting us, and the Christian can say, "Although I feel the Law and sin, in opposition to them I have Christ, the Preacher who heals and consoles me." Christ is greater than Law, sin, and death, for it is His special office not to be conquered by them but to conquer them and help others to be free of them. Therefore you have Christ defined as the Preacher of peace. The *poor* are the afflicted and well-nigh despairing. Thus the human heart can learn where to find refuge, with Christ the Mediator alone. Neither papist nor ungodly man understands these words, and therefore they seek other mediators.

Sermons on John from 1532

Editor's Introduction

Luther was frequently ill at the end of 1531 and the beginning of 1532. He complained of reoccurring vertigo and other symptoms. Despite feeling ill, he continued to climb into the pulpit. He had to. Elector John of Saxony had granted John Bugenhagen, the pastor at Wittenberg, the opportunity to travel to Lübeck to teach and preach there. Since no one else was available, Luther had to continue bearing his university responsibilities while also taking up Bugenhagen's parish responsibilities. In January and February of 1532, Luther's friends believed he was so sick that he would likely die.

Luther's Comments on John 8:34–38

Note: Luther shows the result of one's abuse of Christian freedom, namely, the loss of one's place in the kingdom of God. This reflects a more mature position on Christian liberty that sees just how apt people are to abuse that freedom. They embrace freedom with the ulterior motive of serving themselves as a little "god," all the while neglecting the fact that God will not be mocked.

God gave His promise to His people Israel, yet many turned from the Gospel, still sure of their inheritance. They traded true freedom in the Gospel for a false "liberty" of their own making. That false freedom is really a new servitude to themselves and, through that, to Satan.

Luther comments that the Gospel first draws many disciples, yet the false ones outnumber the true ones ten to one. This is revealed through adversity and other worldly events, as the Gospel becomes distasteful to those who will not remain true to it. Luther makes the growth of the Church contingent on true doctrine, on standing fast to the Lord's words. As there is false doctrine and true doctrine, so there is false freedom and true freedom. Recognizing this difference requires the proper distinction of Law and Gospel. False freedom leads to wrath, not blessing. Christian freedom remains always in Christ, neither contrary to Him, nor to the Word of God. The translation is from LW 23:397–405, 407–413.

Courtesy of the Richard C. Kessler Reformation Collection, Pitts Theology Library, Candler School of Theology, Emory University

Pharisees Reject Freedom

This image from a 1563 edition of Luther's postils shows the scene from John 8:58–59. The Pharisees reject Jesus' claim of divinity, as well as His message of the Gospel. They prefer the bondage of seeking righteousness through fleshly works under the Law (8:15) and are foreign to the faith of Abraham, whom they claim as father (8:37–56). In their spiritual blindness, they seek to kill Jesus.

IOANNES BVGENHAGIVS POMERANVS THEOLOGVS.

Iohannes in Pomerania honefta familia natus,& in omni genere literarum educatus fuit. Vt autem commodius pietati incumberet,fefe monacho rum ordini coniunxit, & eam uitæ cõditionem Lu theri monitu reliquit . Poftea fefe Vuitebergam contulit,& tanta diligentia libris facris incubuit, ut omnium confenfu Theologiæ Doctor crearetur. Erat infuper pietati deditifsimus,& fingulari facun dia ornatus.Itaqȝ factum ut anno 1520 Vuitebergen fis paftor electus fuerit. Eam functionẽ is per mul tos annos optimè adminiftrauit, & Euangelij do ctrinam plurimùm promouit. Cum etiam in Cœ næ negotio cõtrouerfia cum fuperioris Germaniæ Theologis exorta effet,fua mãfuetudine effecit,ut Bucerus,Mufculus, & Fre chius 1536 Vuitebergæ Lutheri fentẽtiæ ferè fubfcripferint.Poftea à rege Chri ftiano Friderici filio in Daniam uocatus eft,ut Euangelicæ doctrinæ initia fa ceret.Ibi is Ecclefias inftituit,& 1538 regem inaugurauit.Cum etiam Iohannes Pomeraniæ Epifcopus eligeretur, ipfe eam dignitatem recufauit, & fua forte contentus fuit.Inde Smalkaldiam à Proteftantibus euocatur anno 1540, ũt cũ reliquis Theologis religionis formam confcriberet, & inftanti Concilio of ferret.Erat hifce actionibus Ioannes ob rerum ufum principibus gratifsimus.

Johannes Bugenhagen (Pomeranus)

Luther's pastor was a valued colleague and friend to him throughout his life. However, when Bugenhagen exercised his freedom to teach in Lübeck, the decision harshly burdened Luther.

These words offend and inflame them anew. They feel insulted by His statement that they are to be set free by His doctrine and by the truth, as though they were captives and slaves. They say: "We are not bondsmen; we are free, for we are Abraham's seed. And Abraham's seed has the promise of God to be the head, yes, not the tail but the head (Deut. 28:13), which is to soar above in the world and not cower on the ground." Thus Rebecca had been told (Gen. 25:23): "The elder shall serve the younger." These words they understood and took to heart, interpreting them to mean that the whole world should be nothing compared with them, and that the whole world should serve them. Therefore even when the prophets warned them: "You will be led into captivity by the Babylonians and the Assyrians; wait and see"—they did not believe, but called the prophets heretics. They lived and did as they chose, and the prophets had to hear them say: "We are the seed of Abraham." Thus here they also rub this under Christ's nose and say: "You may claim to be able to do this, but You might as well cross out Your words. To be Abraham's seed involves blessing, kingdom, government, and inheritance. We shall reign and rule. And now You come along as a heretic who joins the false prophets in disputing the reality of our freedom. You are causing many to fall prey to this heresy when You deny that we are Abraham's seed and imply that the promise given to Abraham does not pertain to us." They alone want to emphasize that they are free men. And since Christ will not proclaim this, they soon take offense at Him—especially the mighty among them—and fall away, although they had believed in Him before.

So it happens. At first people adhere to the Gospel, expecting to become great popes, bishops, princes, and lords. They want to yield to no one and to be as free as the birds. But when they recognize the truth, one after another falls away. These are disgraceful disciples; they flock to the Gospel for carnal freedom and temporal benefits. And when they do not find what they are looking for, they abandon it. For example, our peasants now disdain the Gospel, for they have discovered that it brings them no earthly goods.[28] And the noblemen now have the effrontery to wipe their feet on the clergy and chase them from their homes. The burghers observe this and copy their ingratitude toward the Gospel. But Christ says here: "If you continue in My Word, etc." Christ sets His disciples apart from other hearers of the Gospel, saying: "If you believe in Me, then you are My disciples. To be sure, you are My disciples now, and I have gained pupils. This looks promising." In John 6:26 we read: "You believe in Me, not because you saw signs, but because you ate your fill of the loaves." This is promising indeed! He says, as it were: "To be sure, I am a great Teacher now and have many pupils; but what will they do in the end? O God, how few of you will pass the test! For you have no good foundation and no stamina. You will seek something in Me that you will not find; and when you fail to find it, then it is all over." The scene before us here resembles the spring, when all the branches are covered with blossoms. Then we wonder what to do with all the apples and pears we will harvest. But if rain or a wind hits the blossoms, they drop to the ground in profusion. About nine tenths of the blossoms are lost; barely one tenth of them matures into fruit, and some of this may be worm-eaten.

---

28 An echo of the Peasants' War of 1525.

This also happens to the Gospel. At first everybody listens to it; it sounds precious, and it has many disciples. But if things go contrary to man's wishes, if we do not preach what the people would like to hear, then they say: "All our misfortune is due to the Gospel." Therefore the Lord Christ declares: "You are My disciples, but at the same time you are knaves. Only if you continue in My Word are you truly My disciples. It is not sufficient to begin to believe; no, it is necessary to continue and to persevere in adherence to the Word." I, too, would like to be a Christian and accept the Gospel if it were not for the danger attending it, if one could enjoy only good days with it; for hatred, envy, contempt, and ingratitude are not to everyone's liking. That is why the devil and everybody else act in opposition as soon as a person wants to become this Man's disciple. Hold fast at such a time. Stand fast. Do not flee. Do not retreat. If you have begun to believe, persevere in it. There are many who endure, shed their blood, and boldly venture and dare. Such steadfast people are the true disciples. But these are outnumbered tenfold by those who at first joined us in our faith and to whom our doctrine appealed, but of whom not one tenth remained constant. Yet this does not matter. Let him who stands remain standing, and let him who will not stand fall away. There will still be some who will remain loyal, and these are the[29] true disciples. They will endure whatever befalls them. The others, who seek only carnal freedom and their own advantage, are nothing but mouth-Christians, liars, false disciples, and illegitimate children.

The Jews, too, would have welcomed the Gospel under those conditions if it had meant freedom from the cross, a free and comfortable life at home, exemption from taxes, and subservience to no one. If the Gospel were such a doctrine, I would be able to convert the whole world in one hour. If Christ had given everyone a sack filled with gold coins, plus a castle or a city—who would have deserted Him then? If He had given everyone a thousand guldens, or even only one gulden, with a guarantee to be able to spend it in peace, all the people would have flocked to Him. If He had given them freedom for fornication and adultery, for usury, robbery, and theft, without jeopardy or fear of punishment by death, then He would have been acclaimed a fine king. But He declares: "People will be your enemies and hate you for

---

29   We have changed "My" to "the" in this sentence.

My sake. Because of Me the world will revile, defame, and kill you, and begrudge you even a morsel of bread or a moment of life." Then flesh and blood reply: "Let the devil be a Christian in my stead! Go ahead and be a Christian. There is too much of a stench here for me. This is paying too high a price for steadfastness, that one must put everything at stake." People say: "I am quite willing to make the beginning, but I will not remain." Christ wants to say: "He who is bold and reckless will be called a true disciple of Mine."

What will be the reward and comfort of such a person? He will find the true God; he will be endued with strength and power to remain with God's Word. Thus he will be Christ's disciple and know the truth, for Christ says: "I will reveal the real and absolute truth to you, so that you will not only see what the first disciples saw, those who deserted Me, but will also experience and see that My promise, given to you and My other disciples, is true and will be certified in you." . . .

We experienced this miracle ourselves. A year ago, at the Diet of Augsburg, the opinion was general that everything would go topsy-turvy within four weeks, and that all Germany would founder. One could neither see nor feel how things would end or from what source help and counsel might come. The situation baffled and defied all reason and wisdom, and one was constrained to say: "It all depends on God's power, and it is all staked on His Word." We must progress to the point where we say: "God has promised." If we rely firmly on the Word, then we need have no fear. Even though we find ourselves at our wits' end and see no escape, God will nonetheless let us find out that His Word is true, because He promised that none who trust in Him will be disappointed. This we, too, will find in all the trials and temptations of the future. Hypocrites do not experience that God is true; only those who cleave to the Word have this experience. Take note of this, that a person who abandons the Word sinks into a bottomless pit in days of temptation, poverty, and other tribulations; such a person is driven to despair. Therefore Christ wants to say here: "If you can hold on to My Word, then stand firm; for you remain a true disciple of Mine by holding staunchly to the Word. Not only to know, learn, read, and hear the Word but also to experience it—this makes you a genuine disciple." . . .

It is proper to argue that there is a twofold freedom. The first is a false freedom of the false disciples, who seek a carnal freedom and are motivated by it to become Christians. Thus the Jews here became Christians because they heard that the Christians were pious, kind, patient, gentle, not vindictive, liberal with their alms, and generous; furthermore, that they have a gracious God, not an angry one. This they hear, and it appeals to them that Christians give to others and serve them. Therefore they say: "I shall gladly have others donate to me, serve me, and forgive me. God will also accord me forgiveness and help me into heaven." They are eager to receive, to be presented with things, and to possess. But they are and remain knaves for all that. They refuse to give up their idolatry and their abominations and to give to others. They want to keep on whoring and being knaves as before, and at the same time they want to be regarded as evangelicals. Those are the false disciples, who seek only the freedom of the flesh. They praise the Gospel fulsomely, and in the beginning they seek it with great earnestness. But they are not sincere, and they do as they please. They indulge their evil lusts and will, become viler than they were, turn out to be much more licentious, smugger, wilder, greedier, and more addicted to thievery and robbery than others. Thus our knaves, our peasants, our burghers, and our noblemen are more miserly and lecherous than they were under the papacy. They are becoming much worse than they were before; they refuse to repent and be converted. Therefore they cannot escape being hurled into the abyss of hell.

But the others—who remain loyal to God's Word, endure, suffer, bear, and venture what they must—will be freed. As time goes on, they become stronger. They know the truth that Christ will make them free. The former do not know what truth is. Therefore they give God cause to explain His concept of truth more clearly. For the statement that they did not understand the truth is blunt and curt. They will never comprehend these things with their reason, but to the end of their days they will remain as they were before; in fact, they will be seven times worse. Everything they do is vain and false. They stagger along in a deceiving, drunken daze. Everything they believe is a fiction. They have never tasted Christ; they do not know what Christ is; they have never suffered for Christ's sake. For this reason they are like drunkards who do not know the way home. Everything they believe is false and amounts to nothing. They are not capable of doing one good work. Whenever they do something good, they are motivated by a selfish ambition for honor, money, and goods. Thus if a prince, a nobleman, or a peasant does a good work, he expects to derive honor and benefit from it. And if that does not follow, he grows furious and foolish, and stops doing good. This proves that there is no truth there. One finds no true word on their lips and no true work in their hands. Their one concern is honor and wealth, as is still evident from the example of the pope and his bishops.

But here is the truth: Christ will truly make you free—not in a physical manner, but He will free you from sin. Here Christ wants to state: "I am not a beggar preacher who discourses on paltry things, such as temporal riches, honor, might, and pleasures." For all these are nothing but sow dung and filth, dropped into the straw by swine. Riches are nothing but the fish bones and other bones, leftovers from the masters' tables and thrown to the dogs (Matt. 15:27), the crust cut away from the bread. Such preaching, which pertains to the physical belly, we leave to the lawyers. But Christ is speaking here about true, eternal, and spiritual freedom. The Jews do not understand this correctly. They say: "We are Abraham's children; hence we are not bondsmen." Christ does not use the word "servant" in the sense in which we Germans do, for our customs differ from those of that day. He is referring to slaves, to the relationship which makes a man the absolute property of a master, to persons whom the master may eject from his estate at will. It was the rigorous rule of the time that if the master gave the slave a wife, then their children, too, became the master's property. The master appropriated them. Furthermore, the earnings of their work did not belong to the slaves but to the master. Such were the harsh measures of that day. Milk is not the property of the cow, nor the calf the property of the cow; and the farrow does not belong to the sow but to the mistress of the house.

Thus men were the property of others at that time. Whatever a slave, his wife, or his children acquired and earned belonged to the master. A severe master kept it all, doling out to the slave and his wife and children no more than food, drink, clothing, and shoes. The Turk does that to this day, making people his slaves, who are subservient to him with all their goods. Their status is like that of a cow. When a maid gets much milk from her, this belongs to the mistress, not to the cow. That is the bondage of a sow, a horse, or a cow. Whatever a horse achieves and earns with his work is the master's property. All that the master gives for it to the horse is fodder, feed, and drink, and little enough at that. Thus the slaves of Jesus' day, in bondage like animals, were given food and drink, shabby and torn garments, and then were cruelly driven to work. Our servants today are lords and ladies in comparison. It would seem more appropriate to call them lords and ladies than servants. The Turk, however, still subjects people to slavery. . . .

Truly, truly, everyone who commits sin is a slave to sin.

These words promise to be a text and sermon on the essence of true Christian freedom. Christ does not plan to alter secular kingdoms or to abolish serfdom. What does He care how princes and lords rule? It does not concern Him how a man plows, sows, makes shoes, builds houses, or pays tribute or taxes. Such work was ordered in Gen. 1:28, when God created the world and specified that we should beget children and occupy and cultivate the world. Here Christ is not speaking about these external matters; rather He is speaking of a freedom which lies outside and above this outward existence and life. Here He deals with freedom from sin, death, God's wrath, the devil, hell, and eternal damnation. A cow can free herself and give her master or mistress no more milk. A bondsman can redeem himself from service to his master by paying a ransom.

This Christian freedom may be enjoyed both by one who is free and by one who is a bondsman, by one who is a captive and by one who takes others captive, by a woman as well as by a man, by a servant and a maid as well as by a lord and a lady. We are speaking of the freedom before God, the freedom we have when God pronounces us free from sin. This freedom is extended to all. Christ directs the Jews away from their carnal conception of freedom. It irritates them that He will not lead them to a physical freedom of the flesh. They are incensed because He speaks about a captivity of the people; He implies that they are not free. This is why they call the Lord Christ a heretic and say that the devil is speaking through Him to mislead the people and take them captive.[30] . . .

---

30   This is the end of the eleventh sermon on John 8, which was delivered on the first Saturday in Advent, December 9, 1531.

Such a fate [captivity and exile] will also overtake us Germans. We commit sin and are slaves of sin. We live in carnal lusts and wallow up to our ears in license. We want to do as we please and whatever serves the devil. We want to be free to do whatever we desire. There are but a few who devote themselves to the real problem: how to get rid of sin. The majority is content to be free from the pope, from officials, and from other laws; but they are not concerned about serving Christ and being delivered from sin. Therefore it will come to pass that we, too, will not continue to live "in the house," since slaves do not abide in the house forever. We will have to be evicted, and we will lose the Gospel and freedom again.

What will you wager that we Germans will not be driven out, will not lose our temporal government and the Gospel, will not fall into the clutches of devils worse than the pope, and will not be in bondage to them? They will mislead us as blind fools, and they will scatter us over the whole world, just as the Jews were dispersed. This is God's policy. He applied it to the Jews, and He will apply it to all despisers of His Word. God dispersed the Jews and took away their kingdom and their synagogue. If we blunder, and fail to appropriate this chief doctrine—how to be rid of sin—He will also disperse us so thoroughly that we will not know whether there will be any other true Christians anywhere. At one place a schismatic spirit will arise, at another a sect; and every nook and cranny will crawl with fanatics, heretics, and fluttering spirits. Then our adversaries will exclaim: "Oh, such are the fruits of the Gospel! May the devil lay about among them! Why do they not believe?" The Jews reproached Paul and the other apostles similarly; they said: "What good has come from the preaching of the Gospel?" But it serves them right; it is your own fault. If you do not want to be pious and free from sin, you will not remain in the house; but you will be evicted. And if you then wander hither and yon and have as many pastors as you have beliefs, you are only getting your just due. That is what happens when God begins to disperse the people; then gross confusion ensues, and many factions and sects arise. . . .

Note well that the real freedom is freedom from sin. Without this the temple at Jerusalem will not help you; neither will the pope with his whole train, whether it be indulgences, papal bulls, fasting, rosaries, prayers, or anything else. Neither Jews nor the pope will make us free; only the Son can do this. How does it come about? When we hear

His Word—for instance, that Christ was born of Mary, suffered, was crucified, died, was buried, rose from the dead on the third day, etc. "Oh," it is said, "I know all this very well! It is an old story. The pope, cardinals, and bishops are also familiar with it." Indeed, they do know it. But learn this lesson of the children, for these words tell us how we are redeemed and set free. "Yes," they say, "these sayings and words are so common that they do not do the work." The children are to be highly commended for praying these words and also for understanding them sooner; for the more learned and the smarter we old fools claim to be, the less we know and understand about this subject. To become free implies that you fix your thoughts on something else than that which lies in you, in the papacy, in the saints, or in Moses. You must direct your thoughts to something more exalted than all this, namely, the Son of God. Who is He? In the Creed we say: "Conceived of the Holy Spirit, born of Mary, died, etc." Note well that you will really be pious and free from sin if you believe that Christ makes you free by dying for you, shedding His blood, rising from the dead, and sitting at the right hand of God.

These statements of the Creed point me to the Son, who makes me free. Whoever fails to learn this, to believe it, and to cling to the Son must remain in sin; whatever else he may undertake is all lost effort. This is a message which must be preached again and again to fill and satisfy people with this doctrine. My hunger, however, has not yet been appeased. This doctrine is like bread, of which the body does not weary. We can be surfeited with other food, but not with bread, unless a person is sick and unable to eat. A healthy person does not tire of bread. Likewise, to the end of his days a Christian never finishes with the study of the Creed. Neither will you or any saint, whether it be Mary or John the Baptist.

Therefore it is fitting that we sit down beside the stove with the children and learn this lesson. Of course, some among us have learned from one sermon all there is to know! But when they are confronted with trials, these people are in sore need of having someone recite these words to them and of having a four-year-old child recite the Creed to them. In the meantime they pray psalms as the monks and nuns read and memorize the Psalter. But in the anguish of death monks, nuns, and priests do not know a single letter with which they might comfort themselves. Such persons are called great theologians, even though in the hour of greatest distress they cannot match their knowledge with that of a four-year-old child. Well, you great, learned, and holy saint, are you ignorant of this? Christ knows that much depends on this knowledge, that people disdain this article of faith, that they finish the study of it too soon, that they become doctors too fast, and that when they have heard it, they assume that they know it by heart and really master it. But they are mistaken. . . .

St. Paul also glories in, and rejoices over, his bonds and is really confident, saying, as it were: "Another man might say that he is a prisoner and that the judges in Rome are his masters. But I reverse the order completely and say: 'Dear hangman, dear government, you are my servants, and I am your lord. You are furthering my cause with all that you do to me and inflict on me. I cannot thank you enough, for you make my faith prouder and more glorious.'" Against such a slave one must pray as against a mad and crazy dog. And what else is such a tyrant doing when he resorts to fire, water, sword, and all other tortures and torments to kill and completely suppress me than to lift me up and take me to heaven? That is the lot that awaits him who previously possessed this freedom. . . .

This is a sublime sermon. The Holy Spirit presents and submits it to the children and to the simple-minded. Old fools like me learn this with great difficulty. Little children learn it best. Others learn this wisdom too well, assuming that when they have heard it once, they know it all. I, however, feel that I cannot understand it. St. Paul has the same complaint, saying that he would like to believe and accept this as the Word of God, but that in his flesh there is someone who wars against it and will not accept it (Rom. 7:18–19). Therefore the central fact of this freedom must be proclaimed daily. Then the other freedom will surely follow. But if you want to begin with, and treat of, physical freedom, you will become so muddled and confused that you will lose both freedoms. You must bear this in mind. "Everyone who commits sin is a slave to sin." Both hell and death are his masters. He cannot escape them. How, then, can I become free? Men answer: "I will erect a chapel, endow an eternal Mass, go on pilgrimages, fast, become a monk, etc." But Christ says: "That is just the right way! No, let Him who is called the Son of God deliver you from sin; then you are free. If you give yourself to Him and let Him set you free, all is well. Otherwise everything will be vain and futile, no matter what else you do."[31]

---

31 This is the end of the twelfth sermon on John 8, which was delivered on the Saturday after St. Dorothy's Day, February 10, 1532. The original edition adds this note to the date: "When Luther became well again after being seriously ill in the meantime."

LECTURES ON GALATIANS
FROM 1535

———•◆•———

EDITOR'S INTRODUCTION

Luther's 1535 publication of the *Lectures on Galatians* actually reaches back to 1531, when he originally delivered them to students in the university lecture hall. The lectures followed after significant historical and doctrinal events: the publication of John Eck's *Four Hundred Articles for the Imperial Diet of Augsburg* (May 1530), the presentation of the Augsburg Confession (June 1530), and the Confutation of the Augsburg Confession (August 1530) by Eck and other imperially appointed theologians. In other words, Luther's lectures responded to this new series of confrontations with Roman theologians, which represented an intensity not felt since the early 1520s. On July 3, 1531, in Luther's opening statement about the *Lectures on Galatians*, he acknowledged that the circumstances weighed on his mind. He said, "There is a clear and present danger that the devil may take away from us the pure doctrine of faith and may substitute for it the doctrines of works and human traditions."[32]

LUTHER'S COMMENTS ON GALATIANS 2:19

Note: In order to understand Christian freedom, Luther engages the underlying paradigm of the doctrine of justification and the proper distiction of Law and Gospel.

---

32 LW 26:3.

> He delivers the Law in its full severity in order to "kill off" any hope of self-reliance in the sinner and to "raise" the only hope left, namely, the sweet consolation of the Gospel. After that, one relies so little on works of the Law as a measure of righteousness that one is dead to the Law. One then does good works that are in accord with the Law, but not because of motivation by the Law or the desire for self-created righteousness. Therefore, Christian freedom includes the freedom to do good works as a justified believer. The translation is from LW 26:159–63.

This is a strange and unheard-of definition, that to live to the Law is to die to God and that to die to the Law is to live to God. These two propositions are utterly contrary to reason; therefore no sophist or legalist understands them. But you must learn to understand them correctly. Anyone who strives to live to the Law, that is, wants to act in such a way that he is justified through the Law, is a sinner and remains a sinner; therefore he is dead and damned. For the law cannot justify and save him; but because it rightly accuses him, it kills him. To live to the Law, therefore, is to die to God; on the other hand, to die to the Law is to live to God. And to live to God is to be justified through grace or through faith for the sake of Christ, without the Law and works. Therefore if you want to live to God, you must die to the Law. But if you live to the Law, then you are dead to God.

If a Christian is defined properly and accurately, therefore, he is a child of grace and of the forgiveness of sins. He has no Law at all, but he is above the Law, sin, death, and hell. Just as Christ is free of the grave and as Peter is free of the prison, so the Christian is free of the Law. The relation between Christ raised from the grave and the grave, or the relation between Peter delivered from prison and the prison—such is the relation between the justified conscience and the Law. And just as Christ by His death and resurrection dies to the grave, so that it has no jurisdiction over Him and cannot hold Him, and He rises and goes away freely, now that the stone and the seals have been broken, and the guards have been terrified; and just as Peter dies to his prison through his deliverance and goes where he pleases—so by grace the conscience is liberated from the Law. "So it is with everyone who is born of the Spirit" (John 3:8). But the flesh does not know whence this comes or whither it goes, for it cannot judge except according to the Law. But the spirit says: "Let the Law accuse me; let sin and death terrify me. I do not despair on their account; for I have a law against the Law, sin against sin, and death against death." . . .

We are pronounced righteous solely by grace or by faith in Christ, without the Law and works.

The blind sophists do not understand this. Therefore they dream that faith does not justify unless it does the works of love. In this way the faith that believes in Christ becomes idle and useless, for it is deprived of the power to justify unless it has been "formed by love." But you set the Law and love aside until another place and time; and you direct your attention to the point at issue here, namely, that Jesus Christ, the Son of God, dies on the cross and bears my sin, the Law, death, the devil, and hell in His body. These enemies and unconquerable tyrants press in upon me and now create trouble for me; therefore I am anxious to be delivered from them, justified, and saved. Here I find neither Law nor work nor any love that can deliver me from them. Only Christ takes away the Law, kills my sin, destroys my death in His body, and in this way empties hell, judges the devil, crucifies him, and throws him down into hell. In other words, everything that once used to torment and oppress me Christ has set aside; He has disarmed it and made a public example of it, triumphing over it in Himself (Col. 2:14–15), so that it cannot dominate any longer but is compelled to serve me.

From this it can be sufficiently understood that there is nothing to be done here but to hear that this has been done in this way, and to take hold of it with an undoubted faith. This really is a "formed faith." Afterwards, when Christ has thus been grasped by faith and I am dead to the Law, justified from sin, and delivered from death, the devil, and hell through Christ—then I do good works, love God, give thanks, and practice love toward my neighbor. But this love or the works that follow faith do not form or adorn my faith, but my faith forms and adorns love.

This is our theology; and when it is said that I am not only blind and deaf to the Law and free from it but completely dead to it, these are paradoxes strange to reason and absurd. And this statement of Paul's, "I through the Law died to the Law," is full of comfort. If it could come to a person's mind at the opportune time and cling firmly to his mind with genuine understanding, he would stand bravely against all the dangers of death and the terrors of conscience and of sin, no matter how much they attacked him, accused him, and wanted to drive him to despair. Of course, everyone is tempted, if not during his life, then at his death. Then, when the Law accuses and manifests his sin, his conscience immediately says: "You have sinned." If now you hold to what Paul, the apostle of Christ, teaches here, you will reply: "It is true. I have sinned." "Then God will punish and damn you." "No." "But that is what the Law of God says." "I have nothing to do with this Law." "Why is that?" "Because I have another Law, one that strikes this Law dumb. I am referring to liberty." "What liberty?" "That of Christ, for through Christ I am liberated from the Law." Therefore the Law which is and remains a Law for the wicked is liberty for me, and it binds the Law that damns me. Thus the Law that once bound me and held me captive is now bound and held captive by grace or liberty, which is now my Law. The accusing Law now hears this Law say: "You shall not bind this man, hold him captive, or make him guilty. But I will hold you captive and tie your hands, lest you hurt him who now lives to Christ and is dead to you."

This knocks out the teeth of the Law, blunts its sting and all its weapons, and utterly disables it. Yet it remains a Law for the wicked and unbelieving; it remains also for us who are weak, to the extent that we do not believe. Here it still has its sharpness and its teeth. But if I believe in Christ, regardless of how sin may trouble me to the point of despair, I shall rely on the liberty I have in Christ and say: "I admit that I have sinned. But my sin (which is a sin that is damned) is in Christ (who is a sin that damns). This sin that damns is stronger than the sin that is damned; for it is justifying grace, righteousness, life, and salvation." And so when I feel the terrors of death, I say: "Death, you have nothing on me. For I have another death, one that kills you, my death. And the death that kills is stronger than the death that is killed."

Thus the believer can raise himself up through faith alone and gain a comfort that is sure and firm; and he need not grow pale at the sight of sin, death, the devil, or any evil. The more the devil attacks him with all his force and tries to overwhelm him with all the terrors of the world, the more hope he acquires in the very midst of all these terrors and says: "Mr. Devil,[33] do not rage so. Just take it easy! For there is One who is called Christ. In Him I believe. He has abrogated the Law,

[33] Cf. LW 13:262–63.

damned sin, abolished death, and destroyed hell. And He is your devil, you devil, because He has captured and conquered you, so that you cannot harm me any longer or anyone else who believes in Him." The devil cannot overcome this faith, but he is overcome by it. For "this," says John (1 John 5:4–5), "is the victory that overcomes the world, our faith. Who is it that overcomes the world but he who believes that Jesus is the Son of God?"

With exceeding zeal and indignation of spirit, therefore, Paul calls grace itself "Law," even though in reality it is nothing else than the very great and boundless liberty of the grace that we have in Christ Jesus. Then he also assigns this most shameful name to the Law for our comfort, to let us know that it has now been baptized with a new name, because it is no longer alive but is dead and damned. It is a very pleasing sight as he sets forth and produces the Law as a thief or a robber who has already been condemned and sentenced to death. For by personification he represents the Law as being held captive, with its hands and its feet bound and shorn of all power, so that it cannot exert its tyranny, that is, accuse and condemn. With this most pleasing picture he makes it contemptible to the conscience, so that the believer in Christ now has the courage to insult the Law with a certain holy pride and to say: "I am a sinner. If you can do anything against me, Law, go ahead and do it!" That is how far the Law now is from frightening the believer.

Luther's Comments on Galatians 5:1

Note: In this key biblical passage on freedom, Luther contrasts political and sinful "freedom" with true freedom in Christ: from the wrath of God; from the power of sin, death, and the devil; and from hell. Christian freedom is clearly understood in a world that culminates in the final judgment and the final states of eternal life in heaven and eternal death in hell. In such a world, resisting the yoke of slavery to the Law means losing oneself and taking hold of Christ. Freedom does not point to individuality or to autonomy; it points to Christ. This freedom is not contingent on keeping the Law, but on believing that Christ alone has won for each one of us eternal life and salvation and offers it alone through faith as attested to by

the sole authority of Scripture. The translation is from
LW 27:3–6.

As he approaches the end of the epistle, Paul argues vigorously and passionately in defense of the doctrine of faith and of Christian liberty against the false apostles, who are its enemies and destroyers. He aims and hurls veritable thunderbolts of words at them to lay them low. At the same time he urges the Galatians to avoid their wicked doctrine as though it were some sort of plague. In the course of his urging he threatens, promises, and tries every device to keep them in the freedom achieved for them by Christ. Therefore he says:

1. For freedom Christ has set us free; stand fast therefore.

That is: "Be firm!" Thus Peter says (1 Peter 5:8–9): "Be sober, be watchful. Your adversary the devil prowls around like a roaring lion, seeking someone to devour. Resist him, firm in your faith." "Do not be smug," he says, "but be firm. Do not lie down or sleep, but stand." It is as though he were saying: "Vigilance and steadiness are necessary if you are to keep the freedom for which Christ has set us free. Those who are smug and sleepy are not able to keep it." For Satan violently hates the light of the Gospel, that is, the teaching about grace, freedom, comfort, and life. Therefore as soon as he sees it arise, he immediately strives to obliterate it with all his winds and storms. For this reason Paul urges godly persons not to be drowsy and smug in their behavior but to stand bravely in the battle against Satan, lest he take away the freedom achieved for them by Christ.

Every word is emphatic. "Stand fast," he says, "in freedom." In what freedom? Not in the freedom for which the Roman emperor has set us free but in the freedom for which Christ has set us free. The Roman emperor gave—indeed, was forced to give—the Roman pontiff a free city and other lands, as well as certain immunities, privileges, and concessions.[34] This, too, is freedom; but it is a political freedom, according to which the Roman pontiff with all his clergy is free of all public burdens. In addition, there is the freedom of the flesh, which is chiefly prevalent in the world. Those who have this obey neither God

---

34 The Donation of Constantine, which purported to be a deed of gift from Constantine to the pope, had been exposed as a forgery by Lorenzo Valla in 1440.

nor the laws but do what they please. This is the freedom which the rabble pursues today; so do the fanatical spirits, who want to be free in their opinions and actions, in order that they may teach and do with impunity what they imagine to be right. This is a demonic freedom, by which the devil sets the wicked free to sin against God and men. We are not dealing with this here although it is the most widespread and is the only goal and objective of the entire world. Nor are we dealing with political freedom. No, we are dealing with another kind, which the devil hates and attacks most bitterly.

This is the freedom with which Christ has set us free, not from some human slavery or tyrannical authority but from the eternal wrath of God. Where? In the conscience. This is where our freedom comes to a halt; it goes no further. For Christ has set us free, not for a political freedom or a freedom of the flesh but for a theological or spiritual freedom, that is, to make our conscience free and joyful, unafraid of the wrath to come (Matt. 3:7). This is the most genuine freedom; it is immeasurable. When the other kinds of freedom—political freedom and the freedom of the flesh—are compared with the greatness and the glory of this kind of freedom, they hardly amount to one little drop. For who can express what a great gift it is for someone to be able to declare for certain that God neither is nor ever will be wrathful but will forever be a gracious and merciful Father for the sake of Christ? It is surely a great and incomprehensible freedom to have this Supreme Majesty kindly disposed toward us, protecting and helping us, and finally even setting us free physically in such a way that our body, which is sown in perishability, in dishonor, and in weakness, is raised in imperishability, in honor, and in power (1 Cor. 15:42–43). Therefore the freedom by which we are free of the wrath of God forever is greater than heaven and earth and all creation.

From this there follows the other freedom, by which we are made safe and free through Christ from the Law, from sin, death, the power of the devil, hell, etc. For just as the wrath of God cannot terrify us—since Christ has set us free from it—so the Law, sin, etc., cannot accuse and condemn us. Even though the Law denounces us and sin terrifies us, they still cannot plunge us into despair. For faith, which is the victor over the world (1 John 5:4), quickly declares: "Those things have nothing to do with me, for Christ has set me free from them." So it is that death, which is the most powerful and horrible thing in the world, lies conquered in our conscience through this freedom of the Spirit. Therefore the greatness of Christian freedom should be carefully measured and pondered. The words "freedom from the wrath of God, from the Law, sin, death, etc.," are easy to say; but to feel the greatness of this freedom and to apply its results to oneself in a struggle, in the agony of conscience, and in practice—this is more difficult than anyone can say.

Therefore one's spirit must be trained, so that when it becomes conscious of the accusation of the Law, the terrors of sin, the horror of death, and the wrath of God, it will banish these sorrowful scenes from its sight and will replace them with the freedom of Christ, the forgiveness of sins, righteousness, life, and the eternal mercy of God. Although the consciousness of these opponents may be powerful, one must be sure that it will not last long. As the prophet says (Is. 54:8), "In overflowing wrath for a moment I hid My face from you, but with everlasting love I will have compassion on you." But this is extremely difficult to bring about. Therefore the freedom that Christ has achieved for us is easier to talk about than it is to believe. If it could be grasped in its certainty by a firm faith, no fury or terror of the world, the Law, sin, death, the devil, etc., could be too great for it to swallow them up as quickly as the ocean swallows a spark. Once and for all this freedom of Christ certainly swallows up and abolishes a whole heap of evils—the Law, sin, death, the wrath of God, finally the serpent himself with his head (Gen. 3:15); and in their place it establishes righteousness, peace, life, etc. But blessed is the man who understands and believes this.

Therefore let us learn to place a high value on this freedom of ours; not the emperor, not an angel from heaven, but Christ, the Son of God, through whom all things were created in heaven and earth, obtained it for us by His death, to set us free, not from some physical and temporary slavery but from the spiritual and eternal slavery of those most cruel and invincible tyrants, the Law, sin, death, the devil, etc., and to reconcile us to God the Father. Now that these enemies have been defeated and now that we have been reconciled to God through the death of His Son, it is certain that we are righteous in the sight of God and that all our actions are pleasing to Him; and if there is any sin left in us, this is not imputed to us but is forgiven for the sake of Christ. Paul is speaking very precisely when he says that we should stand in the freedom for which Christ has set us free. Therefore this freedom is granted to us, not on account of the Law or our righteousness but freely, on account of Christ. Paul testifies to this and demonstrates it at length throughout this epistle; and Christ says in John 8:36: "If the Son makes you free, you will be free indeed." He alone is thrust into the middle between us and the evils that oppress us. He conquers and abolishes them, so that they cannot harm us any longer. In fact, in place of sin and death He grants us righteousness and eternal life, and He changes slavery and the terrors of the Law into the freedom of conscience and the comfort of the Gospel, which says (Matt. 9:2): "Take heart, My son; your sins are forgiven." Therefore he who believes in Christ has this freedom.

Reason does not see how great a matter this is; but when it is seen in the Spirit, it is enormous and infinite. No one can realize with language or thought what a great gift it is to have—instead of the Law, sin, death, and a wrathful God—the forgiveness of sins, righteousness, eternal life, and a God who is permanently gracious and kind. The papists and all self-righteous people boast that they also have the forgiveness of sins, righteousness, etc.; they also lay claim to freedom. But all these things are worthless and uncertain. In temptation they vanish instantly, because they depend on human works and satisfactions, not on the Word of God and on Christ. Therefore it is impossible for any self-righteous people to know what freedom from sin, etc., really is. By contrast, our freedom has as its foundation Christ, who is the eternal High Priest, who is at the right hand of God and intercedes for us. Therefore the freedom, forgiveness of sins, righteousness, and life that we have through Him are sure, firm, and eternal, provided that we believe this. If we cling firmly to Christ by faith and stand firm in the freedom with which He has made us free, we shall have those inestimable gifts. But if we become smug and drowsy, we shall lose them. It is not in vain that Paul commands us to be vigilant and to stand, because he knows that the devil is busily engaged in trying to rob us of this freedom that cost Christ so much, and to tie us up again in the yoke of slavery through his agents.

Luther's Comments on Galatians 5:13

Note: Here, Luther presents the doctrines of faith and good works. He warns that a failure to preach faith, that is, the Gospel, results in no one being saved, while preaching the Gospel gives ample opportunity for people to misinterpret that Gospel in sinful ways. Luther is clear that the devil works especially hard to corrupt the truth of Gospel freedom and turn it into self-serving imprisonment to sin. Luther echoes Paul's clear message that such forms of corruption are contrary to both Law and Gospel. The translation is from LW 27:48–51.

This evil is very widespread, and it is the worst of all the evils that Satan arouses against the teaching of faith: that in many people he soon transforms the freedom for which Christ has set us free into an opportunity for the flesh. Jude complains of this same thing in his epistle (ch. 4): "Admission has been secretly gained by some ungodly persons who pervert the grace of our God into licentiousness." For the flesh simply does not understand the teaching of grace, namely, that we are not justified by works but by faith alone, and that the Law has no jurisdiction over us. Therefore when it hears this teaching, it transforms it into licentiousness and immediately draws the inference: "If we are without the Law, then let us live as we please. Let us not do good, let us not give to the needy; much less do we have to endure anything evil. For there is no Law to compel or bind us."

Thus there is a danger on both sides, although the one is more tolerable than the other. If grace or faith is not preached, no one is saved; for faith alone justifies and saves. On the other hand, if faith is preached, as it must be preached, the majority of men understand the teaching about faith in a fleshly way and transform the freedom of the spirit into the freedom of the flesh. This can be discerned today in all classes of society, both high and low. They all boast of being evangelicals and boast of Christian freedom. Meanwhile, however, they give in to their desires and turn to greed, sexual desire, pride, envy, etc. No one performs his duty faithfully; no one serves another by love. This misbehavior often makes me so impatient that I would want such "swine that trample pearls underfoot" (Matt. 7:6) still to be under the tyranny of the pope. For it is impossible for this people of Gomorrah to be ruled by the Gospel of peace. . . .

We know that the devil lies in wait especially for us who have the Word—he already holds the others captive to his will—and that he is intent upon taking the freedom of the Spirit away from us or at least making us change it into license. Therefore we teach and exhort our followers with great care and diligence, on the basis of Paul's example, not to think that this freedom of the Spirit, achieved by the death of Christ, was given[35] to them as an opportunity for the flesh or, as Peter says, "to use as a pretext for evil" (1 Peter 2:16), but for them to be servants of one another through love.

As we have said, therefore, the apostle imposes an obligation on Christians through this law about mutual love in order to keep them from abusing their freedom. Therefore the godly should remember that for the sake of Christ they are free in their conscience before God from the curse of the Law, from sin, and from death, but that according to the body they are bound; here each must serve the other through love, in accordance with this commandment of Paul. Therefore let everyone strive to do his duty in his calling and to help his neighbor in whatever way he can. This is what Paul requires of us with the words "through love be servants of one another," which do not permit the saints to run free according to the flesh but subject them to an obligation.

Of course, it is impossible to teach or persuade unspiritual people of this teaching about the love to be mutually observed among us. Christians comply with it voluntarily. But when the others hear this freedom proclaimed, they immediately draw the inference: "If I am free, then I have the right to do whatever I please. This thing belongs to me; why should I not sell it for as much as I can? Again, if we do not obtain salvation on account of good works, why should we give anything to the poor?" In their great smugness such people shrug off this yoke and obligation of the flesh, and they transform the freedom of the Spirit into the license and lust of the flesh. Although they will not believe us but will make fun of us, we make this sure announcement to these smug despisers: If they use their bodies and their powers for their own lusts—as they are certainly doing when they refuse to

35 Jerome, *Liber interpretationis hebraicorum nominum*, Corpus Christianorum, Series Latina, LXXII, 64, and *passim*.

153

help the poor and to share, but defraud their brethren in business and acquire things by fair means or foul—then they are not free, as they loudly claim to be, but have lost both Christ and freedom, and are slaves of the devil, so that now, under the title of "Christian freedom," their state is seven times as bad as it used to be under the tyranny of the pope (Matt. 12:43–45). For when the devil who has been cast out of them returns to them, he brings with him seven spirits more evil than himself. Therefore their last state becomes worse than the first.

We for our part have the divine command to preach the Gospel, which announces to all men, if only they believe, the free gift of freedom from the Law, from sin, from death, and from the wrath of God, for the sake of Christ. We have neither the intention nor the authority to conceal this freedom or to obscure and cancel it once it has been made public through the Gospel; for Christ has granted it to us and has achieved it by His death. Nor are we able to compel those swine, who are rushing headlong into the license of the flesh, to be servants of others with their bodies and their possessions. Therefore we do what we can. That is, we diligently admonish them that this is what they should do. If we do not accomplish anything with these warnings of ours, we commit the matter to God, to whom it belongs anyway. In His own time He will inflict just punishment on them. Meanwhile, however, we are comforted by the fact that our labor and our diligence are not in vain among the godly, many of whom have undoubtedly been rescued by our ministry from the slavery of the devil and have been transferred to the freedom of the Spirit. These few—who acknowledge the glory of this freedom, who at the same time are ready to be the servants of others through love, and who know that according to the flesh they are debtors to the brethren—give us a happiness that is greater than the sadness that can be caused by the infinite number of those who abuse this freedom.

Paul speaks in clear and precise terms when he says: "You were called to freedom." To prevent anyone from imagining that he means the freedom of the flesh, he explains himself and says what kind of freedom he has in mind: "Only do not use your freedom as an opportunity for the flesh, but through love be servants of one another." Therefore every Christian should know that in his conscience he has been established by Christ as a lord over the Law, sin, and death, and that they do not have jurisdiction over him. On the other hand, he should know also that this external obligation has been imposed on his body, that through love he should serve his neighbor. Those who understand Christian freedom differently are enjoying the advantages of the Gospel to their own destruction and are worse idolaters under the name "Christian" than they used to be under the pope. Now Paul shows beautifully on the basis of the Decalog what it means to be a servant through love.

LECTURES ON GENESIS FROM 1536

EDITOR'S INTRODUCTION

In 1535, Luther stated his intention to spend the last years of his life expounding on the Books of Moses. Luther had preached a series of sermons on Genesis and Deuteronomy in 1523, Exodus in 1524, Leviticus and Numbers in 1527, and Deuteronomy again in 1529. He also continually preached on the Ten Commandments that Moses heard from God and carried down from Mount Sinai. At times, Luther wrote forcefully against "Moses" and his accusations that afflict the conscience. Yet it is also clear that Luther valued Moses' counsel, turned to it repeatedly, and determined to share it with his hearers and readers. He saw the need to explain the place of the Books of Moses in the canon of the Church and their use in pulpit, society, and Christian life. Luther's *Lectures on Genesis* (1535–45) are the last great embodiment of his thought.

LUTHER'S COMMENTS ON GENESIS 13:13

Note: While explaining the story of Abram and Lot, Luther describes the apparent favor that God shows the ungodly. He then engages the matter of following one's vocation in a godly manner. A Christian is not free to be ungodly, even when living among the ungodly, for in all matters that engage what God either commands or forbids, a Christian is not free. The translation is from LW 2:345–49.

Beautiful indeed was the praise of this excellent land. Moses called it the Paradise of the Lord and compared it to Egypt. But who are the people who inhabit it? Wicked men and great sinners. Thus in God's Paradise there live the sons of the devil, and the richest places contain the most detestable men in the entire world.

Why is this? No doubt in order that you may learn that it is God's custom to give the best to the worst. This is a most serious offense; by it the patience even of the saints is troubled, not to mention the wise men of the world and the philosophers. It is for this reason that Ps. 73:3–6 states: "I was envious of the arrogant, when I saw the prosperity of the wicked. For they have no pangs; their bodies are sound and sleek. They are not in trouble as other men are; they are not stricken like other men. Therefore pride is their necklace." "But all the day long I have been stricken, chastened every morning" (Ps. 73:14).

Thus God gave the rule of the world to Alexander and the Greeks, the worst of men. After the Greeks He gave it to the Romans, who were Epicureans. Similarly, we see that the Turks are most successful. After the Epicurean Romans were punished, there are nations in Europe which inhabit the richest region, truly a garden of God, although they surpass all the others in the worst vices—pride, envy, and cruelty.[36] Thereby God causes great consternation for human reason. As a result it concludes that human affairs are of no concern to God.

Yet we must not maintain that these situations come about by chance or without a reason. It is the will of God; by these means He makes the world foolish, so that it debates whether the things that are good, profitable, and delightful are actually good. . . .

Reason cannot cope with the offense of such extreme disparity. Since it is a fact that this place is a garden of God, reason is of the opinion that the Sodomites should not be put into it, but honorable and very good men. It considers it unfair that the wicked are shown favor by God, and it leans toward the opinion that these good things are not actually good. . . .

We see how many people are depraved by their affluence, but this is not the fault of the blessing of God. A harlot adorns herself with gold and jewels; yet the gold and jewels are good gifts of God, and it is a mistake to attribute the shame of the harlot to them. This is the

---

36   This seems to be aimed against Italy and perhaps against Spain.

Moses Presenting the Law

As the prophet who received the Ten Commandments from God, Moses' name was sometimes used to represent the Law and its severity. This image from an early Reformation catechism has Moses propping up the massive stone tablets of the Law.

general rule by which we must judge about the things or creatures of God, because the entire fault lies with your lust and your depraved will and reason.

A woman is beautiful. Very well, this is a gift of the Lord and Creator. But I am inflamed with desire. Does this make beauty an evil thing? Not at all! It is you who are evil because you are unable to make good use of a good thing. Thus the good things which are called useful and delightful convict us of the corruption of our nature, because neither the will nor the intellect is right; otherwise we would make good use of good things.

Grates is extolled among the philosophers because he threw a large amount of gold into the sea and thereafter supported himself by begging. But does he not thereby convict himself of having a corrupt heart, since he declares that he is unable to make the right use of his gold?

Furthermore, what good, I ask you, did he achieve? Hollow ambition took the place of the greed he had seemingly driven away; that is, after one devil had been driven out, seven others, who were worse, took his place (Matt. 12:45).

Let us, therefore, learn what Holy Scripture asserts: that this region near the Jordan was very fertile. Hence there was at that place a superabundance of useful and delightful good things, given by God for men to enjoy and not for committing sin. But nature, which is corrupted by original sin, is unable to enjoy without abuse the things created and given by God, not because this is the nature of created things but because the heart of him who uses them is evil. But if the heart has been reformed by the Spirit, it makes use of both the useful and the delightful things in a holy manner and with thanksgiving.

Paul similarly states (Rom. 14:6, 8): "He who eats, eats in honor of the Lord. He who marries, marries to the Lord. Whether we live or whether we die, we are the Lord's." For he who believes, has everything and is lord of all; he can make use of all things in a holy manner.

Therefore it is an error when the philosophers condemn things because of their abuse. For it is obvious that as natural reason has no knowledge of God, it also has no knowledge of God's creation. The thought of the heathen poet is more correct. Things, he says, are like the heart of him who uses them.[37] Thus there is a difference among human beings: one has plenty, another is in want. But if the one who is in want has an upright heart, he is wealthier than the rich man; for he is satisfied with a little and gives thanks to God for the most important possessions, that is, the knowledge of God and the grace revealed in Christ. But the rich man, as the tragic poet says,[38] is poor among his accumulated gold; and in the midst of the greatest abundance he feels want.

Where does this difference come from? Obviously not from the nature of the things we use but from a difference in the heart, as St. Paul states in Phil. 4:12: "We know how to be abased, and we know how to abound."

So much about this account, which presents to us this general truth that the ungodly spend their lives in the uninterrupted misuse of the best things, while those who live in righteousness and faith make good use even of evil things, and whatever they do is good.

The Holy Spirit fails to say anything about Lot's activity in prayer, fasting, alms, and other works that strike the eye and evoke admiration. He informs us solely about matters concerning the household. These the masses consider unimportant and of no great benefit. "What does it matter," they say, "that Lot and Abram separate, and that Lot chooses the best part of the land for himself?"

But the learned theologian does not look at the bare works. He considers the person and the heart; and if the heart is full of faith, he concludes that everything he does in faith, even though in outward appearance it is most unimportant—such as the natural activities of sleeping, being awake, eating, and drinking, which seem to have no godliness connected with them—is a holy work that pleases God.

All godly people have some definite times at which they pray, meditate on holy things, and teach and instruct their people in religion; nevertheless, even when they are not doing these things and are attending either to their own affairs or to those of the community in accordance with their calling, they remain in good standing and have this glory before God, that even their seemingly secular works are a worship of God and an obedience well pleasing to God.

---

37   Terence, *Heautontimorumenos*, I, 2, 21.
38   Seneca, *Hercules*, 168.

Courtesy of the Richard C. Kessler Reformation Collection, Pitts Theology Library, Candler School of Theology, Emory University

Philip Melanchthon (1497–1560)

Philip Melanchthon wrote the first edition of his *Loci Communes* in 1521. Following Luther, he pointed out how philosophy caused the Church to depart from the biblical doctrines of sin, grace, and human will. Concerning the Gospel, Melanchthon showed that the Gospel alone is the source of grace. All Scripture consists of Law and Gospel. The proper work of the Law is the revelation of sin, even as the proper work of the Gospel is giving comfort to the conscience.

Melanchthon on Christian Liberty

SELECTED FROM THE CHIEF
THEOLOGICAL TOPICS: *LOCI PRAECIPUI* 1559

Introduction

Luther's closest colleague and fellow reformer, Philip Melanchthon (1497–1560), was likewise interested in the topic of Christian freedom. However, after Luther's death, Melanchthon was strongly criticized by fellow Lutherans due to his involvement with the Augsburg and Leipzig Interims (1548), when political pressure caused him to agree to the restoration of some Roman ceremonies in Lutheran territories. Melanchthon never fully admitted that he had erred. But once political pressure was removed, he returned to an approach that was more compatible with Luther's. The section below on freedom from rites of human authority reflects Melanchthon's recovery from the days of the interims.

Luther admired Melanchthon's ability to state things in a simple, concise way that emphasized understanding. We include Melanchthon's thoughts on Christian freedom as an effective summary of Reformation teaching on the topic of Christian freedom and to demonstrate the unity of the Wittenberg theologians.

The text is drawn from Locus 24 of the 1559 *Chief Theological Topics (Loci praecipui theologici)*, the last edition of the *Loci Communes* that Melanchthon edited. Various editions of the *Loci* served as standard textbooks of Christian doctrine at Wittenberg from 1521 to 1610.

LOCUS 24
CHRISTIAN LIBERTY[1]

[INTRODUCTION]

If one of the princes of Babylon had heard the Jews in exile glorying in the fact that they had been divinely given their liberty, he would have said that this was a sign of their insanity. So also in our time, in the midst of these tragic ruins, when slavery is on the increase in many places, when thousands of godly people are being carried away daily by the Turks before our very eyes, and when in many places unjust savagery is being inflicted on pious people, I think we would be ridiculed by people when we still speak of our liberty and make glorious statements about our freedom. Therefore, we must first confess that we also mourn over the plight of the church of God, which is being oppressed in these fierce and tyrannical times, and in the midst of this confusion of kingdoms.

And even when the church has been supported by more favorable governments, it has always been tormented by the devil and still is burdened down with many calamities and death, even in this life. How great were the sorrows of Adam and Eve when they saw the murders and crimes of their offspring, even though royal empires and tyrants had not yet arisen! The church of God has always been under oppression and in great miseries, and it will continue to be until the resurrection.

What is this thing which we call liberty? Is it merely an empty word, like some paradox of the Stoics or some foolishness of those who say

---

1 *Corpus Reformatorum* 21:1037–50.

that only the wise are free? Far different is the doctrine of the Gospel concerning freedom, of which Christ speaks when He says [John 8:36], "If the Son shall make you free, you shall be free indeed." Indeed, He says, you shall be free not with some empty title or the appearance of liberty, but with true freedom. When sin is destroyed, the wrath of God appeased, death abolished, and all human calamities removed, you will be given eternal righteousness, light, life, and glory.

Christ includes the concept of complete liberty, which He Himself brings and prepares for His church by His death. To be sure, this pure freedom does indeed begin in this life, but in the resurrection it will be complete. When all evils have been destroyed, then the church will enjoy an eternal and beautiful relationship with God and our Savior, Jesus Christ. We must keep in mind this eternal and complete liberty whenever we hear the word "liberty," and at the same time remember that this begins in this life. But we must get rid of the dreams of political and physical liberty, of worldly empires, as the Jews still hold regarding the liberation and restoration of the kingdom in Palestine. These dreams have nothing to do with this doctrine which the Gospel sets forth when it talks of liberty.

Although the church in this life not only is held in bondage by governments but is also tormented with great calamities of other kinds, yet the doctrine of liberty gives the greatest comfort in these evils. Hercules, Priam, Agamemnon, Palamedes, Cato, Cicero, Brutus, and countless others who did not know God were afflicted. But they succumbed to their troubles, and they did not have God mitigating the outcomes or strengthening their minds. They were pressed down under eternal despair and eternal darkness regarding the providence and the righteousness of God. But Joseph, David, Jonathan, Hezekiah, Jeremiah, John the Baptist, and Paul, even when they were afflicted, could still discern the presence of God, who strengthened their minds and often softened the outcome for them. And whenever they were pressed down, their sufferings were sooner or later of benefit to the church, since they knew that after this life in the resurrection they would have eternal glory. Thus in this life they have the beginning of liberty, because they have been accepted by God, are guided by Him, defended and aided, and realize that after this life they will have complete liberty. Now understand how great a blessing it is, what great liberty it is—even

Blessings of the Holy Spirit

In this early representation of Luther, the artist celebrates God's gift of the Holy Spirit to Luther, whose teaching from Scripture led to a renewal of Christian freedom.

in the midst of troubles and in the midst of death—to have a God who is favorable toward us—our helper, our guide, and our protector. This statement about liberty sets forth true and certain things which have clear testimonies in the church and which the church, you and I, and all the godly experience. It does not offer to us the empty dreams of the Jews or the Stoics or the Anabaptists, or of Struthius, who tried to free the people from paying taxes.

I am dividing the subject of evangelical liberty into four degrees or grades, in keeping with our common way of speaking.

[Free Inheritance of Everlasting Life]

The first is: Just as the greatest evils are sin and the wrath of God, so it is necessary to speak first about this degree and how we are to be liberated from these evils. Therefore the first degree of liberty is that, for the sake of the Son of God, there is freely given to us the remission of sins, reconciliation, justification or imputation of righteousness, acceptance to eternal life, and the inheritance of everlasting life.

This is liberty because, for the sake of Christ, these great blessings are freely and surely given to us. God wants us to determine for ourselves and to believe that when we repent, we are received into His grace, our prayers are heard, and we are freely saved for the sake of His Son, even if the Law and our own reason accuse us and hold us back so that we do not accept these blessings. Therefore, we are liberated from sin, from the wrath of God, from eternal damnation, from the Law which accuses us, and from the condition of merit. And another thing has been set forth and given to us, on account of which we receive the remission of sins and are justified, that is, we are pronounced as accepted by God. That other thing is the Son of God, the Mediator, not the Law, and not our merits. Those who have been reconciled are declared as righteous, that is, accepted by God to eternal life, even if they fall far short of the perfection of the Law, but for the sake of Christ and by faith. What a great blessing that though the remnants of sin still cling to those who have been reconciled, and though we are weighed down by a great mountain of shameful sins, yet we are pleasing to God for the sake of Christ, as if we had absolutely and perfectly satisfied the Law.

Paul is preaching about this degree of liberty when he says [Galatians 3:13], "Christ has redeemed us from the curse of the Law, having been made a curse for us." This is a short statement, but it far surpasses the wisdom of all men and angels. The true, great, and unspeakable wrath of God against sin is signified when the Son upon whom this wrath was poured is called a curse. He was made for us a ransom and a victim. We must give thought to this blessing and this liberty every time we call upon God, and determine in faith that for the sake of our Lord Jesus Christ our sins are truly forgiven, covered, and buried, and that He truly wills to save, receive, and hear us for the sake of the Mediator. In these exercises of prayer, our understanding increases daily regarding this liberty of which we have spoken under the first degree, which contains the doctrine of justification, which we have fully described above.

[The Bestowal of the Holy Spirit]

The second degree or grade is the bestowal of the Holy Spirit, who kindles new light in our minds and new movements in our will and heart, guides us, and begins eternal life in us. Although this second degree is connected with the first, for the sake of clear teaching I am making a distinction so that as often as we speak about liberation from the Law, we may understand not only help, as Augustine says repeatedly, but also the free imputation of righteousness.

Augustine often says that we are liberated from the Law, meaning that by the bestowal of the Holy Spirit we are helped so that we are obedient to the Law, nor do we any longer strive in vain under the coercion of the Law. He is correct when he speaks about this help, but it is necessary that we also see a second benefit, namely, the free remission of sins and the imputation of righteousness which is given to us for the sake of Christ. This enormous gift must be seen, so that honor may be given to Christ and our consciences may hold on to true and firm comfort and can invoke God.

Moreover, Christ speaks about both degrees of liberty when He says [John 8:36], "If the Son shall make you free, you will be free indeed." Indeed He is talking about the complete benefit: the Son assuages the wrath of God, takes away sin and death, gives righteousness and eternal life, and raises us to eternal glory and joy which we enjoy in the comfort of God, the angels, and the whole church. This total liberty is the blessing of which Christ is speaking, which also here in this life must be begun.

While we are still in subjection to the cross and mortal death, we are being exercised in great calamities, and sins and great darkness still cling to us. We are under attack by the devil, who constantly ties us up in his evil traps. And no one is so careful, so diligent, that he does not from time to time wander into thoughts about these things. And we ourselves cannot govern the very difficult and perilous course of this life and our calling only by human actions and diligence, as Jeremiah says [10:23], "I know, Lord, that the way of man is not in himself."

Although we see ourselves still shut up in this sad prison, yet we are free, first because it is a certainty that we, for the sake of Christ, have a God who is propitious toward us and our defender, as the first degree of liberty teaches us. Then, because we are helped and guided by the Holy Spirit. David was caught in an evil from which he could not extricate himself when he was exiled from his kingdom, and yet in this he sustained himself with the sure comfort that he had not been cast off by God. And he remembered the word of Nathan [2 Samuel 12:13], "The Lord has taken away your sin." Then he sought the aid and guidance of the Holy Spirit, and experienced the fact that he was indeed helped by God. But Themistocles, when he was exiled from Greece, knew none of these consolations, and to the extent that he did have some place of refuge and human protection, he endured his exile with a peaceful mind.

All the saints have learned the second degree of liberty in times of danger, when they experienced the fact that they were helped and strengthened by God, just as Stephen in his confession and in the agony of death, Lawrence, and many others in their confession.

Therefore, when we consider our weakness and our dangers, we also should give thought to this second degree and we should seek the aid and guidance of the Holy Spirit, as Christ commands when He says [John 16:24], "Ask and you shall receive." Again, [Matthew 11:28], "Come to Me, all you who labor and are heavy laden, and I will give you rest." When we call upon Him without any doubting, we are assured that we are being aided, guided with His counsel, our death protected, dangers dispelled, and our troubles alleviated.

These exercises in prayer will teach us about this second degree of liberty. Now, these two grades teach us how great the blessings of God are. For they are liberations from the greatest of evils, from sin, from the wrath of God, and from eternal death. They include the giving of righteousness and eternal life, defense against the devils, guidance in all matters and dangers, with the Holy Spirit ruling our heart and kindling in us the understanding of the Word of God. Finally, they include the presence of the eternal God, who holds us in His arms for the sake of His Son, our Lord Jesus Christ. There is nothing greater or better than these gifts.

And thus this liberty imparted to us through the blood of Christ, which offers the Gospel, is a great and immeasurable gift. It is not a mere empty word or some product of Stoic imagination, as ungodly men think.

Nor is it difficult for sound and godly minds to see the distinction between this liberation from sin and the wrath of God on the one hand, and civil liberty or liberation from tribute on the other. For nothing is being said about external political tranquility or servitude in these first two degrees. Joseph had these two degrees of liberty of soul even though he had been convicted and put in prison. Daniel had them while he sat among the lions. Lawrence did, too, while he was lying on the gridiron. For political liberty or servitude in no way pertains to these two degrees any more than the strength or weakness of the body, as it says in Galatians 3[:26, 28], "You are all sons of God through faith in Christ Jesus . . . there is neither Jew nor Greek, slave or free man." But it is easy for godly people to understand this: some things are a blessing for the soul, and other different things are good for the body.

[FREEDOM FROM THE CIVIL ORDER OF MOSES]

The third grade or degree of liberty deals with our outward or political life, namely, that Christians are not bound to the civil order of Moses or that of any other nation, but in our various places we owe obedience to the present rulers and the laws, as long as the laws are in harmony with the law of nature and do not compel us to do something contrary to the commandments of God. Just as we observe the intervals of days and nights in other regions, so it is permitted to use other forms of the office of rulers, governments, and laws, so long as the laws, as I said, do not prescribe things to be done which are in conflict with the mandates of God.

The uneducated should be instructed in regard to this third kind of liberty, because it has often happened that very pernicious rebellions have been created by the unlearned who have contended that Christians must be governed by the laws of Moses. This error must be opposed, for the prophets, Christ, and the apostles clearly teach that the end of the Jewish political state would come after the suffering and death of Christ. And the very ruins of Jerusalem bear witness that the political nation of the Jews was destroyed 1,470 years ago. On this basis, this rule instructs us that the ceremonial laws of Moses have been abrogated and that the civil laws of Moses do not pertain to the church of Christ. These civil arrangements pertained to a particular race and were to continue for a specific time, but they do not pertain to other races or to other times. These points are confirmed by many passages of Scripture, such as Acts 10[:35] and Galatians 3[:28] and 5[:6], "In Christ Jesus, neither circumcision or non-circumcision is of value, but faith which works through love."

But this question is being asked: when we speak of the abrogation of the Law, is the entire Law said to be abrogated, or only two parts, namely, the ceremonial and the civil? And the moral law is a heavier burden and a harsher prison than those external ceremonies.

My reply is that in regard to the ceremonial and civil laws the response is not difficult. Just as at Athens the tables of Solon or at Rome the laws of the decemviri [councils of ten Roman magistrates], which were changed by the Republic, were ultimately abolished, so the ceremonies and civil laws which were laid down by Moses endured for a specific time, but when the political nation of Moses was destroyed, they were no longer binding on anyone, and now have become extinct. We have spoken above regarding the distinction of the old and new covenants, and why this civil state was established.

But in regard to the moral law, the answer which Christ and the apostles gave is more difficult, and worldly men who live without repentance do not understand it. For the moral law is not something changeable, as the ceremonial laws or the laws of the decemviri, but the moral law is the eternal and immutable rule in the divine mind which commands that certain things be done and not done, and which punishes infractions against it.

Just as this proposition is eternal and immutable: God is wise, good, and just, so these propositions are eternal and immutable: God judges that it was just or righteous for Him as the Creator to be loved by a rational creature and placed above all other things; God judges that the roving lusts of men are evil; God approves obedience which is in accord with His commands; God is angry at refusal to obey.

Therefore, this rule always remains: both that the moral law always remains as the order of the divine mind, so that the creature is to be obedient to it; and that the entire Law obligates men either to obedience or punishment.

Since men did not render this obedience, it was necessary either that they become subject to punishment, or that another person pay their penalty or ransom. Thus with marvelous and indescribable wisdom the Son of God paid the ransom for us and intercedes for us and takes upon Himself God's wrath, which we were obligated to endure. Thus it was not without payment that God mitigated His Law, but rather He preserved His justice in requiring that the penalty be paid. And therefore Christ says [Matthew 5:17], "I have not come to destroy the Law but to fulfill it," that is, by enduring the punishment for the human race and teaching and restoring it [the Law] in believers. It is difficult to explain this matter, but I pray the godly that they spend time considering these things which I am saying. And since Christ has paid this ransom, we are free from the Law for His sake, that is, that we should no longer remain under the curse as long as we apply His benefit to ourselves by faith.

Therefore, Paul explicitly says that we are freed from the curse of the Law, that is, that Christ has paid the ransom. Our sins have not been remitted by some change in the will of God without cause, but a great compensation has intervened because of the righteousness of God. Thus the first patriarchs, even before Moses—people such as Abraham, Isaac, Jacob, and then Moses, Samuel, David, and the Baptist—all believed that their sins were remitted to them and that they were accepted by God for the sake of the Son of God and not because of the Law. They believed that they had been reconciled (even though they were still not without sins) and were pleasing to God because they had been freed from the Law for the sake of the Son, who they knew was going to pay the ransom, just as the Baptist said [John

1:29], "Behold the Lamb of God, who takes away the sin of the world," that is, the victim who has been destined by God. This is the abrogation of the moral law, of which Paul is speaking so clearly when he says that through Christ we have been redeemed from the curse of the Law. Thus we are liberated, if we take to ourselves by faith this benefit of Christ.

This teaching instructs us about two matters—about the wrath of God against sin, which is not remitted without payment, and about the marvelous benefit of Christ. God has always hated sin, but because He has poured out His wrath upon His Son, He receives us. For the Law requires, as I have said, that the obedience to the Law or the punishment for our disobedience be paid by the Son.

Now I shall reply to the principal question. We have been liberated from the curse of the moral law because the Son paid the ransom, and for the sake of the Son we are received by God. God's eternal and immutable order remains in force, that the creature is to render obedience to God the creator. The Law does not accuse or condemn those who have been reconciled, but the order or arrangement remains in the mind of God and in our mind that we are to render obedience to God. In regard to this statement it is said: the Law has been abrogated as it pertains to the curse, but not as it pertains to obedience. Therefore, the Holy Spirit is given, in order that emotions may be truly kindled in our hearts which are in agreement with the Law of God, as it says in 2 Corinthians 3[:18], "We with unveiled face behold the glory of the Lord and are transformed into the same image from glory to glory, just as by the Spirit of the Lord."

From these points it is possible to understand the statement of Paul [Romans 6:14], "You are not under the Law, but under grace." Because the punishment has been transferred onto Christ, believers are liberated from wrath and now for the sake of Christ are righteous and have been accepted by God, even if the remnants of sin by which they contend against the Spirit still cling to them. This is said [1 Timothy 1:9], "The Law was not laid down for a righteous person," where it is clear that Paul by this statement is speaking about discipline, and is saying that the Law was laid down for the unrighteous, adulterers, murderers, etc., so that they might be held in check by it, accused, and punished. By this discipline and this forcible control the righteous man, that is, the person who has been born again of the Holy Spirit, is not to be held in check, but he is governed by the Holy Spirit, through the light of the Word of God, to whom he understands that the rational creature has been placed in subjection. And in this passage by Paul the stress is on the words "laid down." The Law does not press down or run over a righteous man.

[FREEDOM FROM RITES OF HUMAN AUTHORITY]

The fourth degree or level of liberty, which the Gospel calls rites that have been developed by human authority in the church, pertains to matters of adiaphora which do not merit the remission of sins. It does not refer to the righteousness of the Gospel, and these [rites] must not be observed out of an idea of necessity, since they can be omitted without any cause for offense. This is clearly taught in the statements [Matthew 15:9], "In vain do they worship Me with the commandments of men," and again [Colossians 2:16], "Let no one accuse you in matters of food, drink. . . ."

I have spoken above of the errors which the hypocrites add to these human traditions, errors which we must refute and which pertain to this degree or level of liberty in the church. God wills that He and His will be understood from His Word, and He does not grant to us permission to think up ideas by our own volition, as the Gentiles and idol worshipers in all ages have done. For this is the source of many errors—when men think that it is permitted to them to devise notions about God and zealously (in their opinion) to establish worship forms concerning God. The Thebans thought that it was a godly thing to seek from God a rich grape harvest, and therefore they established the Bacchanalian rituals. The Sicilians thought it was a godly thing to ask that there be favorable harvests, and thus they worshiped Ceres and her daughter. The Romans thought it was a godly thing to ask for victory in wars, and therefore they worshiped Mars. And these cults piled up.

All these errors come from one source. Men think that they are permitted to devise for themselves of their own free choice opinions about God, and worship Him according to those opinions, just as Aaron thought when he set up the worship of the image of the calf, and as Jeroboam did when he brazenly led the people of Israel away from the temple of God to his own sacrifices.

The wise men cry: what is wrong about this? Why should honest practices not be permitted? What else did the Gentiles or Aaron or Jeroboam want than that the knowledge of God be kept alive, so that the people might be invited to invoke Him and become accustomed to good spiritual exercises which lead to godly works? These specious and logical-sounding arguments have always deceived, do so now, and always will deceive the human race.

Thus in our own time the wise men are reasoning: what is wrong with the idea that Christ is offered by many and by individuals? Or that we offer prayers for the living and the dead? Or that a part of the Sacrament is carried around? The prayers of the people are increased and the Sacrament given more honor. What is wrong with asking the dead, who are living in the presence of God, to intercede for us? There is surely no doubt that the entire church in heaven and on earth always joins together in prayer. These are beautiful arguments and can be ornamented with much eloquence.

But these lovely rationalizations and specious arguments lead people away from the Word of God. Indeed, games of this kind are forbidden by God. For with the same audacity they dream up their heretical errors—some, one kind, and others, other kinds. Indeed, despite their conscience struggling over the remission of sins and the will of God in times of great calamities, they become so accustomed to following these rationalizations and opinions that they lose the true consolations which have been given us by God.

Men in civil life tell us that conflicts which are destructive for inexperienced people are often caused by very simple things. Discords hang on and increase by reason of the zeal and hatreds of factions. Men do not disagree with moderation. Therefore, they say, why do you stir up such sad tragedies about things like milk, eggs, and the eating of meat? Why do you not put the public peace and tranquility ahead of these minute things?

The answer is true and solid. We are not contending about unimportant matters, but about many very important things, namely, the true knowledge and worship of God, which must be put ahead of our very life, all our physical comforts, governments, and the public concord, so that we do not look for opinions about God and His will outside of the Word which He has given us, as the Gentiles have done and all fanatic spirits, such as Paul of Samosata, Arius, the Manichaeans, Pelagius, and Mohammed.

This kind of uproar when people set forth these controversial matters is reprehensible, and yet it is common. From these same dark corners arise the Bacchanalia, the errors of Paul of Samosata, the rules of the Manichaeans regarding food, the law of the papists regarding the celibacy of priests, and the brazen temerity of the sacrificial system with its sale of Masses and the invocation of the dead.

God wills that our minds be bound to His Word, and when we depart from this, unspeakable madness and idolatry follow. Thus we must contend regarding this rule so that there be no departure from the Word of God. Therefore, we need to give instruction to the church about this matter, which is most important of all and indeed is given by divine mandate. Note the statement [Galatians 1:9], "If anyone teaches any other Gospel, let him be anathema."

Furthermore, the civil leaders in their wisdom select things which appear to be unimportant, such as the eating of meat or eggs, and they assert that the public concord ought to be placed above these matters. But we are not contending only about such minutia as the eating of meat and the like. I have said that the church needs to be instructed regarding the source of these errors, that is, regarding the audacity of mankind departing from the Word of God and devising not only laws about foods (though these by themselves have spawned a multitude of errors) but also about much more evident idolatry, such as the saying of Masses for the living and the dead, the invocation of the dead, the laws of celibacy, and other things. Nor is this the end of the insanity. Now the Anabaptists are thinking up still more new opinions and rituals. Thus the doctrine of this fourth degree or level of liberty is necessary for the church, and the church must carefully consider the reason why this admonition is necessary, and why it must not depart from the Word of God. "Your Word is a light to my feet," says the prophet [Psalm 119:105].

It is easy to fall into this. In the beginning it is not noticed when our minds begin to depart from this light and take up human opinions which strengthen idolatry and seek compelling reasons for their actions. Paul himself says they have the appearance of wisdom, while actually they are false. What forbids, they say, the whole church in heaven and on earth from joining with us in praying to God that He would not allow the true doctrine to be snuffed out, but rather that He would gather the church for Himself and rule it, call His saints [in heaven]—who rejoice in their happy relationship with God—together before His throne, and encourage them to join their prayers to ours. Surely they know that this is the will of pious men. They say these things very plausibly, but what great evil this idea produces!

To hear the prayers of individuals and to behold the movements of their hearts belongs to God alone, or to His almighty nature, as is clearly stated in 2 Chronicles 6[:30], "You alone know the hearts of the sons of men." To the dead they attribute the honor of calling together the individual saints. Then they add an even greater lunacy: they dream up the notion that the dead themselves are our helpers, and they attribute different gifts to some of them, just as the Gentiles seek riches from Juno, wisdom from Pallas Athene, happy love affairs from Venus, victories from Mars, and other favors from other gods. In this way we pile up sins, when at the beginning we seem not to have departed far from the Word of God because of their very plausible line of reasoning. But it is evident that there is no example of the invocation of the dead in the writings of the prophets and apostles. We must use these rules in opposition to the beautiful excuses with which certain very astute people in our time are painting idolatry, just as in ancient times at the festivals they painted the statues: "The dwarf-elders drip with Bacchanalian blood and are reddened with wine" [Virgil, *Eclog.* 10.27].

I have said that we must carefully instruct the learned, so that they do not allow themselves to be carried away by these specious excuses and depart from the truth into idolatry. For if these outrageous tricks are permitted to lead us into excusing our idolatry, what confusions there will be in our religion! I shudder to think of these tricks of the devil. And because no amount of human diligence can sufficiently guard against this witchcraft, I pray our Lord Jesus Christ, who was crucified and resurrected again for us, that He Himself will defend the purity of His Gospel and destroy every idol and guide our minds that we may teach and contend for true and salutary things.

[The Usual Objection: Civil Obedience]

Now to the common argument I reply to the usual objection:

We must be obedient to the necessary power.

The power of the church has instituted rites for both matters of indifference (adiaphora) and for other things.

Therefore it is necessary that we observe these rituals, especially in matters of adiaphora.

We must respond to the major premise, which is not true when the power commands that we teach ungodly things or do them. For then it is necessary to oppose these rules [Acts 5:29], "We must obey God rather than men." In the first place, therefore, when the traditions openly command those things which cannot be performed without sin, it is evident that they are the doctrines of devils and we must not be obedient to them, but come back to the commands of God. Such are many of the traditions of the pope, such as the abuses of the Lord's Supper, the invocation of the dead, and the law of celibacy. These traditions must be rejected and we must be obedient to the commandments of God. The First Commandment says [Exodus 20:3], "You shall have no other gods." Therefore do not invoke the dead, but call upon the almighty God, the creator of all things, who has revealed Himself in the giving of the Gospel and the sending of His Son, our Lord Jesus Christ, who was crucified and raised again for us. Thus you are to invoke Him, as He Himself teaches us to pray in confidence in the Son, our mediator.

Then, when the traditions speak about things which by nature are matters of adiaphora, these matters still become the ungodly doctrines of devils because of the errors which are set forth and defended at the same time with them. One error is that they merit the remission of sins or are the worship of God, that is, works by which God judges that He is being honored. Also, the error is defended that bishops have the power to establish such worship. We must attack these errors. For example, we must oppose them in order that the church may understand that we must not depart from the Word of God nor let down the reins of human brashness, so that men get the notion that they can devise opinions and forms of worship according to their own free choice. For these reasons Christ absolves the apostles of violating the tradition of the Pharisees in Matthew 15.

This first solution to the matter is perfectly clear and plain. But we must also cling to the second solution, which is also true and well-founded. The major premise is true as it pertains to the obedience that the Gospel teaches. In those things which are matters of the divine Law, the conscience must be obedient to the pastors [the seventy] according to the statement [Luke 10:16], "He who rejects you rejects Me." But in regard to rites which are matters of adiaphora established for the sake of good order, the Gospel prescribes that we should not believe that these things are worship or necessary things. But it does permit us to observe them without the idea of righteousness or necessity. Human authority cannot abolish this divinely given belief. Therefore, when the bishops give us a precept, it must call for the kind of obedience which does not destroy a belief required of us by God.

These replies are correct and immovable, and they are not in conflict with the Word of Christ [Matthew 23:2–3], "The scribes and Pharisees sit in Moses' seat. All things which they command you, do."

For this statement does not command that you do or believe something contrary to the commandment of God. Indeed, in another passage [Matthew 16:5] He commands, "Beware of the leaven of the Pharisees." And in Matthew 15 human traditions which are corruptions of the divine laws are expressly rejected. Paul says [Galatians 1:9], "If anyone teaches any other Gospel, let him be anathema." In no way were they to embrace the interpretations of the Pharisees, which had the idea that the Levitical sacrifices merited the remission of sins, or that the Messiah was not going to be a sacrifice for sins but rather would take hold of the empires of the world and would bestow the governance of them upon the Jews. They surely were not to take up such ridiculous notions. And we must not disregard the statement of Christ concerning traditions or opinions which are in conflict with the Word of God.

But now these things are being described as some kind of detraction from the authority of ministers and pastors of the Gospel. Actually their authority is being strengthened. We affirm that of necessity we must render obedience to those teachers who teach correctly in all the matters which are matters of divine Law, as it is said [Luke 10:16], "He who hears you hears Me." But this statement cannot be transferred to opinions or laws which are in conflict with the Gospel, or which establish a kingdom outside of the Gospel. Then we also add this point when, for the sake of good order, they divide up the seasons of the church year and the readings, and say that these must be observed as a rite in order to avoid scandal. But especially we who are in churches which have been reformed must remember to whom the honor is owed by the ministry of the Gospel.

[THE MINISTRY OF THE GOSPEL]

This ministry is the chief blessing of God, and it has been restored with marvelous miracles of God and defended among the human race. God wills that His Gospel be proclaimed in the public assembly and honorable meetings, as it is written [Psalm 149:1], "His praise in the congregation of the saints." He wills that His name be invoked in that place and celebrated in regular meetings. And He adds the promise to the congregation [Matthew 18:20], "Where two or three are gathered together in My name, there am I in the midst of them." And again [v. 19], "If two of you on earth shall agree on a certain matter which you shall ask, it shall be done for you by My heavenly Father." For He wills that these public meetings themselves be public testimonies of your confessions. He also wills that we all understand the difference between the true church, which retains the Gospel, and the meetings of other sects.

And the public gatherings of the church are necessary for the retention of the ministry of the Gospel. Thus in the churches which teach correctly, all must both love and support the public meetings, and be obedient to their pastors who teach correctly, who observe the church year and the readings. As often as you come into the church building, you should think of the marvelous blessing of God, who gathers to Himself the eternal church by means of the ministry and the Word of the Gospel. At the same time instruct yourself regarding the whole doctrine of the creation and redemption of the human race, and remember the promise given regarding the presence of God. In this gathering God wills to be invoked and to answer our prayers. Here you should show in your worship and in the use of the sacraments that you are a member of the people of God and a hearer of Christ. And at the same time repeat to yourself the word which I wish were inscribed on the walls of all church buildings [Romans 8:30]: "Those whom He chose, He also called." None have been elected outside this assembly of the called. Do not seek the people of God anywhere except among those who have been called.

Moreover, the called are the members (*socii*) of this assembly which hears the Gospel, and who through the sacraments are joined to this gathering. What a great comfort it is for the pious mind to know that only in these assemblies are the heirs of eternal life—nowhere else! Therefore give thanks to the eternal God, the Father of our Lord Jesus Christ, that He has called you to the knowledge of the Gospel and to these gatherings and meetings. And in every work of these assemblies or congregations you should give frequent help and protection. Love those pastors who teach correctly, and give them reverent obedience in their performance of their office. Be kind to them, and support their bodily needs where this is necessary. Pious people should think about these matters and be truly eager to perform them.

Likewise, with regard to the schools in which the Word of the Gospel is proclaimed, we should believe and know that God wishes that they be gatherings of those who teach and those who learn. They are a part of the church, in which many have been chosen as heirs of eternal life. Taken from this very assembly are the teachers through whom God preserves the public ministry of the Gospel. Christ reigns at the right hand of the eternal Father in order that He may give gifts to men, pastors, and teachers; therefore He is present also in this very gathering of godly scholars, and from this number He chooses and prepares by the Holy Spirit godly students, that they may serve His church and promote the spreading of the Gospel. Therefore, we should love and support these congregations and help their meetings, which truly give us instruction concerning eternal life.

For measureless eternity will be the normal place where the church will gather to hear the wisdom of God and of our Lord Jesus Christ, and for mutual conversation with the first patriarchs, the prophets and apostles, and the others in whose preaching we have rejoiced. Indeed, as often as we are present in the meetings of the church or the schools, we should be hopeful that as quickly as possible that most happy day will dawn in which the Son of God, our Lord Jesus Christ, will raise the dead and show to us this universal gathering of His church and His school.

APPENDIXES

Appendix A

Use of "Man" in Christian Freedom

Luther's use of the term "man" has several meanings that sometimes overlap. The broadest sense of "man" refers to humans in general, as reflected by the Latin *homo* and German *Mensch*. This corresponds also to historic English usage, such as phrases in the Nicene Creed: "for us men and for our salvation . . . [He] was made man." Both instances of "man" rest on Greek and Latin words encompassing both genders. Modern readers may be used to inclusive language and to associate the term "man" with a male person. Taking cues from Luther's own pattern of usage, some masculine references in the original have been modified to meet inclusive expectations when the objects of consideration are human beings in general. A good rule of thumb is that sinners needing salvation in Christ may be described in gender-neutral terms. Yet one simply cannot translate every instance of "man" with "person" in Luther's treatise, as the following cases illustrate.

"Man" can also apply to Luther's expressed or implied references to a man called to the office of the public ministry, such as theologians, "priests," and bishops. The words of Scripture remain clear that Christ established the public ministry of preaching the Word and administering the Sacraments by calling men into it. Christ left no words of mandate or promise to the Church to do otherwise than to follow Him in this regard, and that certainly was the case in Luther's day. We must respect such usage and let "man" refer to the male incumbents of the pastoral office.

Luther also uses "man" when he refers to the human nature that is embodied in either Adam or in Christ. One sees this in the Large Catechism as the "old Adam" or "old man" and "new man." By extension, we see this here in the terms "inner man" and "outer man." This is not a metaphor, but a spiritual incorporation into one of two alternatives: Every human is either a member of the body that fell from being the son of God (Luke 3:38) to being the man of sin and death (Romans 5:12–14), or one is a member of the body that gives eternal life (Romans 5:15–21; 12:5), the Son of God.

The maleness of both Adam and of Christ is a concrete reality that has importance in God's order of creation and His plan of salvation. Here we follow the clear, consistent witness of Scripture. Sin and grace are not abstract moralities or psychological events, as modern religious philosophy would have it. They are concrete in flesh and blood, in Adam and Christ. One therefore must ground such references to "man" in the two men, Adam and Jesus Christ. Yet these specific male references comprehend the blessings of the God-ordained female in the proper order of creation and salvation. Eve came from Adam and was included as flesh from his own (Genesis 2:23). Christ was "incarnate," given human substance: a human body and a rational human soul, "by the Holy Spirit [out] of the Virgin Mary." Mary, the blessed God-bearer, is of Eve, whose womb was the doorway of Adam's salvation in Christ.

Finally, Luther occasionally uses the term "person" in a strict, philosophical sense meaning "a self-subsisting intelligence attached to a substance," where a "substance" is the concretized instance of an "essence," the definition of what something is, without becoming something else. In other words, the human essence is "having a human body and rational soul," regardless of height, weight, age, IQ, race, and so on, but not "with an elephant's trunk" and the like. Human substance is the specific body and rational soul of a tangible human being; that is what Christ received from Mary through the Spirit's work. A human being's person is the rational soul that subsists within the body from conception. Where these definitions are expressed or implied, it would be incorrect to translate "man" with "person."

In some cases, these uses may overlap. The result has been to translate "man" with the common meaning of "person" or with some other gender-neutral term where no ambiguity might result. By keeping mindful of the cases above, the instances of "man" will become clear to the reader. For the sake of readability, pronouns dealing with human beings remain in the masculine. The context will dictate their meaning.

Appendix B

English Editions
of Luther's *Christian Freedom*

The following timeline does not seek to catalogue every English edition of *Christian Freedom*. Using editions that appear as milestones in the history of the translations, the timeline illustrates how the Reformation differed in Germany and England. It also illustrates how Luther's most famous treatise was understood and misunderstood over the centuries.

First, England had developed a strong central government in which church and state were part of a power structure that entangled all branches of government. Even after the separation of the Church of England from Rome, the English use of church figures as political leaders continued. In contrast, the Holy Roman Empire's system of government was decentralized and the church often had to compete with other local interests. In England, someone declared a heretic, such as Martin Luther, would have been killed within a year or two. In contrast, Luther lived a long life and died of natural causes in Germany. Publishers in Germany did not experience the kind of censorship that became common in England. Thus, the dynamics of "freedom" in Germany differed significantly from the English context.

Second, the interpretation of Luther's treatise differed over time as modern worldviews developed. Even though the early English translations had a political dimension in Reformation England, they always focused on Luther's doctrine of justification as the theme of the treatise. In later editions, one sees a trend away from a worldview that generally accepted Christian truth to one that treated religion as a matter of personal conviction. Later editions focused almost exclusively on the historical impact of the treatise while neglecting its theology. They read modern ideas about nations, philosophy, and genre into the treatise. In the twentieth century, a secular strain of interpretation developed that paid little heed to the theological content. Interpreters often made Luther a hero of Western civilization rather than a servant of the Holy Gospel.

1515–29 Cardinal Thomas Wolsey is English Lord Chancellor, archbishop of York, and later, papal legate known as "the other king." Wolsey holds executive, legislative, and judicial power, in contrast to later constitutional developments and to Luther's Germany.

1520 Martin Luther publishes three major writings that gain notice across Europe: *To the Christian Nobility of the German Nation, On the Babylonian Captivity of the Church,* and *On Christian Freedom.*

1521 For his opposition to Martin Luther's writings, Henry VIII receives from Pope Leo X the title "Defender of the Faith." Thomas More assists Henry in writing the *Assertio,* directed against Luther. Subsequent events reveal that Henry's religion can be altered by his politics.

1528–29 John Tewkesbury reads William Tyndale's 1526 New Testament and 1528 *Wicked Mammon.* He is converted to the evangelical faith and sells Tyndale's books. His story forms the background history for the first English edition of *Christian Freedom.*

1529 Henry VIII forces the resignation of Wolsey for failing to get an annulment for Henry and Catherine of Aragon. More succeeds Wolsey as Lord Chancellor.

April 21: Tewkesbury appears before Cuthbert Tonstal (Tonstall), Bishop of London, and other bishops at a heresy trial. He is placed in church custody and ordered to do penance, which he starts on May 8. Nevertheless, he remains committed to evangelical doctrine.

December 21: Tewkesbury is martyred, the sentence being read at the home of More, who orders Tewkesbury's death at the hands of two sheriffs.

1534 March: Henry VIII is declared Supreme Head of the Church of England through the Act of Supremacy. Separation from Rome is fundamentally political, not theological.

1535 July 6: More is beheaded for refusing to swear the Succession Oath to Henry VIII. After this time, Henry allows selected Protestant writings to be printed. Thomas Cromwell, Henry's chief political minister, and Thomas Cranmer, archbishop of Canterbury, spearhead reforms.

1538–46 Increasing censorship of the English press occurs through successive acts of Parliament. Whether Lutheran, Roman Catholic, or sectarian, many books are banned. Only those books deemed fit by the government and the Church of England (or the Catholics under Mary) can be printed and sold without fear of punishment. Such approved books contain variants of the Latin note *cum privilegio regali* (with royal favor). This form of censorship through government licensing lasted until the Glorious Revolution of 1688, when John Locke's ideas about individual autonomy and reason provided a new framework for freedom of the press.

1544 *De Libertate Christiania (The liberty of a christian Man), Cum privilegio regali* is printed by John Byddell, its translation attributed to John Tewkesbury. It is clear that this work is not seen as a political manifesto or a call to autonomy, as its royal *privilegium* suggests.

1547 Henry VIII dies on January 28. Then follow the short reigns of Edward VI (1547–53) and Mary I (1553–58). Elizabeth I is crowned in 1559.

1579 James Bell translates *A Treatise Touching the Libertie of a Christian* from the Latin. It bears the marks and provenance of Elizabethan England. Its patroness is Anne Dudley, Countess of Warwick. She is the niece of Jane Seymour, the third wife of Henry VIII, and the mother of Edward VI. Bell's dedication picks up the motif of persecution and sees the pope, styled "execrable Nimrod of Rome," as the general source for such misery. Bell points to Anne and other Protestants as the deliverers of "poor Christians" as moved by the Holy Spirit in the freedom of grace. Although there is a clear political dimension, there is also a profoundly spiritual one.

1817 A reprint of the Bell translation is published in Georgian England. Its patron is Augustus Frederick, Duke of Sussex, Duke of Saxony, and son of George III. The dedicatory letter by William B. Collyer points to the centrality of justification in the work. Collyer's subsequent preface, however, also brings in the post-Enlightenment era as a counterpoint to his mention of continued papal opposition to Bible societies, general knowledge, and progress. We therefore observe a trend of secularization in the interpretation of this work.

1826 Henry Cole translates *Concerning Christian Liberty* from the Latin in his edition of selected Luther's works. He sees the interpretive context for *Christian Liberty* in Melanchthon's introduction to the second Latin volume of the Wittenberg edition of Luther's works, which Cole translates in part. This context is that all people hear God's voice in Scripture, the source of faith, and that they are free to worship God and serve their neighbor. Cole emphasizes the doctrine of justification as he seeks to remain faithful to the original, religious meaning of Luther's treatise.

1838   A quasi-academic evaluation of Luther reads, in part, "With this [miner's] sledge [of Hans Luther's coat of arms, Martin] was destined to dint the papal tiara and shiver the pastoral staff of the catholic hierarchy:—the same instrument, which, in the course of time, passing through the hands of [Oliver] Cromwell, Robespierre and Napoleon, hammered regal crowns and regal baubles into fragments."[1] The author of the article, indicated only with a Greek letter *lambda*, also remarks that the "usefulness and influence [of Germans] are restricted to university walls." Immigrant German Lutherans encountered similar attitudes when they settled in Georgia, Tennessee, Missouri, and other southern and border states.

1883   R. S. Grignon produces *Concerning Christian Liberty* (translated from the Latin). He uses the text from the Frankfurt edition of Luther's Works. The translation appears in *First Principles of the Reformation*, edited by Henry Wace, whose theological introduction properly understands the treatise as a theological work. Buchheim's historical introduction, however, speaks of tension between Roman and German cultures, between state and church. It tends to paint Rome and Italy with a broad, negative brush and depicts a German culture under foreign tyranny that is cast off by Luther the liberator. One sees the influence of nineteenth-century philosophy in this evaluation.

1910   The Grignon translation appears in the Harvard Classics volume *The Prince*, a political treatment. The Harvard volume gathers together Machiavelli's *The Prince*, Thomas More's *Utopia* (Graeco-Latin for "nowhere land"), Grignon's translation of Luther's *Ninety-five Theses*, Buchheim's translation of Luther's *Address to the Christian Nobility*, and Grignon's *Concerning Christian Liberty*. It incorporates much of the *First Principles of the Reformation*, while secularizing and politicizing its context.

1915   W. A. Lambert translates *A Treatise on Christian Liberty* from Latin, with German interpolations, in the Philadelphia edition of Luther's Works,

---

1   "Rankings of the Study, No. I: Martin Luther, His Character and Times," *Southern Literary Messenger* 4/9 (September 1838): 596–602 (specifically p. 597).

which Grimm indicates is based on the Weimar edition. Lambert consults both Grignon's translation and Lemme's 1884 German translation of the Latin. The historical introduction engages the interaction among Luther, Miltitz, Cajetan, and others. It speaks to Protestant and Roman Catholic reception of the document, but it avoids theological observations. It sees *Christian Freedom* as an outgrowth of German mysticism.

1957   Harold Grimm revises Lambert's text for volume 31 of the American edition of Luther's Works as *The Freedom of a Christian* (translated from the Latin, he adds the German dedication). Grimm also mentions other modern translations and commentary. His historical introduction seems to be a pared-down revision of Lambert's that speaks to the context of writing and to the publication history of the original without engaging points of theology.

2008   Mark D. Tranvik of Augsburg College in Minneapolis, MN provides a new translation titled *The Freedom of a Christian*. It is based on the Latin text with the assistance of the Lambert translation. His introduction helpfully relates Luther's treatise to the theology of the Small Catechism.

Appendix C

Melanchthon's Advice
for Reading Luther[1]

Let us therefore give thanks to God, the eternal Father of our Lord Jesus Christ, who willed, that by the ministry of Martin Luther, the filth and poison should again be cast out of the fountains of evangelical truth, and the pure doctrine restored to the church. Accordingly, it is fitting for us and for all good people throughout the world to think of this and to unite in prayers and desires. It is good to cry penitently to God with fervent hearts, that He would confirm what He has worked in us, for His holy temple's sake. This is Your word[2] and promise, O living and true God, eternal Father of our Lord Jesus Christ, the author of all things in Your Church. "For My name's sake I will have mercy upon you. . . . For My own sake, for My own sake I will do it, that My name not be blasphemed" [Isaiah 48:9,11]. I pray to You with all my heart, that for Your own glory, and for the glory of Your dear Son, that You would always gather to Yourself from among us, by the preaching[3] of Your Gospel, an eternal Church. And [I pray] that, for the sake of Your dear Son Jesus Christ our Lord, who was crucified for us and rose again [to be] our Mediator and Intercessor, Your Holy Spirit may in all things rule our hearts, that we may call upon You in truth, and serve You acceptably.

---

1   This comes from the concluding paragraphs in Melanchthon's biographical preface to the second volume of Luther's Latin writings in the Wittenberg edition (1546). The text appears translated in Henry Cole, *Select Works of Martin Luther* (London: Simpkin and Marshall, 1826), 1:iv–vi. The text has been updated for current usage and read against *Corpus Reformatorum* 6:168–70. Some text has been translated also from *CR*.
2   Literally, "voice" (Latin: *vox*, as in the "living voice of the Gospel").
3   Again, literally, "by means of the voice."

[Likewise guide the study of doctrine, and also govern those servants in the political estate and their disciples, who are the hosts of Your Church and those who study theology.][4] You have created mankind with the goal that You be acknowledged and called upon by all people. For that purpose, You have revealed Yourself in so many clear testimonies that have given witness to You. Because of this, do not permit this army of witnesses to fail, from whom Your word of truth sounds forth. Your Son, our Lord Jesus Christ, prayed for us just before His final agony, saying, "Father, sanctify them in the truth, Your Word is truth" [John 17:17]. To these prayers of our High Priest we desire to join ours, and beg You, together with Him, that Your word[5] of truth may always shine among people, and that it may be our guide.

And these were the prayers that we used to hear Luther also pray daily, and it was in the midst of such prayers as these, that his peaceful soul, about the sixty-third year of his age, was called away from his mortal body.

Posterity possesses many monuments both of his doctrine and of his piety. First, he published his *doctrinal works*, wherein he set forth that doctrine which encompasses salvation and all that is indispensable to man to attain it, and which instructs the upright concerning repentance, faith, and the true fruits of faith; concerning the use of the sacraments; concerning the difference between the Law and the Gospel, and between the Gospel and philosophy; concerning the dignity of the political order; and finally, concerning all the chief articles of that doctrine, which must be set forth and maintained in the church. He then published his *works of refutation*, in which he disproved and exposed many pernicious human errors. He published moreover his *works of exposition*, which contain many commentaries on the prophetic and apostolic Scriptures. In these works even his enemies confess that he surpasses all the commentaries extant.

All good people well know that these are works of great merit. But truly, based on usefulness and craftsmanship, all these works together

---

4   Cole omits this sentence, which reflects the Lutheran exposition, based on Scripture, of the threefold estate of family, state, and church, all of which serve the proclamation of the Gospel and the growth of the Church. See AC XVI on civil government (*Concordia*, 39–40). The different understandings of Church, state, and society have colored the English versions of *Christian Liberty* and their Anglo-American interpretation since 1544.

5   Literally, Latin *sermo*, from which we get *sermon*. This portrays a living and active Word.

are surpassed by his version of the Old and New Testament, in which there is so much clearness that the German text itself supplies the needed commentary. Yet that version is not quite alone. Annotations of great learning are added to the text, together with descriptions of the subject headings, which give a summary of the divine doctrines contained in them, and instruct the reader in the kind of language that is used in that passage. [This helps the] honest and good heart to draw the firmest testimonies of the true doctrine from the very sources.

For it was the great aim of Luther not to let any remain merely engaged in his own writings, but to lead the minds of all to the fountainhead [that is, Scripture]. He would desire all of us to hear the voice of God. He wished to see, by that voice, the fire of genuine faith and [the routine act of] calling upon God kindled in people, that God might be worshiped in truth, and that many might be made heirs of eternal life.

It is therefore good for us to proclaim publicly with grateful hearts his anxious desire and his labors. Taking him for an example, we remember that it is our good duty to strive to adorn the Church of God, according to each person's ability. For the whole of our life, its studies and designs, should be directed toward these two goals: First, to promote the glory of God. Second, to benefit His Church. Concerning the first goal, St. Paul says, "Do all to the glory of God" [1 Corinthians 10:31]. Concerning the second, it is said in Psalm 122[:6], "Pray for the peace of Jerusalem." To that exhortation there is added, in the same verse, the sweetest promise: Happiness and blessing be to those who love the Church.[6] These commands and promises from above invite all to receive the true doctrine of the Church, to love the ministers of the Gospel and wholesome teachers, and to unite in desires and devoted endeavors [in order] to spread abroad the doctrine of truth, and to promote the harmony of the true Church of God.

Reader, farewell. Wittenberg, June 1, 1546.

---

6   This is Melanchthon's paraphrase.

GLOSSARY

absolve. To set free from sin. By virtue of his office, in the name and stead of Christ, a pastor absolves those who have confessed their sins, affirmed their faith in Christ, and promised to amend their lives (Matthew 16:19; 18:18; John 20:19–23). The Lutheran Church retains private Confession and Absolution as "the very voice of the Gospel," declaring that it would be impious to abolish it (AC XI; Ap XI 2; SA III VIII; SC V). Absolution may be called a Sacrament (Ap XIII 4).

accident (Latin: *accidens*). That which does not exist by itself essentially but subsists in another self-existent essence (FC Ep I 23; FC SD I 54; *see also* substance).

adiaphora (singular: *adiaphoron*). From the Greek, meaning "indifferent things." Church rites neither commanded nor forbidden by God (e.g., making the sign of the cross; bowing during the Gloria Patri). Church rites cease being indifferent when by their use or disuse they compromise the confession of faith (FC Ep X; FC SD X).

administer; administration. To faithfully deliver God's Word and Sacraments to the intended recipients.

alms; almsgiving (Greek: *eleemosyne*, "mercy, pity"). *Alms* means "gifts to the poor," but in some sectors of the Early Church alms were divided into four parts: for the bishops, for other clergy, for the poor, and for the repair of churches. Idea imported from the Apocrypha that giving alms was meritorious; Luther restored almsgiving to its New Testament status as a work of the new life of faith.

anathema. In the New Testament and in Church terminology a solemn curse, pronounced in God's name on heretics and the ungodly (Galatians 1:8–9; 1 Corinthians 16:22). Designates eternal separation from God (Romans 9:3); also used as a formula for sinful cursing (1 Corinthians 12:3; Acts 23:14).

apostle (Greek: *apostolos*, "sent one"). One of the Twelve, or St. Paul, who was chosen by Jesus to guide the mission of the Early Church.

article. Sections of a document or other piece of writing indicated by specific numbers or letters.

atonement (Greek: *katallage* [Romans 5:11]; often otherwise "reconciliation" [Romans 5:10; 2 Corinthians 5:19]). Look at the word: *at-one-ment*. It properly reflects a mutual exchange, or a drawing together of parties previously separated. God's action in Christ to forgive sin in order to restore the relationship between Himself and His fallen creatures.

attrition. Term used by Roman theologians: hatred of sin arising from love of the offended God is called "perfect *contrition*," while other motives such as fear of hell and of punishment, or realization of the heinousness of sin, is called "attrition." The Roman Church teaches that attrition alone does not justify, but that it prepares the penitent to receive grace, and that if people properly receive the Sacrament of Penance, they are justified.

benefit. Mercy or kindness resulting in spiritual or temporal blessings.

bishop (Greek: *episkospos*, "overseer"). Used in the New Testament for those who governed and directed the Christian communities. The New Testament does not distinguish between bishops and presbyters (Acts 14:23; 20:17, 28). The Lutheran Symbols recognized the rank of bishops and described their true function as preaching the Gospel, administering the Sacraments, and using the Keys (AC XXVIII; Ap XXVIII; Tr 60–82; SA II IV 9; III 10).

call; calling. A person's occupation or duties before God. Every baptized Christian has been called to at least one area of service with specific responsibilities, whether as mother or father, son or daughter, engineer, teacher, citizen, employee, and so on. Through the Church, God calls men into service as pastors. Also referred to as *vocation*.

catechism (Greek: *katechein*, "to teach"). Primarily a manual of religious instruction often published in question-and-answer format.

Catholic (Greek: *katholikos*, "universal," or "general"). A term first applied to the Christian Church as a whole in a letter of Ignatius (ca. AD 110): "Where Christ is, there is the catholic Church." In Lutheran theology (as in early Christendom), the word is often used of the one, holy, catholic ("Christian"), and apostolic Church united to Christ by faith, and transcending time, space, and all other barriers.

Christendom. Properly, Christianity as exemplified by its distinct teachings concerning Jesus of Nazareth; secondarily, areas where such teachings corporately or institutionally appear.

cloister (Middle Latin: *claustrum*, "room in a monastery"). 1. A monastery or convent. 2. A covered passage on the side of a court with one side walled and the other open, usually connecting buildings around an open court.

conciliarism; councils. Revival of Ancient Church practice of holding synods (*see also* synods) to combat papal and secular corruption.

197

The conciliar movement gained strength in 1409 at the Council of Pisa. Since the papacy was "captive" in Avignon, the "Babylon" under the influence of the French kings, many in the church looked to the ancient ecumenical councils as models to see the bishops as collective rulers of the church. At Constance (1414–18) and the opening of the Council of Basel (1431–49), conciliarism reached a high point in authority over the papacy. The Council of Basel split, however, and the papacy was able to divide and conquer, cementing its authority over the fractured Council of Basel, which was moved to Ferrara and then to Florence. There was no doubt regarding papal power by the Fifth Lateran Council (1512–17). The Council of Trent (1545–63) undertook reforms on the pope's terms and silenced centuries-old traditions as well as criticism within Roman Catholicism, thus creating the monolithic sort of Catholic Church that lasted until the Second Vatican Council (1962–65). Vatican I (1870) marked the ultimate triumph of the papacy with the doctrine of papal infallibility.

condign merit. See *meritum condigni.*

confess. 1. To profess or openly acknowledge one's faith in anyone or anything, especially in Christ and His Gospel (Matthew 10:32; Luke 12:8; 1 John 2:23; 4:15). 2. To express agreement with that which is confessed: creed, confession, or symbol. 3. To acknowledge, admit, or disclose one's own sins, either publicly or privately.

confessor. 1. One who avows faith. 2. A martyr in the early Church. 3. One who is known for a holy life, especially under persecution. 4. A pastor who hears private Confession and pronounces Absolution.

confirmation. A Church rite associated with post-baptismal instruction in the basics of the Christian faith.

congruent merit. See *meritum congrui.*

contrition. Movement of the heart prior to conversion, namely, "that the heart perceive sin, [and] dread God's wrath" (FC SD II 70). Scripture teaches two truths about contrition: (1) Contrition always precedes genuine conversion (FC SD II 70). Fear of God's wrath and damnation always precedes faith (Joel 2:12; Mark 1:15; Luke 15:18; 18:13; 24:47; Acts 2:37; 16:29; FC SD II 54, 70). True contrition is not active, that is, fabricated remorse, but passive, that is, true sorrow of the heart, suffering, and pain of death (SA III III 2). It should not be concluded from this that contrition is a cause of forgiveness (Romans 3:28). (2) Contrition in no way brings about, implements, or occasions justification through faith (FC SD II 30–31).

covenant. A formal, binding agreement between two or more parties promising the fulfillment of some act. In the Bible, covenants with God are generally associated with God's initiation of the covenant, His promise of some action associated with the covenant, and the shedding of blood. By virtue of His cross, the Lord's Supper is the "New Covenant" for the forgiveness of sins (Matthew 26:26–28; Mark 14:22–24; Luke 22:19–20; 1 Corinthians 11:23–26).

Curia. In Roman Church usage, the departments and officials used by the pope to administer the affairs of the church, although in a broader sense the term includes all dignitaries and officials forming the immediate entourage of the pope.

Decalogue (Greek: *deka logoi*, the "ten words"). The fundamental moral Law given by God to Moses at Sinai: the Ten Commandments (Exodus 19; Deuteronomy 5).

Diet (Latin: *dieta*, "daily food allowance," "parliament"; originally from Greek for "lifestyle"). In medieval times, the term *dieta* falsely was believed to come from *dies*, "day." In German, "day" can mean both a weekday and an appointed day of gathering. *Dieta* came to mean the *Hoftag*, an *ad hoc* gathering of the emperor and his chieftains that met since at least Charlemagne's reign. In 1489, this practice was formalized as a legislative body, the *Reichstag*, the general assembly of the Imperial Estates of the Holy Roman Empire of the German Nation. It consisted of lay and clerical leaders who generally supported estates' rights over the central government and authority of the emperor.

doctrine (Latin: *docere*, "to teach"). The teachings, principles, or tenets held and spread by a group.

dogma (Greek: *dokein*, "to seem"). A doctrine or doctrines (usually of the Church) considered authoritative on their own merits.

ecclesiastical (Greek: *ekklesia*, "assembly"). Having to do with the Church, its leadership, ritual, or members.

ecumenical (Greek: *oikoumene*, "the inhabited world"). Worldwide, or universal in nature and scope (*see* Catholic).

essence. The definition of the basic, unchangeable elements that make something what it is. The human essence is the possession of a human body and a rational soul. *See also* substance.

Evangelical (Greek: *euangelion*, "good news"). Term meaning "loyal to the Gospel of Jesus Christ." The Lutheran Reformation was evangelical in that it emphasized the doctrine of Christ's atonement for sin.

faith. 1. The body of truth found in creeds (objective). 2. The human response to divine activity (subjective); the personal appropriation of divine truth (itself a "gift," not a "work" [Ephesians 2:8–9]).

foreordained. Predestined; selected, determined, or planned in advance.

Gospel. 1. The Gospel of Jesus Christ, in its proper and narrow sense, is the glad tidings of forgiveness, peace, life, and joy, the eternal divine counsel of redemption, of which Christ Himself ever was, is, and will be the living center, the very heart and soul. The Gospel (a) imparts the forgiveness of sin; (b) produces true joy and the zeal to do good works; and (c) destroys sin both outwardly and inwardly. 2. In the broad sense, the term *Gospel* may also refer to the sum of Christian teaching, including both Law and Gospel. 3. The word *Gospel* also designates a particular account of Jesus written by one of the four evangelists.

grace. God's good will and favor in Christ toward sinners who can plead no merit. Grace implies mercy or compassion for one who has by every right forfeited his or her claim to love. God's grace to the sinner is "free" because it is not grounded in any worthiness of mankind (Romans 11:6). In the Roman Church, grace is more of a power given by God to do good works ("infused grace") so as to earn righteousness.

heresy (Greek: *hairesis*, "act of choosing," then "chosen opinion"). Stubborn error in an article of faith in opposition to Scripture.

holy. Without sin, perfect in goodness or righteousness, or set apart for a divine purpose.

image of God. The knowledge of God and holiness of the will, which was present in man before the fall (Colossians 3:10; Ephesians 4:24). This image is to be restored fully in believers only at Christ's second coming.

indulgences. Roots of the Roman doctrine of indulgences reach back to the ancient practice of penitential discipline. As the penitential system changed its character and the Roman sacrament of penance evolved, penance was no longer regarded as a mere expression of sorrow for sin or even as the discharge of church penalties, but as pleasing to God, meritorious, and compensatory for sin. It was held to remove, according to the degree of its merit, a portion of that temporal punishment of sin (chiefly purgatory) that could not be removed by Absolution. Commutations of penance, or indulgences, became commutations of divine punishment and were gained by giving money to churches and monasteries, by pilgrimages, and sometimes by direct payment to the priest. *Contrition*, or at least *attrition*, was in theory necessary to gain indulgence.

institute. To set up, establish, or begin.

jurisdiction. Ecclesial power, authority, or responsibility granted to pastors and/or bishops either by divine or human right (Tr 60–82).

justification. Judicial act of God consisting in the charging of our sin to Christ and the crediting of Christ's righteousness to us. This justification is received through the gift of faith. The Lutheran Confessions call the doctrine of justification the most important teaching of divine revelation (Ap IV 2, 3; FC SD III 6). Justification is both objective (won by Christ for all people) and subjective (applied personally through the Means of Grace).

Law. God's will, which shows people how they should live in order to please God (e.g., the Ten Commandments), condemns their failure to fulfill His will (sin), and threatens God's wrath because of sin. The preaching of the Law is the cause of contrition. Although the ceremonial laws of the Old Testament have been abolished (Colossians 2:16–17), the Moral Law (*see* Decalogue) is in force until the end of time (Matthew 5:18).

Levitical. Having to do with the Levites, the biblical Book of Leviticus, or (in general) Jewish ceremonial laws.

liturgy (Greek: *leitourgia*, "public service"). In a narrow sense, *liturgy* means the order of service for the celebration of Holy Communion. In a wider sense, the term means the whole system of formal worship.

Mass (Latin: *missa*, perhaps from the concluding words of public worship, *Ite, missa est,* "Go; it is the dismissal"). An older name for the Lord's Supper; in the Middle Ages, *Mass* became the most common name for the service in the Western Church. Lutherans kept the Mass, though purified from certain abuses (AC XXIV 1, 40; Ap XXIV 1).

meritum condigni (Latin: "condign merit"). According to Roman Church teaching, the reward people gain for themselves by grace. God rewards the actions of believers out of a sense of justice, as holding a debt, for the work performed. The Confessions reject the distinctions of condignity and congruity as screens for Pelagianism (Ap IV 19), robbing Christ of His honor, giving it to people (Ap V 195–197), and leading eventually to doubt and despair (Ap V 200).

meritum congrui (Latin: "congruent merit"). According to Roman Church teaching, the reward people gain for themselves by their own power. God rewards the actions of believers on the basis of His own liberality. See *meritum condigni*.

nature. The essence or inherent attributes of a thing; *see also* essence; substance.

office. 1. A particular position or area of responsibility having certain prescribed duties. 2. Any number of religious services (i.e., a "choir office").

pagan (Latin: *paganus*, "of the country"). A religious, or nonreligious person who is opposed to Christianity. Since Christianity first came to cities of the Roman Empire, those who lived in the country adhered longer to non-Christian religions; hence the association of the word *pagan* with the concept of unbelief.

papacy; papal. The office of the Roman pope. Having to do with the pope, his authority, or the Roman Church in general.

parish. Territory of a congregation in which it exercises its usual functions; part of a diocese.

pastor (Latin: "shepherd"). Christ continues His prophetic work through the ministry; men called by Christian congregations or groups of congregations are Christ's undershepherds, Christ Himself being the one Lord and Master (Matthew 23:8; 1 Peter 5:4). The Means of Grace were given to the Church by God, who calls certain men through her to administer them to the congregation. Also referred to as bishops (or overseers), presbyters (or elders), teachers, and ministers (*see* Acts 20:28; 1 Corinthians 4:1; 12:29; Ephesians 4:11–12; 1 Timothy 3:1–13; Titus 1:5).

person. A self-subsisting intelligence attached to a substance. In the doctrine of God, three persons (Greek *prosopa*; later *hypostases*) subsist in the divine substance (Greek *ousia*).

The use of the Greek words and their Latin counterparts, *persona* and *substantia*, has been contested at times as mere mortals struggle with the infinite, divine mystery. Ecumenical councils worked out the terminology to settle the issues. In the West, Augustine, Anselm, Bede, Thomas Aquinas, and others have engaged the scope and applications of these terms; *see also* substance.

piety. Devout; conforming to a certain belief or standard of conduct, especially in religious matters.

polemical (Greek: *polemos*, "battle"). Controversial discussions or arguments involving attack and/or refutation.

pornocracy. Tyrannical influence of the Theophylact family, the counts of Tusculum, over the papacy in the tenth century. In the Middle Ages, weak popes tended to die of unnatural causes. This time is also known as the "dark age" of the papacy in which simony, sex, nepotism, and murder dominated during a rapid series of weak popes in the decades preceding the creation of the College of Cardinals under Nicholas II in 1059. Other papal reforms resulted after the election of Gregory VII in 1073, working toward what Gregory considered the "liberty of the Church."

praescientia (Latin: "foreknowledge"). The attribute of God whereby He knows in advance all future events.

predestination. The doctrine that God, before the foundation of the world, chose us in His Son, Jesus Christ, out of the mass of sinful mankind unto faith, the adoption of sons, and everlasting life (Ephesians 1:4; 3:11; 2 Thessalonians 2:13; 2 Timothy 1:9). This election is not based on any good quality or act of the elect (those predestined), nor was it made in view of those who eventually would come to faith. Rather, our predestination in Christ is based solely on God's grace, the good pleasure of His will in Christ Jesus. While the Bible does teach the predestination of the elect, it does not (contra Calvin) teach the predestination of the damned, nor does it solve the problem of the human intellect seeking to understand universal grace and predestination (see FC Ep XI 5–7; FC SD XI 14–23).

promise (Latin: "to send forth"). A binding pronouncement granting the right to expect fulfillment of that which is specified. An early Lutheran term for the Gospel.

propitiate; propitiation (Greek: *hilasterion*). Atonement. Hebrews 9:5 translates this word as "mercy seat"; the Hebrew equivalent (*kapporeth* [Exodus 25:17]) means the cover or lid of the ark of the covenant on which the high priest, once a year, would sprinkle blood to propitiate, or make atonement for, the sins of the people. This was a type of the propitiatory sacrifice of Christ on the cross. *See also* atonement.

providence. The activity of God whereby He uninterruptedly upholds, preserves, governs, and directs lifeless creation, plant life, animal life, the world of people and all that concerns people, heaven, hell—indeed, everything (*see* Job 9:5–6; Psalm 104:13–14; 145:15; 139:13; 31:15; Luke 12:6–7; Hebrews 1:1–3).

purgatory. In Roman Church teaching, all who have not been thoroughly perfected in this life will be "purged" by fire in an intermediate state of existence between earth and heaven. Masses, prayers, and good works by the living supposedly aid those suffering in purgatory and reduce its sentence. Those who die with mortal sin unconfessed and unabsolved do not enter purgatory, but hell. *See also* indulgences.

recant. To formally renounce a belief, statement, or writing previously disseminated.

reconciliation. Synonymous with atonement (*see* atonement; propitiation) in the sense of the act of reconciling and so restoring friendly relations.

redeem (Latin: "buy back"). Recovery from sin and death by the obedience and sacrifice of Christ, who is therefore called the Redeemer (Job 19:25; Isaiah 59:20; Matthew 20:28; Romans 3:24). The subject is sinful mankind, under guilt and the curse of the Law and the power and dominion of the devil, servants of sin, liable to death and eternal punishment. Redemption applies to all, but is not free; the ransom paid was divinely sealed by the resurrection (1 Corinthians 15:3–20).

repentance. In a wide sense, change from a rebellious state to one of harmony with God's will, from trusting in human merit to trusting in Christ's merit. Embraces contrition and justifying faith; sometimes the fruit of repentance are included (Ap XII 28). In the narrow sense, faith and fruit are not included. The means to repentance is God's Word (*see* Jeremiah 31:18; Acts 5:31). Sometimes taken as an equivalent to penance and penitence.

righteousness. God's righteousness is the essential perfection of His nature. The term *righteousness* is applied to Christ not only in view of His essential righteousness but also in view of the righteousness that He gained for mankind (Jeremiah 23:6; *see also* justification). The righteousness of the Law is the obedience that the Law requires (*see* Law; Gospel). The righteousness of the Christian is the righteousness of faith (*see* faith; justification).

rite; ritual. Prescribed ceremonial practice, or a specific action as part of a formal worship service.

Sabbath. Day of rest corresponding to the day of rest after creation (Genesis 2:3; Exodus 20:8, 11; 31:17). The Old Testament laws concerning the seventh-day Sabbath have been abrogated by Christ, who is Himself our "Sabbath rest" (Hebrews 4:9–11).

Sacrament (Latin: *sacramentum*; "something to be kept sacred"). A sacred act instituted by God in which God Himself has joined His Word of promise to a visible element, and by which He offers, gives, and seals the forgiveness of sins earned by Christ. By this definition, there are two Sacraments: Holy Baptism and the Lord's Supper. Sometimes Holy Absolution is counted as a third Sacrament, even though it has no divinely instituted element (LC IV 74; Ap XIII 4). In Ancient and Medieval Church usage, the term had various meanings: (1) a secret; (2) the Gospel revelation; (3) a mystery; (4) a means of giving, and receiving, grace (e.g., Baptism and Holy Communion); (5) the Office of the Holy Ministry. According to Luther, the chief Sacrament is Christ Himself (WA 6:97).

saint. The word *saint* in Scripture refers to believers on earth (Acts 9:32; Romans 1:7) and in heaven (Matthew 27:52). Throughout Church history, it has been used to designate one set apart as especially holy (e.g., St. Paul, St. Francis of Assisi). The Lutheran Reformation rejected prayers and devotions to saints. In

Lutheran usage, the title of "saint" is not used for anyone except those who were called such before the Reformation.

sanctification. In a wide sense, sanctification includes all effects of God's Word (Acts 26:18; Ephesians 5:26; 2 Thessalonians 2:13; Hebrews 10:14; 1 Peter 1:2). In a narrow sense, sanctification is the spiritual growth (1 Corinthians 3:9; 9:24; Ephesians 4:15; Philippians 3:12) that follows justification (Matthew 7:16–18; John 3:6; Ephesians 2:10). By God's grace (Galatians 5:22–23; Philippians 2:13), a Christian cooperates in this work (2 Corinthians 6:1; 7:1; Philippians 2:12; 1 Timothy 4:14; FC SD II 65–66). Through the Holy Spirit's work, faith is increased daily, love strengthened, and the image of God renewed but not perfected in this life.

satisfaction. According to Roman Church teaching, temporal punishments (justly due because of sin) can be paid through penance.

schism; schismatics (Greek: *schizein,* "to divide, tear, cleave asunder, open, cut apart"). Used of divergent opinions (John 7:43; Acts 14:4). The church uses the term in the sense of dissension, division, or discord (1 Corinthians 1:10; 11:18; 12:25). Schismatics disrupt church harmony and unity.

see. The seat (center of power and authority) of a bishop; the jurisdiction of a bishop.

simony. Buying or selling the offices, blessings, and benefits of the Church. The term comes from the attempt of Simon Magus to buy the power to give the Holy Spirit (Acts 8:9–24). The practice was condemned by many Early Church synods. Pope Gregory I strongly opposed and combated simony, but the practice increased in the Middle Ages and became entangled with the policy of secular rulers investing bishops with their office. Pope Gregory VII renewed the battle against simony. *See also* pornocracy.

sin. The breaking of God's Law (Romans 4:15; 1 John 3:4). Sin may be divided into original sin (the inherited tendency to sin and God's resultant condemnation) and actual sin. Actual sin (every thought, emotion, word, or act conflicting with God's Law) may be involuntary or may be done ignorantly (Acts 17:30) and includes sins of commission (Matthew 15:19; James 1:15) and sins of omission (James 4:17). Sin arouses God's righteous wrath and deserves His punishment. Willful sin sears the conscience; repeated, it hardens the heart and may lead to, but is not identical with, the unpardonable sin against the Holy Spirit.

sophistry. Subtle reasoning or argumentation designed to deceive.

substance (Latin: *substantia*). The concrete instance of the essence

205

(nature) of a thing, such as a particular human being. Also understood as an application of the term *essence*: that which exists by itself essentially, such as created human nature (FC Ep I 23; FC SD I 21, 54; *see also* accident, essence, person).

synods (Greek: *synodos*, "a meeting of the ways"; from *synoduein*, "to travel as a caravan"). Ecclesiastical assemblies convened for discussion and settlement of questions affecting the faith and discipline of the Church. Traditionally, such meetings were called by the bishop or archbishop within his jurisdiction, or by the emperor or pope for the whole Church as an ecumenical synod. The bishops traditionally had exclusive "seat and vote" at the larger synods. In Lutheran teaching, the theological basis for synods is found in Acts 15. In synods, pastors and congregations converse with one another and express unity in doctrine, order, and life. The authority of synods derives from the activity of the Holy Spirit.

testament. A covenant between God and human beings. A will or expression of someone's desire as to the disposal of his or her property at death.

theologian. A student or practitioner of theology.

union (Latin: *unus*, "one"). The bringing together of two or more things.

vicar. One who substitutes for or represents another. Anciently, a secular cleric who officiated in a church owned by a religious order.

worship. The broadest definition of *worship* is the response of the creature to the Creator. Christian worship can only be defined accurately, however, by further defining "Creator" as "He who revealed Himself in Jesus Christ and makes Himself known through the Holy Spirit." In common usage, *worship* properly designates the reception of the Means of Grace—Baptism, Absolution, Word, and Holy Communion. However, worship also describes mankind's response to God in prayer, praise, confession of faith, and thanksgiving. This is not limited to the worship service itself, but encompasses anywhere and everywhere all that a Christian says and does by faith in Jesus Christ (Romans 12:1).

DESCRIPTION OF PERSONS AND GROUPS

Abraham (d. c. 1991 BC). The first patriarch of Israel (Genesis 11:26–25:18). He received God's promises and blessings by faith (Genesis 12) before the covenant of circumcision or the Law of Moses was given (Galatians 3). In St. Paul's writings and the Lutheran Confessions, Abraham is a shining example of faith.

Adam (ancient history). The first human being, husband of Eve (Genesis 1:26–5:5). Adam bore responsibility for the fall into sin, which cursed all mankind. Christ is called the "Second Adam" because He takes away the sin of all mankind (Romans 5:12–19). The Lutheran Confessions often refer to the "old Adam," our sinful nature that resulted from Adam's fall into sin.

Albert of Brandenburg (1490–1545). Archbishop of Magdeburg (1513). Also archbishop and elector of Mainz (1514), by special favor of Pope Leo X. Cardinal (1518). Leo granted Albert the right to sell indulgences in Saxony and Brandenburg to raise money for St. Peter's Cathedral, Rome. Albert hired John Tetzel for this purpose. These indulgences caused Luther to write the Ninety-five Theses, sparking the Reformation. Albert was open to the Reformation at first, but supported Rome from 1525 onward.

Alexander VI (1431–1503) Member of the infamous Borgia family; nephew of Pope Calixtus III; exemplified debased standards of Renaissance-era papacy; accused of simony by Julius II.

Alexander the Great (356–323 BC). Educated by Aristotle. Conqueror from Greece to India, including the Jewish people.

Amalric of Bène (Bena; died c. 1204/07). Scholastic philosopher who taught at Paris; influenced by Aristotle and John Scotus Eriugena. Amalric held that God is the essence of all and that they who remain in the love of God cannot sin. Pope Innocent III ordered Amalric to recant in 1204; the humiliation hastened his death. His teachings were officially condemned and his followers burned a few years after his death.

Anabaptists. From Greek word for "rebaptize." 1. Fourth-century term for groups that rebaptized (a) people baptized by heretics and (b) people baptized by clergy who later fell from faith during persecution. 2. During Reformation, name of reproach applied to groups insisting on rebaptism of people baptized as infants. Anabaptists were most influential from Switzerland down the Rhine River to Holland. Modern groups include Mennonites, Amish, and Swiss Brethren.

Antichrist. Term used in the New Testament (a) of all false teachers (1 John 2:18; 4:3) and (b) of one outstanding adversary of Christ (1 John 2:18). Characteristics of Antichrist are taken from Daniel 7; 8; 11:31–38; Revelation 11; 13; 17; 18; writings of John; and especially 2 Thessalonians 2:3–12. These passages of Scripture were cited during a thirteenth-century quarrel that arose between strict Franciscan monks (Spirituals) and the papacy on the poverty of Christ versus papal riches. The Franciscans divided between a strict and lax interpretation of the issue. These competing views became politicized, with the papacy, universities, and major bishops supporting lax interpretations, and several emperors supporting the stricter adherents. This tension was further strained by the apocalyptic writing of Joachim of Fiore, who was condemned at the Fourth Lateran Council. Several popes persecuted the Spirituals with the aid of the Dominican monks. The perceived corruption of the Avignon papacy in the fourteenth century added to negative views of the papacy. As a result, a number of voices in the Church called the pope Antichrist. With end-times anxiety and fear of the Black Death, popular contempt for the luxury and immorality of Renaissance-era popes and other high church officials sustained this critique into Luther's time. The Apology shows that the papacy has marks of Antichrist as depicted by Daniel (Ap VII–VIII 24; Ap XV 19; Ap XXIII 25; Ap XXIV 51) and by Paul (Ap VII–VIII 4). It speaks of papacy as part of the kingdom of Antichrist (Ap XV 18). The Smalcald Articles hold that the pope, by his doctrine and practice, has clearly shown his office as Antichrist since it exceeds even the Turks and Tartars in keeping people from their Savior (SA II IV 10–14). The Formula of Concord quotes the Smalcald Articles on Antichrist (FC SD X 20). The papacy has never ceased to be wealthy and powerful since Luther's time, nor has it retracted any of its imperious and unscriptural claims on the church.

Aquinas, Thomas. *See* Thomas Aquinas.

Augustine (354–430). Renowned North African Christian teacher and philosopher. Had a pagan father, Christian mother (Monica). Joined Manichaean sect. Under influence of Ambrose at Milan, Augustine converted during study of the Book of Romans (386). Baptized the following year. Returned to North Africa, sold family inheritance, and founded a monastery with a clerical school. Bishop of Hippo Regius (396).Vigorously fought heresies of Pelagius, Donatists, and others. His writings were the basis of Western theology until overshadowed by Scholasticism. Augustine taught justification by grace, but only for the elect. Luther joined the Augustinian Hermits and studied Augustine's writings. Luther broke with Augustine's theology to emphasize Scripture alone. Augustine's views on predestination greatly influenced John Calvin and Reformed theology.

Baal. The Canaanite storm god, often worshiped by ancient Israelites (see 1 Kings 18). The Lutheran Confessions refer to this history in describing the evil worship practices of the papacy.

Beguines. Semimonastic communities of women in western Europe from the twelfth century onward. Beguines (sisterhood) are the original order. The Beghards became the male counterpart. Celibacy was required as long as one remained a member. They were devoted to contemplation and deaconess work. In the thirteenth century, they were persecuted for heresy and prosecuted for living together outside of marriage. Many joined the tertiaries of the mendicant monastic orders. A few small com-munities of Beguines survive in the Netherlands and Belgium.

Bernard of Clairvaux (1091–1153). Called "Teacher of Flowing Honey." Influential abbot because of his deep piety and eloquence. Joined the Cistercians (1115) and founded a cloister at Clairvaux, France. Wore himself out in severe self-discipline. A pious and humble Christian who diligently read his Bible and loved his Savior. Worked up enthusiasm for the Crusades, though he frowned on using force against heretics. Luther deeply valued Bernard's sermons. His poetry inspired Paul Gerhardt's unforgettable hymn "O Sacred Head, Now Wounded."

Bugenhagen, John (Pomeranus; 1485–1558). Called "pastor of the Reformation." Luther's *Babylonian Captivity* won him permanently for the Reformation. Came to Wittenberg (1521) and lectured on the Psalms. Pastor of St. Mary's Church from 1522. Assisted Luther in translation of the Bible. Celebrated its publication every year with a little festival in his home. His sermons were warm and direct. Motto: "If you know Christ well, it is enough, though you know nothing else; if you know not Christ, what else you learn does not matter."

Cajetan, Thomas de Vio (1469–1534). Italian cardinal and defender of papal supremacy. Admirer of

Thomas Aquinas. General of the Dominican order (1517). Made cardinal (1517). Papal legate to Diet of Augsburg (1518) with task of moving Luther to recant. Confounded and embarrassed by Luther's superior knowledge of Scripture, Cajetan began to study the Bible himself. His commentaries grew more and more critical of Roman doctrine. However, he continued to follow Rome, to serve the papacy, and to oppose Lutheranism.

Carlstadt, Andreas (c. 1480–1541). Revolutionist of the Reformation; professor at Wittenberg; supported Luther's Ninety-five Theses; tangled with John Eck at the Leipzig Disputation (1519); introduced Reformation at Wittenberg by force (1521); preacher at Orlamünde (1523/24); rejected Baptism and the Lord's Supper as Sacraments, and abolished ceremonies in undue haste; expelled by Saxon authorities (1524); wandered from place to place; associated with Zwingli at Zurich and finally with Bullinger at Basel. During Luther's Wartburg retreat, vanity and impulsiveness got the better of Carlstadt, and he rushed reform with ill-advised haste. Even the extreme radicalism of Thomas Münzer found favor in his eyes. Luther returned to Wittenberg and quieted the storm successfully, while Carlstadt went back to teaching. Carlstadt finally with-

drew to a little farm, dressed and lived like a peasant, and wanted to be known as "neighbor Andrew." But his temperament could not endure this either. He returned to the ministry at Orlamünde.

Charlemagne (742–814). Charles I, the first Holy Roman emperor, crowned by Pope Leo III. Conquered and Christianized the Saxons. Through Alcuin, implemented church and educational reforms.

Charles V (1500–58). Holy Roman emperor; elected 1519, crowned 1530. King (Charles I) of Spain (1516–56). He suppressed or tolerated the Reformation based on his political and military needs in his struggle with the French and Turks.

Church Fathers. Recognized teachers of the Church from the close of the apostolic age to dates variously set between the seventh and ninth centuries.

Cicero, Marcus Tullius (106–43 BC). Roman statesman, orator. Slain under second triumvirate. Noted for his orations, eclectic treatment of philosophical and religious subjects.

Constance. *See* Council of Constance.

Council of Basel (1431–49). Last of the councils of the conciliar movement, convoked by Pope Martin V. Its objectives were (a) the rooting out of heresy; (b) the reunion of all Christians; (c) the development of religious instruction; (d) the settlement of disputes among Christian princes; (e) the reformation of the Church; and (f) the reestablishment of discipline. Pope Eugenius IV dissolved the council in 1431, but the council continued and reaffirmed the Council of Constance on the supremacy of councils over the pope. In 1433, Eugenius again recognized the council, but the anti-papal climate of the council brought on many restrictions of the papacy. In 1437, the council granted the Bohemians the right to celebrate Communion in both kinds. When the pope transferred the council to Ferrara (1437) to meet with the representatives of the Greek Orthodox Church, a remnant remained at Basel, deposed the pope, and elected Amadeus VIII of Savoy as Pope Felix V. The Council of Ferrara met 1438–39, then was transferred to Florence, where it met 1439–42; then it was transferred to Rome, where it met 1442–45. In 1448, the rump council moved to Lausanne. After the death of Eugenius, Nicholas V was chosen pope and generally recognized. In 1449, Felix V abdicated and submitted to Nicholas V.

Council of Constance (1414–18). A council intended to bring about a reformation of the Church. The papal schism that began in 1378 was settled, electing Martin V. It excommunicated John Wycliffe posthumously (1415) and had his bones burned (1427) and their ashes thrown into the Swift. John Hus (1415) and Jerome of Prague (1416) were also condemned by this council and burned at the stake. Reforms were urged by lower clergy, monks, doctors, and professors, but the would-be reformers disagreed among themselves and their agitation practically came to naught, largely because the abuses they attacked concerned such matters as papal procedure, administration and income of vacant benefices, simony, indulgences, and dispensations, from which the pope, cardinals, and other Roman Church officials received much of their income.

Council of Trent (1545–47, 1551–52, and 1562–63). Regarded as the nineteenth ecumenical council by the Roman Church. Met in three assemblies. In the first assembly, accepted traditional canon of Scripture (including Apocrypha), authorized the Vulgate, and defined Scripture and tradition as the two sources of religious truth. Rejected Lutheran view of imputed, or forensic, righteousness in the doctrine of justification. In the second, canons were established on the Eucharist, penance, and extreme unction. The last assembly reaffirmed episcopal residencies; agreements concerning the sacrifice of the Mass, orders, and the establishment of seminaries were also reached. Anathemas of Protestant doctrines and affirmations of Roman Church teachings, along with the success of reform decrees, mark the council as one of the most important factors of the Catholic, or Counter, Reformation. This council established the Roman Catholic Church in distinction from medieval catholicism, which Lutherans regard as part of their heritage.

Cranach, Lucas, the Elder (1472–1553). Court painter under Frederick the Wise (c. 1505) and under John the Steadfast and John Frederick. Painted portraits of Luther and practically all important Lutheran reformers. His art shows evangelical understanding of Scripture and Church. Sons Hans (c. 1513–37) and Lucas the Younger (1515–86) worked with their father and continued his style. Lucas took his name from Kronach in Upper Franconia, where he was born. He was influenced by Renaissance painters and humanist scholars while living and studying in Vienna around 1503. Until 1508, Cranach signed his works with the initials of his name. In that year, the elector gave him the winged snake as a emblem, and this emblem, or *Kleinod*, as it was called, superseded the initials on all his pictures after that date. He became a fast friend of Luther and played an important role in arranging for Luther's marriage celebration. He was the baptismal sponsor for Luther's oldest son, Hans. He was a member of the Wittenberg town council and served for a while as mayor of Wittenberg. After the defeat of the Smalcaldic League's armies in 1547, he wrote to Albert of Brandenburg at Königsberg to tell him of the capture of John Frederick the Magnanimous: "I cannot conceal from your Grace that we have been robbed of our dear prince, who from his youth upwards has been a true prince to us, but God will help him out of prison, for the emperor is bold enough to revive the papacy, which God will certainly not allow." During the siege of Wittenberg, Charles V called for Cranach, whom he remembered from his childhood, and summoned him to his camp at Pistritz. Cranach came and reminded Charles of his early sittings for portraits by Cranach when he was a boy, and begged on his knees for kind treatment to the elector. John Frederick ordered Cranach to his side, so he left his prosperous businesses and spent time with his elector in his exile, returning home with him in 1552. Cranach died on October 16, 1553.

Daniel (sixth century BC). Old Testament prophet most often mentioned in the Lutheran Confessions. The Confessions describe his preaching to Nebuchadnezzar, king of Babylon, which resulted in the king's conversion (Daniel 4).

Daniel also prophesied about the coming of Antichrist (Daniel 11).

David (d. c. 970 BC). King of Israel, prophet, and psalmist. The Lutheran Confessions describe David as an example of sincere repentance and faith.

Devil. *See* Satan.

Dominic (1171–1221). Priest; founder of the Dominicans (*see* Dominicans).

Dominicans. "Order of Preachers," also called "Friars Preachers," founded by Dominic while engaged in efforts to convert the Albigenses of South France (1215). Adopted the Augustinian rule and was committed to poverty and dedicated to teaching, preaching, and scholarship. The rule of poverty was soon disregarded and eliminated altogether by 1477. Dominicans were to strengthen faith and combat heresy. Most Inquisitors were Dominicans. John Tetzel and Thomas Aquinas were Dominicans.

Eck, John (1486–1543). Clever dialectician. Professor at Ingolstadt from 1510. Obliged by his superiors to pass judgment on the Ninety-five Theses of Luther, with whom he had stood in friendly relation. The two clashed especially in the Leipzig Disputation (June 27–July 16, 1519). In Rome, Eck was largely instrumental in getting Leo X to issue against Luther, on June 15, 1520, the bull *Exsurge Domine*. Champion of medieval Romanism and papal supremacy at the Diet of Augsburg (1530); was active in this capacity in all later similar religious conventions. Eck never became a noted author but is generally regarded as Luther's ablest opponent.

Enthusiast(s) (from Greek for "one possessed by a god"). The Lutheran Confessions use this term to describe fanatics who believed that God spoke to them without the Holy Scriptures and would save them without the Means of Grace.

Epicureans. *See* Epicurus.

Epicurus (c. 341–c. 270 BC). Greek philosopher; founded Epicurean school of thought. Founded school at Athens (c. 306). Lived with followers in a secluded and austere way. Developed philosophy of pleasure and contemplation.

Erasmus of Rotterdam, Desiderius (1469–1536). One of the most learned men of his age. Guardians forced him into a monastery; he became a priest but never had a parish and never performed priestly functions. Edited an edition of the Greek New Testament, which was published in Basel (1516) and was later used by Luther in his Bible translation. Recognized the many ills of Christendom, but they moved him to laughter rather than to tears. He looked to a humanistic education for a gradual and peaceful reform of the Church. At first sympathetic to Luther's ambitions, he drew farther and farther away from the Reformation because of its positiveness, its emphasis on Scripture alone, and its refusal to submit to Rome. Wrote against Luther in defense of the free will of people, a point of Scholastic doctrine. Luther refuted him in his book *On the Bondage of the Will.* The controversy left Erasmus mistrusted by both Romanists and by Protestants.

Eugenius III (Eugene; d. 1153). Born into the aristocracy of Pisa; became a Cistercian monk; made an abbot by Pope Innocent II. Raised to the papacy without being a cardinal. Friend and pupil of Bernard of Clairvaux, but nevertheless did not meet with Bernard's approval. His weakness prompted Arnold of Brescia (*see* Waldenses) to invoke the old Roman constitution and establish the Commune of Rome. Never resided in Rome; eventually moved to France. Dominated by Bernard in the matter of the disastrous Second Crusade; dependent on the goodwill of the emperor, kings, and the nobility. Held several synods in northern Europe to reform clerical life.

Eugenius IV (Eugene; 1383–1447). Augustinian friar; nephew of Pope Gregory XII. Appointed papal treasurer and cardinal at age 24. Proved useful to both his uncle and to Pope Martin V, whom he succeeded as pope. Embroiled in Italian clan warfare with the family of Martin V; responsible for eroding the power of the conciliar movement. Recognized the Council of Basel as ecumenical due to invasion of the Papal States as a result of his support for Florence and Venice over Milan. Exiled for a decade, then returned in triumph. Made a policy that allowed Christians to enslave non-Christians; this set the stage for centuries of European slaveholding.

evangelist (first century AD). Author of a New Testament Gospel (Matthew, Mark, Luke, and John).

Eve (ancient history). The first woman, wife of Adam (Genesis 1–4).

Faber, John (1478–1541). Called "Hammer of Heretics" after one of his works; vicar-general at Constance (1518); humanist friend of Erasmus; participated in disputations at Zurich (1523) and Baden (1526) against Zwingli; bishop of Vienna (c. 1530); wrote against Luther.

Fathers. *See* Church Fathers.

Francis of Assisi (c. 1181–1226). *See* Franciscans.

Franciscans. Order founded in 1209 by Francis of Assisi. Their early years were marked by strict poverty, limited use of property, begging, humble service to all, and mission endeavors; but the order was wracked for more than a century by disputes about the question of poverty. Bonaventure, Duns Scotus, and William of Ockham were members of the order. In 1517, a split took place between the stricter faction (Friars Minor proper [Observant]) and the moderate faction (Friars Minor Conventual). The Friars Minor Capuchins were founded c. 1528 by an Observant priest; they became one of the most powerful agencies of the Counter-Reformation. The Second Order (Poor Clares) was founded 1212. There is also a Third Order (Tertiaries).

Frederick III, "The Wise" (1463–1525). Elector of Saxony from 1486. Called "The Wise" because of his vision and astuteness, which raised little Saxony to the rank of the most influential power in Germany. At the death of Maximilian I (1519), Frederick was offered the imperial crown, but he declined it. Frederick was largely a nationalist and worked toward strengthening his own government rather than that of the empire and the church. He was a devout son of the church. In 1493, he went on a pilgrimage to the Holy Land and returned with a thumb of Anna, his favorite saint. This he added to the more than 5,000 relics he kept in the Castle Church at Wittenberg. In 1502, he had established Wittenberg University, to which Luther was called (1508). When Luther's reformatory activity began to attract public notice, Frederick protected Luther. He would have no one condemned unheard and unconvicted, nor would he have an offense that had been committed in his country tried at Rome. Frederick and Luther communicated through Spalatin, Frederick's secretary. Gradually the Gospel exerted its power on this devout medieval man and Frederick became a Lutheran in faith—if not in public confession. He abolished the exhibition of his precious relics in 1523 and discontinued Masses in the Castle Church. Two years later, on his deathbed, he received Communion in the Lutheran and scriptural form.

friars (Latin: *frater*, "brother"). Members of a monastic order that lives on almsgiving (mendicant).

Galatians (first century AD). Members of congregation(s) in Asia Minor to whom Paul wrote about justification and the use of Law and Gospel.

Greeks. 1. The ancient Greeks. 2. The Greek-speaking Christians of the East.

Gregory VII (c. 1015–1085). Born Hildebrand in the Italian city of Savona. Influenced by his mentor, Pope Gregory VI, who claimed the papacy in the latter 1040s against Benedict IX, the "boy pope" of the Theophylact family who wanted to marry, and Silvester III. Gregory VI tried to fight extensive corruption, but was himself charged with simony and deposed with the support of Emperor Henry III. Henry took Gregory VI to Cologne with Hildebrand in tow. Hildebrand soon returned to Rome, served as archdeacon and papal legate, and acted as the power behind several popes. In 1073, his sudden, irregular election to the papacy as Gregory VII, with his later ordination as presbyter and bishop, technically violated earlier reforms of Pope Nicholas II. Nevertheless, Gregory moved quickly in 1074–75 to require clerical celibacy and pass strict measures against simony. Gregory rejected aspects of earlier reforms by brushing aside consultation with the emperor and claiming that only the pope could appoint, remove, or move bishops. Gregory's harshness with the weakened Henry IV turned the German bishops against him and helped to spark the Investiture Controversy. Gregory mandated the doctrine that would eventually be adopted as transubstantiation, the substantial conversion of bread and wine into the flesh and blood of Christ. The Fourth Lateran Council (1215) ratified much of Gregory's program. Gregory died in exile, as did his mentor before him, after having attempted to influence every nation in Christendom. His model for a powerful papacy set the stage for later political reactions and different forms of papal corruption.

heathen. *See* pagans.

Henry VIII (1491–1547). Tudor king of England (1509–47); joined Holy League against France (1511); appointed Wolsey lord chancellor (1515); received title "Defender of the Faith" from Pope Leo X (1521) for opposing Luther. In conflict with pope because the latter refused to grant him an annulment from Catherine of Aragon; secured from Parliament the Act of Supremacy (1534), creating a national church with the king as head; closed monasteries and confiscated their property. In 1533, Thomas Cranmer, a prelate with Lutheran leanings, was consecrated archbishop of Canterbury. Henry's actions led to a quasi reform in England by the dissolution of monasteries (1535–36), the promulgation of the Ten Articles (1539), the translation of the Bible with the royal sanction, and even an exploration of the possibility of a working agreement with the reformers on the Continent, especially Luther and his associates. Luther was correct when he remarked that Henry wanted to kill the pope's "body," that is, papal authority in England, but desired to keep the pope's "soul," papal doctrine.

hermits (Greek: *eremites*, "living in the desert"). Religious orders whose members lead solitary lives.

Hugh of St. Victor (c. 1096–1141). Spent most of his adult life in abbey of St. Victor, Paris; combined mysticism and dialectics in treatment of theology.

Hus, John (c. 1370–1415). Forerunner of the Reformation. Studied at University of Prague, became priest (1400) and rector of the university (1402). A follower of Wycliffe, he clearly recognized the need for reformation. He was put under the great ban of the Church of Rome (1412). Refusing to be silenced, he countered by writing his book *On the Church*. Hus taught the sole authority of Scripture and held that the Church is the body of the elect. Though he preached Christ as Savior, he confused Law and Gospel and mixed justification with sanctification. After three public hearings, the Council of Constance condemned him to be burned publicly as a heretic on July 6, 1415, because "no faith should be observed toward a heretic." His ashes were flung into the Rhine.

Hussites. Generic name for followers of John Hus. Fierce indignation aroused throughout Bohemia after the execution of Hus and Jerome of Prague. The Council of Constance (1414–18) condemned Communion in both kinds (Latin: *sub utraque specie*) that had been introduced with the approval of Hus during his imprisonment. The result was a long civil war. The *Devotio Moderna* movement (modern devotion to methodical prayer),

which included Geert Groote and Thomas à Kempis, gave the Hussites a basis for spiritual life, while thoughts that grew from the teachings of John Wycliffe furnished Hussites with an intellectual basis for revolt. The estates rejected Emperor Sigismund as King of Bohemia and ignited the Hussite Wars. Pope Martin V organized a crusade against the dissidents in 1420. Hussite moderates were called Calixtines (from Latin *calix*, "chalice") or Utraquists (from Latin *utraque*, "both"). Taborites were a more radical group gathered around Jan Žižka (c. 1360–1424) that rejected transubstantiation, adoration of the saints, intercession for the dead, and church customs not commanded in the Bible. Taborites demanded that the state regulate its affairs by the Bible, and had chiliastic and communistic tendencies. Horebites were named after a mountain commune they called Horeb; they also gathered around Žižka. All of these groups adopted the Articles of Prague in 1420: (a) freedom of preaching; (b) Communion under both kinds; (c) reduction of clergy to apostolic poverty; (d) severe punishment for mortal sin. The driving force of the Hussites was religious zeal nourished by biblical preaching, frequent partaking of the Eucharist, and rich vernacular hymnody. A crushing defeat of Catholic forces in 1431 forced negotiations with the Council of Basel. The Hussites adopted a modified form of the Articles of Prague in 1433. Communion under both kinds was allowed. Taborites rejected the agreement and were annihilated in 1434 by Hussite moderates and Catholics. Hussite theology found new expression in the Bohemian Brethren. The movement's descendants include Lutherans, Moravians, and parts of the Roman Church in Poland. Communion in both kinds was allowed by Vatican II.

Isaac (c. 2066–c. 1886 BC). Son of Abraham and patriarch of Israel (Genesis 21–28), through whom God promised a Savior would be born.

Isaiah (eighth century BC). Prophet in Old Testament Judah. Cited often in the Lutheran Confessions.

Israel. The Hebrew people of the Old Testament, named for the patriarch Jacob, whom God called "Israel" (Genesis 32:22–32). The Lutheran Confessions regard the good and bad events of Israel's history as examples for warning and teaching the Church.

Jacob (c. 2006–c. 1859 BC). Son of Isaac and patriarch of Israel. God gave him the name Israel (Genesis 32:22–32).

Jeremiah (d. c. 585 BC). Prophet in OT Judah.

Jeroboam I (d. c. 909). The first king of the northern tribes of Israel,

which broke away during the reign of Rehoboam of Judah (1 Kings 12). He reintroduced idolatry in ancient Israel (the golden calves).

Jerome (c. 340–c. 420). Church Father. Baptized at 19 in Rome, where he had gone to study rhetoric and philosophy; traveled, settling finally at Bethlehem. Turned from secular studies to the things of God during his first stay at Antioch; secretary to Bishop Damasus I of Rome. Works include revision of the Latin Bible (Vulgate) and commentaries on books of the Bible. However, he never seems to have clearly understood Christ's redemptive work.

Jerome of Prague (c. 1360–1416). Friend of John Hus, copied *Dialogus* and *Trialogus* of John Wycliffe, whom he championed. Council of Constance condemned him to be publicly burned as a heretic (1416).

Jesus of Nazareth (eternal God, born of the Virgin Mary c. 4 BC). The Christ and Savior of the world. Subject especially of AC III, Ap III, SA II I, FC Ep VIII, and FC SD VIII.

Jews. Descendants of the Israelite tribe of Judah and other Israelites who followed the leadership of Judah. Mary and Jesus descended from this tribe. Because the Jewish leadership rejected Jesus as God, antagonism has long existed between Jewish people and Christians.

Job (second millennium BC). OT figure known for his suffering and patience. The Lutheran Confessions commend him because he sought God's will more than an escape from suffering.

Julian the Apostate (c. 331–363). Roman emperor (361–363). Although reared Christian, embraced paganism; developed strong anti-Christian policy.

Julius II (1443–1513). Nephew of Pope Sixtus IV; pope 1503–13; chiefly military. Founded the Swiss Guard in 1506 and either controlled powerful Italian families or took military action against them. Joined Aragon, France, and the Holy Roman Empire in the first Holy League against Venice in 1508, thereby reducing Venetian power. Wanted to restore Italy as a powerful, unified kingdom. French influence grew in Italy, so he joined Aragon and Venice against France in 1511 (the second Holy League). Convened the Fifth Lateran Council in 1512 to oppose the council at Pisa and Lyon that declared him deposed at the urging of Louis XII of France and Emperor Maximillian I. Was a patron of Italian art and culture. Leo X continued Julius's plans for the council after the latter's death. Lateran V reiterated the principle of "freedom of the Church" established by Gregory VII.

laity. Laypeople. Division of church members into clergy and laity is valid if the words simply distinguish those who have been called into the ministry from those who have not been so called. But with the rise of the priestly system, which culminated in the papacy, the idea that the priesthood formed an intermediate class between God and people became prevalent, and the term *clergy* took on added, hierarchic meaning in that context. The doctrine of justification by faith alone abolished human mediation between people and God. Luther effectively proclaimed the priesthood of all believers (see 1 Peter 2:9). As a result, the laity recovered its proper position and lay representation again became possible.

Lang, John (c. 1487–1548). Reformer of Erfurt. Augustinian monk (1506); priest (1508); friend of Luther; supported Luther at the 1519 Leipzig Disputation. Introduced new order of service in Erfurt (1525). Signed SA (1537).

Lawrence (third century AD). Deacon at Rome; martyr. Cited by reformers as an example of a saint who did not trust in his works.

Leo X (1475–1521). Pope 1513–21; used his influence in the interest of his family; misunderstood the importance of Luther (1519), excommunicated him (1521).

Lot (twenty-first century BC). The patriarch Abraham's nephew who moved his family into the evil city of Sodom (Genesis 13–14). His wife turned into a pillar of salt when she disobeyed the angel's warning about looking back toward Sodom (Genesis 19:26).

Luke (first century AD). Physician and evangelist. Author of the Gospel according to St. Luke and the Acts of the Apostles. An associate of the apostle Paul (Luke 1:1–4; 2 Timothy 4:11).

Luther, Martin (November 10, 1483–February 18, 1546). Born and died in Eisleben, Germany. Luther probably first saw a Bible in Magdeburg, under instruction of the Brethren of the Common Life at the Cathedral School. Entered University of Erfurt (spring 1501). Father wanted him to be a lawyer. Entered Erfurt Law School (May 1505). Then, quite unexpectedly on July 17, 1505, entered the very strict Black Cloister of the local Augustinian Hermits (their black outer coat gave them their name). Later, he often spoke of a severe thunderstorm that terrified him and caused him to pray to St. Anne, promising to become a monk. Luther did not find peace of mind and soul in the monastery, but he determined to keep his vows. Ordained a priest (spring 1507). Celebrated first Mass on May 2, 1507, in the presence of his father, other relatives, and many friends. Continued studies (1507–12); became a doctor of theology in biblical studies, spe-

cifically the Old Testament. The more Luther studied medieval theology, and the more he became involved in the labyrinth of Scholasticism, the more concerned he grew. The main problem that disturbed him was how to find a gracious God. Luther was sent to Wittenberg (1508) to teach moral philosophy, but returned to Erfurt (1509). In November 1510, Luther and another monk set out on foot for Rome to help settle some matters pertaining to the Augustinian Order. They reached Rome in January 1511. Luther was shocked by the worldliness of some Italian clergy. While praying for his grandparents, he climbed the Holy Steps (*Scala Sancta*), said to be the steps Christ had climbed on Good Friday. Shortly after his return to Germany, he was sent back to the University of Wittenberg, where he was trained to succeed John von Staupitz in the chair of lecturer in the Bible as soon as he had earned the doctorate (awarded on October 18–19, 1512, in the Wittenberg Castle Church). While lecturing on Genesis, Psalms, Romans, Galatians, and Hebrews (1512–18), Luther departed from Scholasticism to hold a thoroughly biblical theology. Probably in fall 1514, while lecturing on Psalm 71, he first began to realize that salvation is not based on works but on God's grace. He did not fully understand all its implications but said later that he had found, as he called it, the "Gate to Paradise" (WA 54:186). Eventually won the university faculty to his views. By 1517, the school had become a center of biblical studies. The "New Theology," which was Christ-centered and stressed Scripture alone, was too dynamic to leave the Medieval Church unaffected. Conflict with traditional Scholastic theology began over the sale of indulgences. Luther posted notice of a debate on the school bulletin board (the north door of the Castle Church) on October 31, 1517, listing ninety-five theses for discussion. The theses rapidly spread throughout Germany. Many people agreed with Luther. Financial returns from indulgence sales in Germany were greatly reduced, bringing immediate reaction from John Tetzel (indulgence salesman in Luther's territory), from Tetzel's fellow Dominicans, and from Albert of Brandenburg. (Albert was hoping to pay the "fee" for his appointment as archbishop of Mainz, which made him holder of three church positions simultaneously [contrary to church law].) The uproar pressured Pope Leo X to silence Luther. He instructed the Augustinian order to discipline its recalcitrant member. At the Heidelberg Disputation (April 1518) Luther won new friends. Instead of reprimanding him, the order asked

him to write an elaboration of his original Ninety-five Theses. Under influence of the Saxon Dominican provincial, the fiscal procurator of Rome opened Luther's case, charging "suspicion of heresy." In September 1518, Luther was summoned to appear at Augsburg before papal legate Cajetan. Luther was willing to be convinced on the basis of Scripture that indulgences were biblical. But the differences could not be reconciled. Staupitz released Luther from the vow of obedience to the Augustinian order (mid-October 1518). Cajetan recommended to Frederick III that Luther be either banished or surrendered to Rome. On Luther's initiative, Wittenberg University faculty sent a letter (November 22, 1518) to Frederick III, expressing complete agreement with Luther's views. With this statement of Luther's case and the advice of his court, Frederick III refused to surrender Luther to Rome unless an unbiased tribunal proved Luther was a heretic. Luther hoped for a solution by a general church council. Roman Church leaders on the case included Karl von Miltitz and John Eck, the latter known especially from the Leipzig Disputation (1519). First hopeful of cleansing the church of error, Luther began to realize that no reformation of the existing body, permeated with error in head and members, was possible. After the election of Charles V (1519) as Holy Roman emperor, Rome again focused on Luther. Universities of Louvain and Cologne issued condemnations of Luther's theology (1519). Pope Leo wrote the bull *Exsurge Domine* ("Arise, O Lord"; June 15, 1520), giving Luther sixty days to recant. It also required all his writings to be burned. At Wittenberg, Luther responded by burning the canon law and the bull. Rome's reply was the bull of excommunication (January 3, 1521). Charles was pressured to condemn Luther, so he summoned Luther to appear at the Diet of Worms (1521). There, Luther resisted all efforts to persuade him to recant. Privately and publicly he said he could not recant unless convinced of error by Scripture. Lacking the necessary support of German princes to secure Luther's condemnation, Charles waited until the Diet had been dismissed. Then, in a special session, Charles declared Luther a heretic and outlaw who could be killed on sight. Luther's prince, who left the Diet earlier because of illness, anticipated the outcome and arranged to have Luther placed in "protective custody" at the Wartburg. There, Luther reexamined his position and resolved to remain steadfast in the pure doctrine of the Scriptures. He spent his time at the Wartburg working, especially on a German New Testament. Luther returned to Wittenberg (March 1522) to quiet the confused situation created by the ill-considered leadership of Andreas Carlstadt and Gabriel Zwilling. Luther preached a series of eight sermons on love and restored order. Hymn singing was introduced and the liturgy revised slowly and conservatively, providing greater participation by the congregation. The political situation after the Diet of Worms was confused. The *Edict of Worms* could not be enforced. New economic forces brought on other disturbances culminating in the Knights' Revolt and the Peasants' War (1520s). In both cases, Luther's writings were misunderstood. When he called on forces of law and order to quell the revolt, he was accused by his enemies of turning against the peasants. The Diet of Speyer (1529) nullified an earlier pronouncement permitting a prince to control religious affairs in his realm. Followers of the pope and of Luther prepared for violence. A rift developed between Luther's followers and Zwingli's followers. This divided Protestantism. An attempt to resolve their differences at the Marburg Colloquy (1529) ended in agreement on all points except the bodily presence of Christ in the Lord's Supper. Attempts to reconcile Romanists and Protestants included the 1530 Diet of Augsburg. Luther's teaching from the Ninety-five Theses (1517) to the Small and Large Catechisms (1529) reveals how much Luther grew in his understanding of Scripture and its application. He grew dramatically in the 1520s during the theological struggles with Rome, the Anabaptists, and the Reformed. He changed from an excitable young monk—who did not realize how people would twist his words—to a steady churchman. He married Katharina von Bora (June 13, 1525) and started a family. Eventually they had six children, two of whom died young. In 1527, plague devastated Wittenberg. The Luthers turned their home into a hospital, ministering to the spiritual and physical needs of numerous people. They refused to flee from the plague when so many neighbors were in need. Historians and theologians must keep these events and Luther's growth in mind as they read his earliest writings and sermons. They should compare them with his later texts—especially Luther's texts in the Book of Concord—to gain the clearest understanding of what Luther taught. Luther led an amazingly active and productive life. Works include the Large and Small Catechisms; sermon studies providing materials for the "emergency preachers" who filled pulpits made vacant by conversion of many con-

gregations from medieval Romanism to Lutheranism; a complete German Bible (1534); many tracts, letters, and treatises. In 1535, Luther began his monumental lectures on Genesis, which embody his mature views on numerous topics and took him ten years to produce. During the Smalcald Conference (1537), Luther nearly died from an illness and had to leave matters in Melanchthon's hands. Luther wrote the Smalcald Articles in preparation for a church council that was to meet in Mantua that year. The pope later cancelled the council. In 1539, Luther issued *On Councils and the Church*, a work of profound historical and theological scholarship, written to overthrow the claims of the papacy and define the Church. Luther's many duties and years of rigorous monastic life took their toll. He suffered from numerous physical problems. Late in 1545, he was asked to arbitrate a family quarrel among the princes of Mansfeld. Though old, ill, and loath to undertake a winter journey of about eighty miles from Wittenberg, Luther went to Eisleben. Judging the family quarrel proved hard. While there, Luther also preached four times and helped conduct several services. The quarrel was settled February 17, 1546. That evening, Luther felt severe chest pains. Despite treatment, he died early the following morning in the presence of sons Martin and Paul, two doctors, and others. Testimony of the love and esteem with which he was regarded by the people was the homage given his mortal remains as the funeral cortege returned to Wittenberg, where his body was laid to rest.

Mani (c. 216–c. 277). Founded Manichaeism. Allegedly received divine revelations; claimed to be the last and highest prophet; traveled probably to India and perhaps China; became acquainted with Buddhism; returned to Persia; successfully opposed by Magi; perhaps suffered a cruel death in prison. *See* Manichaeans.

Manichaeans. 1. Religion founded by Mani. 2. Dualistic philosophy of nature, including Gnostic, Zoroastrian, and Christian elements. Held that the kingdom of light and kingdom of darkness were in conflict from eternity. Manichaeism spread over the Roman Empire and was a menace to the Church. Augustine of Hippo was Manichaean in his youth. Manichaeans and Manichaeism are referred to in AC I 5; Ap XVIII 1; FC Ep I 17, 19, 22; II 8; FC SD I 26, 27, 30, 45.

Mark (first century AD). Evangelist; author of the Gospel according to St. Mark. An associate of the apostles Peter and Paul (2 Timothy 4:11).

Mary (first century AD). The virgin mother of Jesus. In the Lutheran Confessions, her name appears most often in quotations of the creeds. She is often called "blessed." Jesus received His flesh from Mary.

Matthew (first century AD). Apostle chosen by Jesus (Matthew 9:9–13). Evangelist; author of the Gospel according to St. Matthew. His Gospel was the most widely used among early Christian teachers.

Melanchthon, Philip (February 16, 1497–April 19, 1560). Born in Bretten, Lower Palatinate (Baden), Germany; educated at Heidelberg and Tübingen; educated in classics and served as corrector in the print shop of Thomas Anshelm at Tübingen (1514); gained praise of Erasmus for style (1515); became known as a humanist; published a Greek grammar (1518); recommended by Reuchlin for University of Wittenberg and arrived there on August 25, 1518. Won by Luther for the study of theology. He abandoned plans to issue an edition of Aristotle; studied and taught theology and other subjects; gave lectures that were attended by hundreds and sometimes outstripped Luther's in popularity. On November 25, 1520, Melanchthon married Katharina, the daughter of a mayor of Wittenberg, Hans Krapp. They had four children and enjoyed thirty-seven years of marriage. The movement of the Zwickau prophets and the Peasants' War in the 1520s emphasized the need for an education program to implement the Lutheran Reformation. Melanchthon devised methods and planned an education process using classic languages and philosophy as the basis for specialized vocational studies. Princes were patrons of the organized program of instruction. Melanchthon was also prominent in the preparation of the Articles for Visitors. (Every parish in electoral Saxony was surveyed and religious and moral life supervised.) Melanchthon's fame spread, and he declined repeated calls, such as those to Tübingen, to France, and to England. He more or less fathered the universities of Marburg, Königsberg, and Jena, while helping to reorganize Leipzig. He set in place widespread education reforms throughout Germany; therefore, he is often called *Praeceptor Germaniae*, "The teacher of Germany." In 1521, Melanchthon issued *Loci Communes*, the first Lutheran work on dogmatics. It was reprinted more than eighty times during his lifetime. Luther himself was greatly impressed by the 1521 edition; he said it should be made part of the canon of the Bible. During Luther's absence at Wartburg, Melanchthon revealed some of his weaknesses. He was a thoughtful leader but was also timid and hesitant. His philosophical tendencies made him overcautious and indecisive. Melanchthon strongly opposed Zwingli's doctrine of the Lord's Supper at Marburg (1529). Melanchthon's timidity and willingness to compromise caused difficulties at Augsburg, however, where the Lutheran laymen and Luther encouraged him to remain strong and steadfast. The 1535 and later editions of *Loci Communes* increasingly reflected Melanchthon's synergism. Melanchthon had a prominent role in the Wittenberg Concord (1536), signed by some Swiss Reformed. The Colloquy of Worms (1540) revealed Melanchthon's tendency to make concession. His alterations of the Augsburg Confession in 1540 caused considerable problems later, when it became apparent that Calvinists felt comfortable with the Augsburg Confession according to the changes made by Melanchthon. These changes were rooted in certain doctrinal differences that Melanchthon began to reveal even during Luther's lifetime, but particularly after Luther's death. Those who espoused these alterations were later called "Philippists." His most harmful compromise was his personal involvement in preparing and supporting the Leipzig Interim (1548). Despite Melanchthon's significant errors in judgment after Luther's death, his gifts and essential contributions to the Reformation must never be underestimated or devalued.

Miltitz, Karl von (1490–1529). Born in Rabenau, Saxony; studied in Germany and Italy, but could not master Latin; went to the Roman Curia c. 1513 with only limited success in his career; became natural choice as liaison between the papal court and Frederick the Wise. Miltitz was appointed nuncio to deliver the Golden Rose to the elector. He met with Luther in Altenburg on January 5–6, 1519, and negotiated a tentative settlement, broken by Luther's opponents. Miltitz investigated and condemned John Tetzel. He drowned accidentally in 1529.

monks. Male members of a monastic order or those who live in solitary retirement from the world to practice asceticism. Many monks followed Luther, but most opposed the Reformation because it attacked their self-righteousness.

Moses (fifteenth century BC). Hebrew prophet from the tribe of Levi who led Israel out of Egypt (the Book of Exodus) and author of the first five books of the Bible (Genesis–Deuteronomy). After Moses received the Law from God, his face shone with divine light (Exodus 34:29–35); Jerome translated this as "horns of light," hence many artists depicted Moses with horns. The Lutheran Confessions sometimes use the name *Moses* to mean the Law.

Münzer, Thomas (c. 1489–1525). Radical enthusiast and fanatic.

In 1520, he became preacher at Zwickau. Always emotionally excitable and disturbed, he felt the urge to become a reformer and on occasion would sign himself "Martin's competitor for the affection of the Lord." Münzer taught that God speaks directly to the soul, without the "dead letter of the Word." This "inner light" persuaded the fanatic to attempt the destruction of all the "ungodly," the overthrow of government, and the establishment of a society along communistic lines. Dismissed from Zwickau, he went to Allstedt and from there to Mühlhausen. After a nightmare regime in this community, he and his duped hordes were defeated at Frankenhausen (May 1525). Münzer was executed.

Muslims. Followers of Islam and the prophet Muhammad. Referred to as Turks. Turks attacked Eastern Europe throughout the Reformation period. Fear of Turkish invasion helped keep the Christian rulers of Europe from war with one another. This gave the Reformation time to develop and spread. Luther wrote the hymn "Lord, Keep Us Steadfast in Your Word" as a prayer against the Turks and the papacy. He researched Islam to prepare a defense against their religion in case the Turks successfully invaded Germany.

Nathan (eleventh century BC). Hebrew prophet and counselor to

King David (2 Samuel 12) who led David to repentance.

nuns. Women belonging to a religious order who live in contemplation and mortification.

pagans (from Latin *paganus*, "of the country"). A religious or nonreligious person opposed to Christianity. Since Christianity first came to cities of the Roman Empire, those who lived in the country adhered longer to non-Christian religions; hence the association of the word *pagan* with the concept of unbelief. Related to *heathen,* meaning "one living on the heath, the uncultivated land," that is, a savage or unbeliever.

Papists. A derogatory title for followers of the pope.

patriarchs. Abraham, Isaac, and Jacob.

Paul of Samosata (third century AD). Bishop of Antioch (260–272); dynamic monarchian; followers called Paulianists, Samosatenes, and Samosatenians.

Pelagians. *See* Pelagius.

Pelagius (c. 354/360–c. 418/420). British or Irish monk. Visited Rome (c. 400), Carthage (c. 410/411), and Palestine. Pelagian Controversy. Expelled c. 418. Disappeared from history. Wrote commentaries on thirteen Epistles of Paul; a book on faith; treatises on Christian life, virginity, and the divine Law; letters. Pelagius and his followers held that a person's nature is not corrupt since the fall but is still in its original state of moral indifference and depends on the individual will to develop the moral germ of his nature and be saved. According to Pelagius, grace and salvation from Christ are not necessary.

Pharisees (from second century BC). 1. A Jewish group known for strict observance of the Law. The Pharisees often argued with Jesus, who rebuked them for self-righteousness (Matthew 23). Later Jewish rabbis continued their teachings and practices. 2. In the Lutheran Confessions, those who trust in good works for their salvation are called Pharisees.

Pius II (1405–64). Pope 1458–64. Before he became pope, he supported the conciliar movement, but in 1460 he condemned it in his bull *Execrabilis.* This is the pope, with Julius, whom Luther refers to as being foolish for his anti-conciliar decree.

Pius III (1439–1503). Pope for less than a month in 1503.

Pontius Pilate (first century AD). Roman governor who ordered Jesus to be crucified (Matthew 27:11–26).

pope (Greek and Latin: "father"). Title was first used for any bishop. In 1073, Gregory VII concluded that the term could be used only for a bishop of Rome.

Romans. 1. Pagans of pre-Christian Rome. 2. Recipients of Paul's letter to the Roman Church (first century AD). 3. Supporters of the bishop of Rome (the pope).

Sarah (twenty-first century BC). The wife of the patriarch Abraham, the mother of the Israelite nation. Sarah showed exemplary devotion to her husband.

Satan. "Accuser" (1 Peter 5:8). Originator of all wickedness (Ephesians 2:2), an opponent of God's kingdom. He is the tempter of the faithful (1 Peter 5:8–9); led Eve into sin and so became the originator and king of death (Hebrews 2:14). Originally created good, Satan and the evil spirits fell through their own fault (2 Peter 2:4). Everlasting punishment was prepared for the devil and his angels (Matthew 25:41).

Saul (eleventh century BC). First king of Israel, from the tribe of Benjamin (1 Samuel 8–10). In the Lutheran Confessions, Saul is an example of despair and unrepentance.

Saxons. The residents of Saxony, Germany.

Scholastics. From Greek for "school." Philosophical movement dominant in the later Middle Ages. Concerned with dogmatics. Accepted the body of doctrine then current as complete. Used dialectics and speculation in discussing and trying to comprehend, harmonize, and prove doctrines through reason. Reasoning patterned largely on Aristotle.

sectarians. Members of a sectarian group, usually defined as exclusive or narrow-minded adherence to a sect, denomination, party, or school of thought. In the Confessions, this term describes the Anabaptists.

Seneca, Lucius Annaeus (c. 4 BC–65 AD). Roman rhetorician, eclectic Stoic philosopher, statesman, poet; tutor of young Nero; later, councillor of Nero, who turned against him; suicide by Nero's order. Held ethical goal to be life in harmony with nature; life is preparation for death. Seneca's apocryphal correspondence with the apostle Paul was known to Jerome.

Spalatin, George (1484–1545). Priest, 1508; tutored John Frederick; served Frederick the Wise in several capacities. He became a firm and faithful friend of Luther, who wrote more than four hundred letters to him. Moved to Altenburg (1525), where he had received a canonry (1511); took part in 1526 Diet of Speyer; active in church visitations; attended the 1530 Diet of Augsburg and wrote an account of it; took Luther home from Smalcald when he became sick (1537); helped reform Albertine Saxony under Henry the Pious; helped install Amsdorf as bishop of Naumburg-Zeitz (1542). Never robust, he aged quickly because of his restless activity. One of Luther's bosom friends, Spalatin is no doubt one of the most deserving and influential characters on the crowded stage of the Reformation period.

Staupitz, John von (c. 1469–1524). Descendant of an ancient noble family of Meissen, Saxony. Became an Augustinian monk and studied theology at Tübingen, receiving the doctor's degree in that subject. In 1502, he helped Frederick the Wise found the university at Wittenberg and became dean of its theological faculty; in 1503, he was made vicar general of Augustinians for the province of Germany. Through Staupitz's influence, Luther was called to Wittenberg (1508) to teach dialectics and ethics, was induced to ascend the pulpit, and became a doctor of theology (1512). From the first, Scripture, rather than Scholasticism, had attracted Staupitz. He himself directed Luther to study the Bible and was, therefore, at first sympathetic to the Reformation. But his disposition was quiet, sensitive, and contemplative. Therefore, he gradually withdrew from the movement, joined the Benedictine order of monks (1519), became abbot of a convent at Salzburg (1522), and died there (1524). His motto is said to have been "Jesus, I am Thine; save me." Just how clearly he recognized the *sola fide* of Scripture and the Reformation is unknown, but both Luther and the Reformation owe him a debt of gratitude.

Stoics (from Greek *stoa*, a porch where Zeno of Citium taught in Athens). Greco-Roman school of philosophy founded c. 300 BC by Zeno; divided philosophy into logic, physics (including religion), and ethics. Earlier Stoics stressed logic; later Stoics stressed ethics. Stoicism is a form of materialistic monism. It is deterministic, regarding God as the all-pervading energy (spirit, *pneuma*), law, and reason (*logos*) that gives order and beauty to the world. In ethics, people must recognize that they cannot change the predetermined course of events. Absolutely self-sufficient, Stoics can practice the virtues: practical wisdom, bravery, justice, self-control. They are not bound to things or life itself.

theologians. 1. People who study theology. 2. In the Lutheran Confessions, a name for the medieval Scholastics.

Theophylact. 1. Surname of dominant noble family, the counts of Tusculum, which controlled the papacy in the tenth century through political, financial, nepotistic, sexual, and violent means. 2. (c. 1050–c. 1108). Also called Vulgarius. Archbishop of Ochrida and metropolitan of Bulgaria (c. 1078 or 1090). Works include commentaries on some OT books and on the NT, except Revelation.

Thomas Aquinas (1225–74). Called "Angelic Teacher." Leading Scholastic theologian, most influential in Roman theology even today. Dominican (1244). Taught at Cologne and Paris (1253). Doctor of theology (1257); called to teach at various places in Italy. His most noted work is *Summa theologiae* (three volumes), left incomplete at his death. Defended the papal hierarchy and the primacy of the pope, teaching the infallibility of the pope and the supreme temporal power of the papacy. Taught that God saves us by infusing sanctifying grace. Dominated largely by the philosophy of Aristotle, yet held that reason is subservient to theology.

Turks. *See* Muslims.

Venus. The Roman goddess of love.

Waldenses (also known as Waldensians). The Waldensian Church grew out of the work of Peter Waldo (c.1140–c.1217) and the "Poor" movement that may have predated him. Marked by lay preaching and voluntary poverty, this movement, with Waldo's aid, commissioned the first "modern-language" translation of Scripture in Europe. The movement preached against papal excess, purgatory, masses for the dead, indulgences, prayers to saints, transubstantiation, and clerical hierarchy. They promoted the universal priesthood of Christians. The movement was condemned in 1179 at the Third Lateran Council. Waldo and others were excommunicated in the 1180s, with perse-

cution throughout the next three centuries. The movement incorporated followers of Arnold of Brescia (c.1090–1155), Peter of Bruys (fl. 1117–31), and others. Arnold was a student of Peter Abelard in Paris and an Augustinian monk who called for the Church to renounce its wealth. He participated in the twelfth-century republic known as the Commune of Rome. He was tried and killed not for heresy, but because of political views that recalled ancient Rome and were forerunners of modern politics. Peter, a defrocked priest, rejected all Scripture except the Gospels, in addition to rejecting clerical hierarchy. Waldensians became part of the Reformed Church at the time of the Reformation. They were granted civil and religious liberty in 1848.

Wycliffe, John (1320–84). "Evangelical Teacher." Connected with Oxford University as student or teacher most of his life; parish priest, last at Lutterworth, a small market town near Birmingham. Wycliffe's repeated opposition to the pope's meddling in English affairs of state and church and his other anti-Roman activities caused his citation before ecclesiastical tribunals. This failed to silence him. He trained and sent out itinerant preachers. With Nicholas of Hereford, he translated Bible from Latin Vulgate and issued complete English Bible. His attack on transubstantiation aroused bitter controversy with mendicant friars. At times, he seemed to teach the Lutheran doctrine of the Lord's Supper, but then again spoke of the bread and wine as being "Christ's body and blood figuratively and spiritually." Ascribed a certain degree of merit to the good works of a Christian. Upheld separation of church and state and taught that the Church is the congregation of the elect. Considered enforced celibacy immoral and apparently also thought it unscriptural. Maintained that Christ is only Head of Church and that pope is Antichrist, yet never left the Roman Church. Excommunicated (1415) by the Council of Constance; bones burned and ashes thrown into the Swift (1428).

Zeno of Citium (c. 336–264 BC). Greek philosopher; founder of Stoicism.

Zephaniah (seventh century BC). Judean prophet; author of Book of Zephaniah.

Scripture Index

Topical Index

Muhammad, 126–27, 179
Müntzer, Thomas (c. 1489–1525), 16
Murner, Thomas (1475–1537), 3, 16
Muslims, 32, 104, 125, 136–37, 158, 167
mysticism, 4

Nathan, 172
nature, human, 50, 69, 86, 94, 101, 160. *See also* reason
neighbors, service to, 13, 70–78, 93, 102, 105–8, 110–13, 145, 153–55
New Testament, 53, 126
noblemen, 132, 135–36
nuns, 7n3, 109, 139

obedience
    to authority, 76, 173, 102–8, 173, 181–83; as benefit of faith, 53–55; of Christ, 72; to God, 65, 101, 120, 175–76; to the Law, 52, 171, 175–76; of love, 48; of outer man, 64–65; pleasing to God, 161; to pastors, 182–84; to the will of others, 76
offending the weak, 75, 81–83, 93, 107
Old Testament, 52, 57–58
Ottoman Empire, 125
outer man, 43–44, 48–49, 63–86, 137. *See also* body

Palamedes, 168
Pallas Athene, 180
papacy
    abuses of, 122–24, 126; authority of, 2, 120–21; bankruptcy of, 21, 23; Hutten's pamphlets against, 16; Luther's attempts for peace with, 22, 24, 32–38; Luther's criticism of, 31, 106, 123, 128, 135, 151; *See also*

Roman Curia; Rome; pope
Paradise of the Lord, 158, 160
paradise, 10, 65, 158
paradox
    both free and slave, 7, 13–14, 43, 48, 71–76, 106–7, 110–13, 115, 153–55; both free from and dead to the Law, 145; Stoics and, 167
passive righteousness, 10, 43. *See also under* righteousness
Paul (apostle), 80
Paul of Samosata, 179
peace, 11, 93, 127, 128; through faith, 52–53, 117; flatterers and, 35, 36, 38; Luther's attempts for, 32–38; Luther's preaching and, 97; public, 103–5, 178–79
Peace of Augsburg, 17
peasants, 132, 135–36. *See also* Peasants' Revolts; Peasants' War
Peasants' Revolts, 5–6
Peasants' War, 16, 115, 132n28
Pelagius (c. 354/360–c. 418/420), 179
persecution of Christians, 120, 133-34
Petrarch (1304–1374), 5
Pharisees, 126, 130, 181–82
philosophers, 158, 160–61
philosophy, 162
Pius II, Pope (1405–64), 27
plagues, 5, 9, 29, 38, 91, 148
Ponet, John (c. 1514–1556), 17
pope, 30, 119; as Antichrist, 123 (*see also* Antichrist); commands of, 98, 100, 106–7, 123–24, 181; concern with honor and wealth, 120–21, 136; salvation through works and the, 118, 138; speculations of divine glory and, 127; tyranny of, 16, 27, 76, 153–54. *See also* Roman Curia; Rome; papacy